Disney Devotionals

100 Daily Devotionals Based on the Walt Disney World Attractions

Albert Thweatt

Theme Park Press
The Happiest Books on Earth
www.ThemeParkPress.com

Editor: Bob McLain
Layout: Artisanal Text

ISBN 978-1-68390-217-1
Printed in the United States of America

Theme Park Press | www.ThemeParkPress.com
Address queries to bob@themeparkpress.com

This book is dedicated to my wife, Susan and our three boys, Carter, Max and Griffin. I love you all!

Susan: Thank you for introducing me to what it truly means to be a Disney fanatic. More importantly, thank you for being my strongest spiritual influence and for encouraging me through all our ups and downs.

Carter and Max: You are what make our Disney trips so magical. I am so proud and honored to be your dad.

Griffin: I love and miss you more than you'll ever know. Thank you for giving me just one more very important reason to strive for Heaven. I can't wait for you to introduce me to Jesus one day. See you soon, buddy.

Proverbs 3:5-6

Contents

Introduction

It's very simple. I work nights. Our family devotionals work best at night right before bedtime. Therefore, I couldn't be there for our family's nightly time with God. So what could I do? Allow me to give a little background information.

As a teenager, I had a dream. I wanted to work in the health profession. I decided to start college pre-med. It didn't go exactly as planned. My freshman Biology course got the better of me. I still had the dream, but not the drive. The summer after my freshman year, I was asked to teach a 4th grade class at our church. I was very hesitant but complied. I quickly fell in love with teaching and decided to make it my career. It was my life for 16 years. I taught mainly 6th grade History and loved it. However, I still had that dream in the back of my mind. I still had the itch to do something health care related. I finally decided to go for it. It was the scariest thing I've ever done. I left the classroom as a teacher and went back to the classroom as a student. I was going to make a drastic life change.

Who knew I would be starting over in my 40's and following a dream as I began a new career as a paramedic? I sure didn't, but there I was, starting a new job and beginning a new chapter in my life. I absolutely loved it. The only downside is that the new job required that I work some nights shifts, so I would at times miss our bedtime routine which includes family devotionals. I hated that. I really wanted to be there as our family helped each other grow closer to God, but how could I possibly do both? I thought about this a lot and decided to write a series of brief devotionals that my family could read on the nights I was away. As I finished each one, I emailed them to my wonderful wife to share. She read and discussed them with our boys. She also came up with the idea to email me any feedback they had. I so looked forward to hearing back from them each time, and I cherished those return emails.

As I began writing, I knew I needed a main topic. I needed something I could center all of the devotionals around. It didn't take long for me to come up with that. As a kid, I went to Disney World maybe three times. I enjoyed it of course, but never really knew the place. My parents' preference was to travel to many different places which I also enjoyed. When I found my incredible future wife, I had no idea she had an addiction. I didn't really discover it until we were married, and after that there was no going back. She influenced me to be an addict as well. Now I'm completely hooked. She and her family went to Disney World every single year growing up. She knew Disney. She was a fanatic, and she graciously turned me into one as well. I didn't really know Disney at all until I met her. Now, it's my absolute happy place. There is nowhere on Earth I'd rather be than at Walt Disney World. Of course, I'd settle for Disneyland if I had to. In our 18 years of marriage, we have now been to one of the two nearly 30 times together and have taken our two wonderful sons on most of those trips. We are turning them into Disney addicts whether they like it or not. I say all that to say that when I needed a topic for the devotionals I would send, it was quite obvious.

So that's the story. Now you know the background of how these 100 Disney devotionals came to be. I humbly present them to you and hope you will read them, think on them and consider them. I hope you will read the Bible passages presented. You will probably not agree with everything I say, but that's absolutely ok. I welcome your feedback, comments and questions. Please know that if you are reading this book, you have already been prayed for by me and my family. I am so grateful to Theme Park Press for publishing this book. I honestly don't care about profiting from it. I simply wanted an avenue so I could share these thoughts with as many as possible. If you don't read one more word in this book, please read John 3:16 in the Bible. I can't say it any better than that. I promise you God is real. Heaven is real. No matter where you are in life, you can get there. It doesn't matter if you're a sinner. I'm definitely a sinner, but I'm planning to be there. I'm trying hard to help my family get there. I want you there, and I will help you in any way I can. May God bless you all!

DEVOTIONAL #1

"The Welcome Gate"

Hello, family! Here is the first of what I hope will be many nightly devotionals I can send to you. With this new work schedule and working nights, I hate that I can't be with you to share in our traditional devotional time together, but maybe this will be a fun way I can still be involved. I have thought a lot about this and decided to write a series of brief devotionals that you can read on the nights while I am at work. I wanted to center the devotionals around one theme and what better theme for our family then WALT DISNEY WORLD of course, a place we love and where we have shared many wonderful memories together! My plan is that when I am working the night shift, I will email mom a short devotional based on certain rides, attractions and shows that we might see when we're at our favorite place on Earth. It will be a fun way to share a little Disney trivia together but more importantly, it will focus our minds and hearts on a positive thought to encourage and inspire us.

So let's start where else but at the beginning and think about the first thing we see when we go to Walt Disney World. I guess you could say that would be the Orlando International airport or the Disney Magic Express but technically, those are not inside Disney property. No, the first real Disney thing you see on property is that gate. Do you know which one I'm talking about? It's the one over the highway that says "Welcome to Disney" with Mickey, Minnie and Cinderella Castle on it and a banner that reads "Where Dreams Come True," It's basically that awesome archway that lets you know you're there! You've arrived! Did you know that there are actually three of those gates? There is one on World Drive between the All-Star resorts and Disney's Wide World of Sports, one on West Osceola Pkwy right next to the Pop Century and Art of Animation resorts and the final one on Epcot Center Drive just south of the Typhoon Lagoon waterpark. I don't know about you guys, but I love these gates. I get so happy and excited when I see one of these archways in the distance and then ride underneath it. It means we're there! We're on the Disney property and the fun is about to begin!

As much as I love seeing that gate, there's another gate I really want to see. Revelation 21 talks about actual gates in Heaven. I want us all to go through that amazing and beautiful gate one day...I'm hoping we can all go through it together, maybe even holding hands. Wouldn't that be incredible? In Genesis 28 right after Jacob flees his family because his brother Esau wants to kill him, he has a dream. He is scared to death and alone and so God sends him a message in his dream and tells him He will take care of him and all his descendants. When Jacob awakes, he actually says in verse 17, "How awesome is this place! This is none other than the house of God; this is the gate of heaven." So even though he was worried and scared, Jacob saw that he was surrounded by the gate of Heaven. God sent him that vision as a comfort and sign of protection. Did you know that He does the same for us? God has His gate open wide for us. We can go through it and feel joyful just like we do when we go through that special Disney gate. Let's all strive to one day go through the Heavenly gate together!

DEVOTIONAL #2

"The Magic Kingdom"

So we've now gone through the huge Disney welcome gate so let's get started at the parks! Where do we go first? Well, unless you know absolutely nothing about Disney, you know where we have to start. We have to start at the beginning of course! What park represents the beginning more than the Magic Kingdom? After all, it's the original park. It's the park that started it all. It's the park with more rides and attractions than any other. It's the park that is very appropriately named (more about that later.) However, before we swipe our MagicBands and enter this most visited theme park in the world, let's talk about the Magic Kingdom in general, shall we?

The Magic Kingdom officially opened on October 1, 1971. In 2017 it was the most visited theme park in the world for the 12th year in a row. It's been the most visited park in North America for at least 15 years and most likely more. It is typically represented in pictures by its main icon, Cinderella Castle, which is based on the 1950 film. Construction on this park began in 1967 after Walt Disney had died in 1966 so although he certainly knew this park was coming, he never got to see the finished product with his own eyes. Walt hated the fact that in Disneyland, there was no way for cast members to get from one area to another without being seen. Therefore, it was his vision for this park to have a secret tunnel system underneath. Since most of Florida is at sea level or lower, it was impossible to have an underground system. Therefore, tons of dirt was moved to the site of the park to raise it up one level. The Magic Kingdom is actually built on a second story. This accomplished two things. It created the Seven Seas Lagoon in front of the park which the monorail and deluxe resorts surround. It also allowed a system of tunnels called Utilidors to be built underneath the park. This allows cast members movement and all operations to take place out of sight. The park itself opened with 23 attractions and 2 resorts. Today there are more than 1000 audio-animatronics throughout the park. Located nearly directly under the castle is the digital animation control station which controls all of these as well as all ride vehicles, sound, lighting, etc, in the entire park.

When the Magic Kingdom officially opened, Walt's brother Roy made the dedication. He announced the park would officially include his brother's first name in the title as a tribute to his vision and hard work. Roy spoke these words on opening day: "Walt Disney World is a tribute to the philosophy and life of Walter Elias Disney... and to the talents, the dedication, and the loyalty of the entire Disney organization that made Walt Disney's dream come true. May Walt Disney World bring joy and inspiration and new knowledge to all who come to this happy place ... a Magic Kingdom where the young at heart of all ages can laugh and play and learn together." Notice that he called the park a "happy place."

Over the years, this park has been most often described with two main adjectives: happy and magical. It is often referred to as the "happiest place on earth" and as a "magical place;" hence the park name. I can vouch for both. Those words truly do describe what a true Disney fan experiences while visiting each and every time. As you will probably be able to tell as you read the following devotionals, Disney World is truly my happy place on Earth. There really is no place on Earth I'd rather be. What about you? What is your happy place? Think about it. What place on Earth truly makes you the happiest? Is it Disney World? The beach? The mountains? Your home? There is nothing wrong with being happy on Earth. In fact, in Ecclesiastes 3:12-13, it reads, "I perceived that there is nothing better for them than to be joyful and to do good as long as they live; also that everyone should eat and drink and take pleasure in all his toil—this is God's gift to man." Happiness is a gift from God. He gives us laughter, pleasure and joy while we are here on Earth; and while it is fine and healthy to have a happy place of your own, I hope your true happy place is not of this Earth.

I made sure above that when talking about Disney as my happy place, I mentioned "on Earth." My true happy place will be in Heaven with my Father, His Son, and my family. That's where I truly want to be. That's when I'll truly be happy forever. So how do we get there and be truly happy? In the famous "Sermon on the Mount" spoken by Jesus in Matthew 5-7, he begins with what are called "The Beatitudes." Each one of these starts with the words "blessed are the...." If you look at the Greek from which this was translated, the word "blessed" could also be translated "happy." So we are given a list here by Jesus of what makes us happy here on Earth. The list ends with Jesus stating, "Rejoice and be glad for great is your reward in Heaven." As long as we follow the words of Christ and try to live just as He did, He will show us how to get there and be truly happy forever with Him. We'll talk more in future entries about Heaven and how to get there. One thing is certain—Heaven is the true "Magic Kingdom" that we all can hope for thanks to the sacrifice of Jesus.

DEVOTIONAL #3

"Cinderella Castle"

Ok, let's scan our bands and finally get into this park! As I mentioned in our last devotional, there truly is something "magical" about entering the Magic Kingdom, especially for the first time. One of the most magical things about it is seeing the icon of that park which I mentioned in the last devotional. It is the sight that for anyone and everyone just represents what this park is all about. It could be argued that this icon represents not just the Magic Kingdom, but Walt Disney World in general. Do you know this giant structure? Of course you do. We're talking about that beautiful castle that can't be missed when you take your first steps inside. So let's begin our adventures in this park by talking about Cinderella Castle!

Did you know there are three elevators inside the castle, one for guests to Cinderella's Royal Table restaurant, one for restaurant staff use and the third that goes from the utilidors underneath to the breezeway to the restaurant and then all the way up to the castle suite. Yes, there is actually a suite inside that castle that is used only for special occasions. You can actually spot the windows of the suite on the backside of the castle. Do you know how tall Cinderella castle is? The answer is 189 feet to be exact. Like a few other Disney attractions such as the Tower of Terror and Everest, it is just under 200 feet. Why? Because FAA regulations state that if a structure is 200 feet or taller, it has to have a light at the top to warn aircraft and Disney doesn't really want random lights at the top of their attractions. I've heard many times that the castle is the most photographed icon in the world, and I believe it. Our family alone has taken many photos in front of it. When the castle was built in 1971, it was modeled after several real medieval castles in Europe, one of which was Neuschwanstein Castle in Bavaria, Germany. (You can catch a great view of this castle riding Soarin' Around the World in Epcot but more on that later.) Castles represented strength and power during the many battles of the Middle Ages era.

What comes to mind when you hear the words "strength" and "power?" I don't know about you, but when I think about real strength and power, I think about God. The Bible makes it clear that God, like a castle, is a mighty fortress. Psalm 46 says it twice. There are so many times in life when we may feel weak, weary and tired, but God tells us many times in Scripture to lean on Him and he will make us strong like He is. Psalm 31:24 says "Be strong and let your heart take courage, all you who wait for the Lord!" So not only is God strong and powerful, but He promises to make us those things as well. Have you ever heard Philippians 4:13? It says we can do all things through God who gives us strength. He gives you and me strength!

The next time you see that mighty castle at the Magic Kingdom, think about how strong of a structure it is and how strong of a God we have. Also remember that we are strong because we have Him in our lives. And while we will most likely have times that we don't feel strong, He is always there listening, so ask Him to strengthen you. He promises He will! What an awesome God!

DEVOTIONAL #4

"The Walt Disney World Railroad"

We're still in the Magic Kingdom, and I think we'll just stay here and visit all the attractions at this park before moving on to another. What do you think? We've talked about the park in general and its famous icon. So let's ride something already! As you enter the Magic Kingdom, what's the first ride or attraction you come to? I guess technically you could say the monorail, but that's not an exclusive Magic Kingdom attraction, so I'm not counting that. Maybe we'll do a monorail devotional later. No, the first real attraction you come to is that beautiful train station, one of three for the Walt Disney World Railroad. So let's talk about the WDW railroad for today's devotional!

The railroad attraction has been there from day one. It is a 1.5 mile loop with three station stops. It transports 3.7 million passengers per year. The four train cars are named after Walt Disney himself, his wife Lillian, the original imaginer (Roger Broggie) who helped acquire the train for WDW and finally there is one for Roy Disney, Walt's brother. Obviously this was one of Walt's favorite attractions since he had his own miniature train in his backyard.

This attraction reminds me of one of my favorite verses in the Bible and what I think is one of the most important. As you are aware, the WDW railroad attraction has to stay on a track as do most of the rides. It can't veer off and drive through the park. That would make for some scary moments and dangerous situations. It has a track it has to follow which allows it to make a complete circle and get back to the stations where it belongs. In our lives, we also have a track we have to follow. And it's a very narrow track. We can choose to get off track and follow a much wider and easier path if we want, but it's also very dangerous and won't take us to the station where we belong. In fact, the wider path will take us to a place we really don't want to go, and the Bible says that sadly many will choose to take their own wide path. I want to strongly encourage you to stay on track.

Matthew 7:14 says, "For the gate is narrow and the way is hard that leads to life, and those who find it are few." When that verse says "life," it means Heaven. Isn't it sad that "only a few" will find Heaven? I know it's often difficult to stay on track, but the track is there and God tells us how to stay on it. We just have to focus and constantly be making sure our lives are on track. Are you on track now? Ask yourself that question every day for the rest of your life. If not, find the track and get back on it. It's NEVER too late. When I taught 6th grade, I used to close every day by telling my students the same four words that I'll tell you now. Stay on the path!

DEVOTIONAL #5

"Main Street, U.S.A."

Continuing in the Magic Kingdom past the WDW railroad, we come to what is arguably the most beautiful site in all of Disney World...Main Street, U.S.A.! Once you pass under the railroad, you can see the view down Main Street with the breathtaking castle in the background. It's an amazing view, especially the first time you see it. If you've never explored this section of the park before, it's definitely worth a stop or at least a slow walk. If you're a seasoned veteran like us, you may tend to simply run (or walk fast so as not to get yelled at) through Main Street and not take the time to really investigate. However, there is a lot to see on Main Street!

For example, as you walk down the street, you can see many important names on the windows of the buildings. These are dedications to the many people who made WDW come to life and contributed to the development of the park. Also, did you know that the walk into the park is a little harder than the walk out? The Imagineers intentionally made Main Street slightly uphill on the way in so that people would have a slightly easier time at the end of the day when they are tired getting out of the park. A final fun fact about Main Street is that it is patterned after Walt Disney's childhood hometown of Marceline, Missouri. Walt wanted a place that would remind him of where he came from...his home!

What do you think of when you think of the word "home"? Do you think of your house? Your hometown? Your neighborhood? Or do you simply think of a place that is comfortable and safe? For me, the word "home" makes me think not of a physical building or place, but of family. While I do enjoy being at my own house, the word "home" has more meaning than a simple structure. Home means being with family whether at our house, someone else's house, out to eat at a restaurant, or even at my favorite place...Disney World! When I'm with you guys, my wife and awesome sons, I'm home. What does home mean to you?

Home is a wonderful blessing from God, but if you think about it, we really haven't experienced our real home yet. The Bible makes it clear that, like the famous hymn says, this world is not our home, we're just passing through. This life and our current home are just an incredibly short stop compared to our eternal home with God. Hebrews 13:14

says, "For here we have no lasting city, but we seek the city that is to come." If you enjoy being home in this world as much as I do, imagine how awesome and amazing our real home is going to be! John 14 says that Jesus is preparing a place for us right now, and that God's house has many rooms...one of which is for us! I can't wait to see our eternal home. Can you?

If you haven't noticed, Heaven is my favorite spiritual topic to talk about. I've already mentioned it in a couple of these devotionals, and you'll notice that several of the ones to follow have it as their theme. I just love to study Heaven, think about it and plan for it. After all, it's real, and it's our eternal home! The next time you walk down Main Street, think about how it reminded Walt Disney of his home. I also feel at home walking down that beautiful street. I'm not sure what the Disney executives would think, but I think I could live there. What about you? At the same time, don't forget that street is nothing compared with the beautiful streets that are waiting on us in Heaven. I can't wait! Let's get there together!

DEVOTIONAL #6

"Walt's Apartment"

Before we go any further into the Magic Kingdom, I've decided we're going to make a slight detour here for one devotional...a 2500 mile detour! I fully intended for all of these devotionals to be related to Walt Disney World in Florida since that is the set of parks our family is most familiar with. However, we're going to go to Disneyland in California for just one moment because there is something very special there on Main Street, U.S.A. that you don't see in the Florida counterpart. Disneyland of course was the original park that Walt Disney built in 1955. Disney World wasn't built until 1971. The two parks are 2496.9 miles apart to be exact and it would take approximately 36 hours without stopping to drive from one to the other.

The reason I want to go to Disneyland for this one devotional is that Walt Disney himself decided to build something there that is very unique. He built himself his own apartment right there on Main Street. It is right above the fire station to your left when you enter the park. It is very small but was fully operational with a small bathroom, kitchen and even a quiet patio where his wife, Lillian would entertain guests. If you search "Walt's apartment" on the internet, you can see what is the only known picture of Walt with his family in that very apartment. Walt also had a small wooden desk near the far right window facing Main Street below where he would sit and work. That way, he could look out on Main Street and see what was going on down below. To this day, there is a lamp that sits in that window that Walt used that remains on around the clock as a tribute to Walt and to show that his presence is still felt even though he has passed.

If you ever get a chance to go to Disneyland, look for that lamp. It will be easy to see, especially at night. When you spot it, think about Walt Disney himself looking through that window out over the park he built. That special light reminds me of several verses in the Bible. Jesus is called a light in John chapter 1. In that same chapter it says that John the Baptist was sent to prepare the world for that light. We are also called to be a light in Matthew chapter 5, verse 14. "You are the light of the world," Jesus tells us. That passage even talks about how a city on a dark hill can't be hidden because of its light. It also mentions how one lamp can give light to an entire house. We are then told in the same way to let our light shine. We shouldn't hide our faith from others, but let it shine so others can see how we live and know themselves. We should be a constant good example to those around us.

Just like Walt's light shines in that window each night and reminds us of his work and life, our light should shine every night and day for all to see. Everyone around us should know that we follow God based on our example, our words and our actions. Do people around you know that you follow God and His Son, Jesus Christ? Do they see Him in you? Do they see your light? If not, stop hiding it, turn it on and leave it on! Light up this world and make a positive impact wherever you go.

DEVOTIONAL #7

"Disney Parades"

Let's go back across the country to Disney World and stay on Main Street because there is something else very special that happens here each day. Parades! Each day at the Magic Kingdom, there is an afternoon parade currently called the Festival of Fantasy Parade. There used to be a night parade at the Magic Kingdom called the Main Street Electrical Parade, but sadly they discontinued it in 2016. There are parades at other parks too so we'll just let this devotional topic cover all parades at Disney World.

Epcot used to have a parade called Tapestry of Nations. Hollywood Studios has had a Pixar Parade for many years and the Animal Kingdom at times has had the Jammin' Jungle Parade. All of the parks also have nighttime shows which could be considered types of parades with characters on display. One of my favorite "parades" of sorts has always been the Electrical Water Pageant that runs on the Seven Seas Lagoon in front of the Magic Kingdom. This simple water parade has been running since 1971 when the park opened and continues today. It can be seen from all the Magic Kingdom hotels each night as it moves through the water with its electrical music.

Since our family has been to the parks for many years, we generally skip the parades having seen them many times. That is generally a good time to head for the rides as the lines tend to die down a little as many guests are enjoying the parade. However, I'll admit that I do love to sit, rest, and enjoy a good parade from time to time. There are always surprises in store and the detail in decoration that Disney goes to is always impressive. Years ago, when I ran the Disney Marathon, I had the pleasure of running "backstage" where I got to see these giant floats parked and waiting for their next show. I also recently got to enjoy the Keys to the Kingdom tour at the Magic Kingdom and once again got to see the giant floats for the Festival of Fantasy Parade in the warehouse. This parade is very well done and I have enjoyed getting to watch it the last few times we've visited. One of my favorite parts of the parade was the giant Maleficent dragon that breathed fire from time to time. However, I'm afraid I may have seen it for the last time as it unfortunately caught fire in May of 2018.

These parades at Disney remind me of a parade that took place in the Bible. Can you think of a parade in the Bible? That may be hard to believe, but it's true. I can think of at least two actually. The first one took place in the Old Testament in I Kings chapter 1 when King David was old and close to death. His evil son Adonijah proclaimed himself to be king but God and David wanted Solomon to be king. He told his servants to put Solomon on his donkey and "parade" him around town to show that he was the chosen king. Many years later, a very similar parade took place and is described in all four gospels in Matthew 21, Mark 11, Luke 19 and John 12. In the Bible, this is traditionally called the "Triumphal Entry." Jesus told his apostles to fetch Him a donkey as well and he "paraded" into town to show that He was the chosen one, the King sent by God to show the world how to live. That second parade in particular was pretty simple. One float. Not very decorated. Not very detailed. Not exactly Disney-worthy, but so much more important. I would've loved to have seen that parade. I would've loved to have been in the crowd as they laid palm branches in his path and shouted "Hosanna to the son of David!" as the crowd did.

If you ever get to sit down and enjoy a Disney parade, pay attention to the terrific detail that Disney puts into it. Pay attention to the crowd and how happy they are as they shout out to their favorite characters. Maybe you'll see Goofy or Donald or even Mickey, but you won't see Jesus on the Disney floats. His parade has already taken place. He has shown the world that He is the Son of God, and we are to follow in his footsteps every day so that we can have eternal life with God! Now that was an important parade!

DEVOTIONAL #8

"Dumbo, the Flying Elephant"

So let's get to our first ride at Magic Kingdom, shall we? It feels like we've been standing at the entrance for a while. While I guess we've technically already talked about our first ride with the WDW Railroad, I would never recommend riding that first. That's a pretty easy one to ride anytime with rarely any long lines. So what do we ride first here in the Magic Kingdom? Many choices, possibilities and strategies here, but I'm going to start with an old faithful...Dumbo, the Flying Elephant. While that may not be our first ride anymore, it certainly used to be. When you two boys were little, your mom and I used to run like crazy across the whole park pushing your strollers at maximum speed to get to Dumbo first. Why? Well at that time, it was a much smaller ride and would without a doubt have a long line the rest of the day. It was always very popular, and the line moved extremely slow. These days that's not always the case.

Dumbo is one of the many special rides in Fantasyland, the land I would definitely recommend starting with, especially if you have little kids in the family. From 2010 to 2014, Dumbo and all of Fantasyland underwent major renovations. This included Dumbo making an actual move across Fantasyland. Now there are actually two Dumbo rides put together with a special interactive waiting area. Therefore, Dumbo doesn't have to be our first ride anymore. However, for old time's sake and because of special memories, we're going to talk about it as our first official ride.

Dumbo the ride is based on the 1941 film by the same name. It is said that the Dumbo movie was Walt Disney's personal favorite. The original ride opened in Disneyland 3 months after the park opened in 1955 so this ride has been around for a long time. In fact, one of the elephants from the ride is even in the National Museum of American History in Washington, DC. All of the Dumbos around the world at the various Disney parks spin counterclockwise with the exception of the newer one in WDW. It spins clockwise. Another fun fact about this ride is when President Harry S Truman visited Disneyland in 1957, he refused to ride Dumbo because an elephant symbolized the Republican party which he didn't want to be associated with.

If you've never seen the classic movie, you should check it out. It's a great movie. Through a series of events throughout the film, Dumbo learns he can fly. However, he thinks he can fly because of a feather he holds with his trunk. The feather, of course has no magic powers and is just a psychological trick played by Timothy Mouse to make Dumbo think he can fly. There is a pivotal and climactic scene in that movie where Dumbo is flying after jumping from a high building and he loses the feather. He immediately thinks he's going to crash and Timothy Mouse pleads with him to fly. He tells him that the feather had no power and Dumbo could fly on his own all along. I won't tell you what happens, but you can probably figure it out. (I don't think it would be quite the classic movie if Dumbo crashed to the ground.)

So what about you? What is your magic feather? What gives you power and strength? Maybe you say a good meal or exercise. Maybe you say your family or friends. Maybe you say God's word, the Bible. And while those are all important things, I suggest that the thing that gives us the most power isn't a physical object at all. It's living inside all of us and is a free gift from God. Acts 1:8 says "you will receive power when the Holy Spirit has come upon you." Romans chapter 8 talks about how the Holy Spirit gives us life and frees us from sin. Isn't that an awesome gift from God? And it's free to all people who follow his instructions and stay faithful to Him.

The next time you ride Dumbo, take a look at the center of the ride as you spin around. You'll see Timothy Mouse holding that "magic feather." But everyone, including Dumbo, figured out that the real magic was inside him. We also have "real magic" inside us. We have the Spirit of God living inside us to guide us in this world and to our Heavenly home one day. Listen to the Spirit. Let It guide you and appreciate this special gift God gave you. It is certainly better than some old feather!

DEVOTIONAL #9

"Prince Charming Regal Carousel"

Now that we've ridden Dumbo, let's stay in Fantasyland and move around to the other attractions here, starting with Prince Charming Regal Carousel. We usually just call it "the carousel" but officially it does have that long, fancy name. Now I would never ride this next in real life. The carousel tends to be one of those rides you can avoid until later in the day, or altogether if you've ridden it before. For a first timer, especially the little ones, it's worth a ride. It is another classic with an important history, which is why I've gone to it now. It is the first ride you come to once you go through Cinderella Castle. It has a prominent place in Fantasyland and is a sentimental favorite of many.

There are several fun facts about this carousel. It is the oldest ride at WDW having been originally built in 1917. Walt Disney himself purchased it in 1967 and had it refurbished for Disney World. During installation, Roy Disney noticed it was off-center from the castle and it was moved 8 inches over. There is real gold in the decoration of the horses and 2325 lights on the carousel. Finally, while it has never been officially confirmed, most cast members agree that Cinderella herself has a horse on the carousel. It is in the 2nd row of horses and has a golden bow on its tail.

That leads me to an important thought...do you have a golden bow on your tail? You may think that's a weird question, and you'd be right, but think about the following. There are 90 horses in all on that carousel but only one with a golden bow. There's only one that stands out as belonging to Cinderella. If that bow wasn't there, it would just blend in with the other 89 and we would never know which one belonged to the famous princess. So maybe a better question for you is, how do you stand out?

The Bible makes it pretty clear that we are called to be different. We are called to stand out in the crowd. Romans 12:2 says, "Do not be conformed to this world." We are clearly told not to blend in. John gets even more direct when he quotes Jesus as saying, "...because you are not of the world, but I chose you out of the world, therefore the world hates you." (John 15:19) That may sound harsh and we may not want the world to "hate" us, but if we are truly living like we are supposed to, Christ tells us that's how it should be. The world should see us and know we are different. They should see the golden bow on our tail and know that we belong to someone special, and we don't care how that means we are treated.

So look for that special horse next time you ride. See if you can find that golden bow and even be lucky enough to ride Cinderella's horse! More importantly, when you see it, remember to stand out among the crowds in this world. Be different. Be weird. Be unlike the world because that's what we are told to do. Let the world see Christ in you and know that you are different, because one day we won't be different from those around us. All the "golden bows" will be together in Heaven where we won't stand out anymore. What an awesome day that will be!

DEVOTIONAL #10

"Goofy's Barnstormer"

We're still in Fantasyland of course, and will be for quite a while. There's a lot to do in this land. Our family rarely does all the rides in Fantasyland simply because there's a few that we don't mind missing or that can wait until later if there is time. However, so as not to get too confused, we're just going to go ahead stay in this land for our devotionals before we move on to another land. That being said, let's make our way over to the only true roller coaster in Fantasyland. Let's talk about Goofy's Barnstormer!

The Barnstormer is one of those rides that I think a lot of people probably skip. It can have a long line, especially at peak times, because it is slow loading and doesn't hold many people. It is also a pretty short ride compared to most at WDW. It lasts only one minute! But there is some value in giving it a try, especially for first timers and those with younger children. Did you know that there used to be a petting zoo right where the Barnstormer now sits? The petting zoo was famous for having a cow, named "Minnie Moo", with a natural hidden mickey on its side. The petting zoo was removed in 1996 and the famous cow was relocated to Fort Wilderness. She later died of natural causes in August of 2001. The barn which housed some of the animals was used in the decoration for the new junior roller coaster that was built and named Goofy's Barnstormer. Some theming changes took place in 2011 with the expansion of Fantasyland, but the ride itself pretty much stayed the same.

I mentioned above that this ride is worth doing at least once. For us it has become a classic of sorts, and we try to do it each time we are there. Personally I would be ok with skipping it since I've done it several times, but I understand the fun and nostalgia of it all. For a lot of families, this is their children's very first roller coaster. It doesn't do anything too crazy. It doesn't go super-fast or upside down so most kids of a certain age are able to tolerate it. I'm not sure if it was our boys' very first roller coaster, but it was certainly one of. And they still love it even as teenagers. (Well, love is a strong word, but they do like it a lot.) It's a great way to introduce children to what a roller coaster is. It's a great first!

Can you remember the first time you rode a roller coaster? Were you scared? Were you excited? Did you finish and want to immediately ride it again? There is something exciting and thrilling about the first roller coaster ride, even if there is a little fear that goes with it. How about another first? Can you remember the first time you heard about Jesus? Can you remember the first time you understood what He did for you and for all of us? Can you remember the first time you realized that He gave his life so that we have the hope of eternal life with Him and our Father in Heaven? As fun and exhilarating a first roller coaster is, it doesn't compare to knowing you can spend eternity with your Father in Heaven.

Now, here's the more important question...have you shared that with anyone? Have you given someone else the thrill of hearing for the first time that Jesus Christ loves and died for them? We are all called to be like Jesus who came to seek and save the lost (Luke 19:10). That's not always easy to do, but it's our purpose while we're here on Earth. We are told in Mark 16:15 to go into all the world and tell others the good news! I challenge you and myself to look for those who are lost or those who have never even heard the good news and share it with them. Give them their first! Not only will it give them the excitement of hearing it for the first time, it will give you a thrill as well, to know that you told them about Christ first! Spread the good news!

DEVOTIONAL #11

"The Many Adventures of Winnie the Pooh"

Now let's head over just a short ways to what was quite the controversial ride when it was first built. Do you know why? When this ride opened in 1999, many people were upset. This ride replaced a beloved classic called Mr. Toad's Wild Ride which still exists in Disneyland. However, many were sad to see Mr. Toad go in WDW. We're talking today about the Winnie the Pooh ride, officially called The Many Adventures of Winnie the Pooh (not that anyone ever actually calls it that.) Disney Imagineers did pay a small tribute to Mr. Toad in the Pooh ride by placing portraits of Mr. Toad and Moley in the first room of the ride. You have to look quick but these tribute portraits can be found on either side of the room, on the left as you enter and then on the right as you leave. There is also a tribute statue of Mr. Toad in the pet cemetery outside of Haunted Mansion at WDW.

Even though many were upset at the loss of Mr. Toad's Wild Ride, the new Winnie the Pooh ride has become a beloved classic itself and slowly the controversy has drifted away. Kids of all ages love the creativity of scenes in the ride and especially the bouncing scene with Tigger where your ride vehicle literally bounces up and down several times. Expect to find a long wait at this ride during peak times although the fairly new interactive queue is a lot of fun as well.

So what do you know about this character Pooh? Did you know that he ranks right next to Mickey as the top selling character for the Walt Disney Company? Pooh is famous for many things but probably most well-known for his love of honey. In fact, it has been confirmed that as you exit the ride, there is a distinct scent of honey in the air as you enter the gift shop. It is pumped in through the AC vents. See if you can smell it next time. If you've ever watched a Winnie the Pooh movie or even paid attention during the ride, it's pretty obvious that Pooh will do anything to get his hands on a pot of honey, including getting himself in trouble sometimes. He just can't control his desire for the delicious stuff. It's his #1 love. What about you? What is your #1 love? What do you strive for? What makes you really happy when you get your hands on it?

How about these questions: do you get that happy when you realize you have God on your side? Do you get that happy when you realize that you have the freedom to go to church every week and worship Him? Do you get that happy when you remember that you possess his written Word, a book that was literally inspired by God Himself? Does serving God make you happy? Or is it just another thing in life you have to do? Is it important to you but you still put other things ahead of it because they make you happier?

Here are some facts: God gave us pleasures in life. He gave us things to have on this Earth that make us happy. He gave us wonderful food, like honey. He gave us family. He gave us money and material blessings that we enjoy, like Disney World! It's ok if those things make you happy. But do we forget that God gave us all those things? Do we forget to thank Him for making us happy? Do we forget to put Him before those things? Matthew 6:33 tells us to put God first! He should be our first love. He should be what honey is to Pooh. Our first and greatest commandment is to "...love the Lord your God with all your heart, with all your soul and with all your mind." (Matthew 22:37) If we do that and put Him first in all we do, everything else will fall into place, and we will be truly happy. So what is your honey? What do you love the most? Is it God? I hope so.

DEVOTIONAL #12

"Peter Pan's Flight"

There is still plenty to do here in Fantasyland. Actually we've still got six attractions to go in this land. Can you name them all? For now, we're going to head over to one of my favorites and what I think is the favorite of a lot of people based on wait times. I'm talking about the classic ride that is Peter Pan's Flight!

This is another attraction that has been in operation since day one, even in Disneyland so it's been around for over 60 years! When the ride first opened in Disneyland, guests were very confused and wondered why you never saw Peter Pan on a ride named after him. If you've ever ridden this ride, you know that a unique feature of the ride is that your ride vehicle is up in the air and you are looking down upon the different scenes and characters. Disney Imagineers did this intentionally to make you feel as if you were flying. In other words, you were supposed to be Peter Pan himself and so his character wasn't seen. The ride has since been updated and you can now see Peter's character in the ride several times. There are several hidden mickeys in this ride and even occasional hidden messages. When the ride first begins, check out the blocks in the nursery which often spell out "Peter Pan" and even "Disney." This is one of several rides in WDW that uses an Omnimover which means you walk onto a moving platform while loading which aides in faster loading. Peter Pan in Disneyland stops to load making for a slightly longer load time. Whichever park you are in, be prepared for a long line for this one as it's one of the most popular attractions in the park and should definitely be ridden first thing in the morning unless you can score a fastpass.

I've always loved this ride. I especially enjoy the "flight" part of the ride. To me it is so clever how your ride vehicle goes up at the beginning and you "fly" throughout the ride. I remember as a kid thinking how cool it would be to be able to fly. That would be my superpower. What about you? If you could choose any superpower; such as flight, invisibility, strength, etc,, what would it be? I would choose flight. I've always enjoyed flying in airplanes. I think I would've enjoyed being a pilot. There's just something special about hovering over the Earth with no definite path to follow. And while Peter Pan's Flight is on a track above your vehicle, it doesn't necessarily feel that way. It's easy to imagine you are indeed flying over those detailed scenes from the movie.

I'm guessing I'll never get my superpower. I will never be able to fly, at least not here on Earth. That will just have to continue to be wishful thinking. But there was someone on Earth that had superpowers. You know who I'm talking about? Our Lord and Savior Jesus Christ had superpowers. He walked on water! He healed the sick! He made food multiply! He raised the dead! He even flew! He ascended into the air right before the apostles' eyes in Acts chapter 1. I don't know about you, but I really enjoy all the Marvel movies, also produced by Disney. As a kid, I always wanted to be Spiderman. He was my favorite although I still wanted to fly as well. As cool as all the Marvel characters are, they are all fantasy of course. They aren't real superheroes, but Jesus was! He was the one and only real superhero. He is our superhero! He is the greatest man to ever walk the face of the Earth and guess what? He is waiting for all of us, for you and for me. He is standing with open arms ready to take us into Heaven. I for one cannot wait to see Him. I want to ask Him about those "super" moments, about walking on the water and flying to Heaven. Of course, He did not think of Himself as a superhero. Philippians 2 tells us He humbled Himself like a servant and was therefore exalted and we are told in that same passage to do the same.

We don't have to be a superhero to be like Jesus. We do need to be humble as He was and then our reward will be to one day be united with Christ himself. When you ride Peter Pan next time and get to "fly" for just a few moments, think about that day when we all get to fly to Heaven and be with Jesus. We can all get there to see our superhero. I can't wait to meet Him and I hope you'll join me there!

DEVOTIONAL #13

"it's a small world"

For our next ride, we're going to simply walk out of Peter Pan and across the "street" to the ride facing it. If you can't picture it, I'll give you a hint. It contains a very famous song that will get stuck in your head. Today we're going to ride It's a Small World. I know I've mentioned the word "classic" with a lot of these Fantasyland rides, but this one takes the cake on that word. You haven't really been to Disney World until you've ridden Small World. It's a must-do. For some veterans that have been to Disney many times, it might quickly become a must-don't simply because that song can become annoying I suppose. However, it is still a classic necessity in my book and a trip to WDW is not really complete until I've ridden it once every time we go.

The Small World ride wasn't in the original Disneyland park. It originated at the New York World's Fair in 1964 and was brought to Disneyland soon after in 1966. However, it has been at the Magic Kingdom in Orlando since the park opened in 1971. The famous "It's a Small World" song was written by the Sherman Brothers who wrote songs for many Disney rides and movies. Walt told the brothers that he wanted one song that could easily be translated around the world. It is argued that the song is the single most performed and translated piece of music on Earth, and since it plays continuously for over 12 hours every day of the year, I'd say this is a good argument. This 12-15 minute boat ride is all indoor at WDW while the Disneyland version does venture outside for a portion. There are over 300 audio-animatronic dolls in traditional costumes from around the world singing the "beloved" song in their language. Many veterans of Disney have a favorite room that they look forward to. Do you have a favorite room? If not or if you aren't sure, pick your favorite next time you ride.

So you might be able to figure out the lesson here. It should be pretty obvious. The Small World ride is an attraction that celebrates diversity and highlights many cultures from all over the world. Its message is a simple one that even though this planet is large, it really is a small world because we can all communicate and work together to make the world a better place. At least that's the message I get from it and one I assume was the purpose of the ride and song.

Genesis 1:27 says that we were ALL created in the image of God. God made every single person on this Earth. It doesn't matter who you are, where you were born, what color you are or what you look like...you were created by God and in His image. God loves you just the same as He loves the people in Jamaica, India, Russia or any other part of this world. Revelation 7:9 even says that John saw "a great multitude that no one could number, from every nation, from all tribes and peoples and languages" when he saw his vision of Heaven. James 2 also tells us to show no partiality or favoritism when dealing with others. Jesus certainly didn't in His teaching.

As humans, we are all different. We all look different, act different, speak different and think different. Even identical twins have different personalities. No two people on Earth are the same. That's the way God created us. We are called to celebrate diversity and the fact that we are all different. Wouldn't it be a boring world if we were all the same anyways? As I mentioned in a previous devotional, we are called to spread the good news of Jesus all over the world to all people of all races. As you ride Small World next time, try to get that song out of your head for one minute and appreciate the many different cultures celebrated there. I suggest as you ride to say a silent prayer and thank God that He created diversity and different types of people. Also thank Him that even though we are all different, we can all be the same in the fact that we were all created by Him and can all join Him one day if we follow the right path. We can all be brothers and sisters regardless of how we look or where we came from. With that fact and blessing, it really is a small world after all.

DEVOTIONAL #14

"Mad Tea Party"

For our next ride, we are going to an attraction that I've never done. That makes this a rarity as I've done all but just a couple of attractions at WDW. Even though I've been to Disney World and the Magic Kingdom dozens of times, I've never set foot on this ride, and I don't ever plan to unless someone offers me some serious money. If I were to do it, they would probably have to clean it afterwards. I'm talking about the Mad Tea Party ride. (Insert vomit sound here.) I just can't do those spinning rides. Can you? I could do them as a kid so I guess it's possible I did this ride when I was younger, but I certainly don't remember it. This ride is one we always pass by each time we go, and I always wonder how people do it. It would ruin my day for sure, but hats off to those who can do it and enjoy it.

What do you know about this ride? First of all, this ride actually is famous for making people sick (shocking!) due to its speed and motion. Secondly, it is based on a scene from the movie Alice in Wonderland. The original version of this ride in Disneyland is open on top and therefore cannot run if it's raining due to the fact that the cups won't spin if they get too wet. This is why other versions of this ride in WDW and around the world are covered. The original version also wasn't limited on how fast you could spin making it possible to spin as fast as you could turn it. This was modified in 2004 due to the fact that a disabled rider lost his balance, slipped from the teacup and was injured.

So what is the message from this ride? The message is DON'T RIDE IF YOU GET MOTION SICKNESS! That's obvious, but let's try to turn that into a spiritual message. I mentioned above that this ride, like some others we will talk about later, is famous for making people sick. Also like I said, I have no doubts that if I rode this ride, I would be out for a while. I would have to sit down (or probably lay down) and recover for several minutes or even hours. So let's go with this lesson...SPIN = SIN!

What do I mean by spin equals sin? No it's not a sin to spin. If you want to ride this ride and spin all day long, and it doesn't affect you, go for it! I won't be participating or probably even watching. What I mean is that the effect that spinning has on me and many others is like what sin does to you. Once you participate in sin, it can have lasting effects.

It can knock you down for minutes, hours, days or even longer. Sin is sometimes addictive. It can cause others to sin. It can lead to other sin. It can severely damage your relationship with others, and it can especially damage your relationship with God. To me, that makes sin very dangerous and can cause spiritual sickness just like the ride can cause literal sickness.

Isaiah 59:2 says that our sin separates us from God. I John 3:4 says that sin is lawlessness which means committing sin is like breaking the law. I could list another hundred verses from the Bible here that talk about how sin damages us and takes us away from God. The good news is that God never takes Himself away from us. Thankfully, He doesn't leave us because we sin. We are also told that we will sin. It's inevitable. It's a fact. What isn't definite is how we handle our sin. Do we get back on that narrow path and make our lives right, or do we stay down, sick on a park bench somewhere, suffering the effects of our sin?

So the next time you ride the Mad Tea Party (or just pass by it like me), think about how spin equals sin. Sinning will knock you down every time and have very negative effects. Don't get caught up in it. Why risk it? Draw near to God so you don't have to suffer those effects. If you do mess up (and we all will), learn from it, get right with God again and don't repeat it!

DEVOTIONAL #15

"Seven Dwarfs Mine Train"

We've still got three more Fantasyland attractions to go before we move on to another section of the Magic Kingdom. Can you believe it? It feels like we've been in this land for quite a while. As mentioned, Fantasyland has more attractions than any other area in WDW. Where are we going today? All I can say is "Hi Ho, Hi Ho, it's off to work we go." Yes, today we're walking over to the newest attraction in Fantasyland, the Seven Dwarfs Mine Train! This is kind of the central point of Fantasyland as all the other attractions can be found around its perimeter. This is also the attraction that takes up the most space. Like Goofy's Barnstormer, it is a type of roller coaster but is definitely unique.

The Seven Dwarfs Mine Train opened in 2014 as a much anticipated new ride. Many were upset when Snow White's Scary Adventure, another Fantasyland attraction based on the same movie, closed down. However, when Disney announced its successor and described this new ride, the excitement level began to grow. It is a roller coaster, however the mine carts you sit in rock back and forth as you move along the track making for a unique experience. This indoor and outdoor ride has several interesting facts. First of all, it has a detailed and interactive queue that is fun to walk through. There are several activities for you to do while in line. Once you're on the ride, the Audio-Animatronics are the first of their kind, very life-like and have become the models for future attractions. On November 1, 2014, this attraction caught fire after some of the sparks from the nightly fireworks landed on the fake grass of the ride causing a fire. The fire began around 10:15pm and was quickly put out by 11pm causing no injuries.

This ride of course is based on the classic movie and Disney's very first animated feature, *Snow White.* If you've never seen this movie, it is an awesome story of good versus evil. The kind and generous Snow White is being threatened by the wicked Queen because Snow White is more beautiful and the "fairest one of all" according to a magic mirror. Snow White is forced to go into hiding to avoid being killed by this queen and comes upon a small cottage that is the home of seven dwarfs. These dwarfs are tiny little men that each have a unique personality which gives them their name. This movie is based on a classic fairy tale by the Brothers Grimm. Their version gave no names to the dwarfs but Walt Disney named them Doc, Happy, Bashful, Sleepy, Sneezy, Grumpy and Dopey. As you can imagine, the dwarfs each act like their name. Doc is the smart one and the leader of sorts, Happy is always happy, etc.

My question for you is this...which dwarf are you most like? Which of those seven names fits you best? If none of them, what would be a good dwarf name for you based on your personality? What if I asked others like your friends and family members to give you a dwarf name? What would they say? Think about how others see you. Think about how you come across to others. Think about who you really are. It doesn't really matter what your outside looks like. It's what's on the inside that is important. The Bible even says in I Samuel 16:7 that God looks at your heart, not your outward appearance. What's on your inside will reflect how you come across to others and ultimately influence them either for good or bad. Proverbs 27:19 says that what's in our heart reflects on us. People can see what's in our heart. So would others describe your heart as Happy or would they see it more like Grumpy?

When you ride the creative Seven Dwarfs Mine Train next time, think about the dwarfs and their different personalities, especially when you see them down in the mine. See if you can identify them based on their names. Then think about your own personality and how you influence others. Do people see you as a good or bad example to them? More importantly, do people see Christ reflected from your heart to your outward appearance, actions and words?

DEVOTIONAL #16

"Ariel's Undersea Adventure"

Still in Fantasyland for two more attractions, let's head over around the Mine Train to the back of Fantasyland and ride a fairly new ride which is officially called The Little Mermaid: Ariel's Undersea Adventure. Ok, that name is way too long, don't you think? We usually just called it the "Little Mermaid ride." This ride is of course based on the 1989 classic movie of the same name. This movie was a very important one. It was the first of a sort-of reboot for Disney classic animated movies. After this movie was made, *Beauty and the Beast, Aladdin*, and *The Lion King* came out in succession and all became hits for Disney. Before *The Little Mermaid,* there were some good movies of course, but it had been a while since Disney had a real blockbuster type movie. I've always enjoyed the movie itself. It is a great story and the show at Hollywood Studios based on the film is always fun to watch as well (more on that one later.)

The Little Mermaid ride opened in WDW in 2012 after the original opened in Disneyland in 2011. They are pretty much identical to each other. I personally enjoy this ride as it is simply a journey through the film as most of the important scenes are shown. I've heard a few people say that it is too simple or boring, but to me it is relaxing and fun. I especially like the scene with Ursula. The audio-animatronic of her is pretty impressive. There are some definite fun facts about this ride. This ride sits on the spot where another classic attraction used to be; 20000 Leagues Under the Sea which was a submarine ride that still exists in Disneyland. As a nod to this former attraction, you can find an imprint of the Nautilus, the submarine from the film, in one of the massive rocks in the queue line. Also, Imagineers bottled up some of the water from the previous ride, held on to it for 18 years and in an official ceremony, poured it into Ariel's waters when opening this Little Mermaid ride. This ride, or actually the queue line, also contains one of the most creative Hidden Mickeys ever. It can only be seen one day a year, on Mickey's birthday which is November 18. On that day, if the sun is out, its rays blasting through the rocks in the queue line form a Hidden Mickey on the rocks below. As usual, I am impressed with the attention to detail and the fact that Imagineers were able to come up with that and make it happen on Mickey's actual birthday.

For today's devotional, let's get back to the story from the famous movie. The film is of course about Ariel wanting to become human instead of a mermaid and she is willing to give up her life under the sea and her voice to become human and meet Prince Eric. So that leads me to my main question for today...what are you willing to give up for God? Ariel was willing to give up a lot to make her dreams come true. What about you? Do you have dreams, goals and aspirations? I hope so. I encourage you to actually write them down, put them in a prominent place and work hard for them. At the same time, I hope your ultimate dream is to see God and be with Him one day. What are you willing to give up to do that? Is anything holding you back right now from being right with God? As I mentioned in another recent devotional, we are all human and make mistakes. We all sin and fall short of God's glory. It even says so in the Bible in Romans 3:23. So what is your sin? You know you have one (or 2 or 3). I know I do. I have things I need to work on and give up for God. Maybe it's not a sin at all. Maybe something we love like money, electronics or TV is taking our focus away from God. When something dominates our life, whether it is sinful or not, and takes us away from time with God, that is not a good thing. Whatever it is, we need to give it up to obtain our goal. I John 2:15-17 basically tells us not to love the world. As great and fun as this world is, as well as a blessing from God, we are not to love it. We are to remember that it is temporary, and we need to give up the world to be with God one day.

I hope you get to enjoy the Little Mermaid ride on your next trip. It is a fun journey with fantastic scenes and great music. As you ride, remember Ariel's story and how she gave up a lot to make her dreams come true in the end. Are we willing to do the same? Matthew 16:25 says, "...but whoever loses his life for my sake will find it." This was Jesus talking and He means if we are willing to give up our life here on Earth, we will one day find life in Heaven. So can you do that? Can you really give up your life here and all the fun things that go with it? It's so important that you do. I'm trying really hard myself to do just that. I hope you'll join me.

DEVOTIONAL #17

"Mickey's PhilharMagic"

It's time for our last attraction in Fantasyland! Did you remember which one we hadn't talked about yet? It's another one of my personal favorites that I try to do each trip. It's called Mickey's PhilharMagic. It is not a ride per se but more of a show or movie, and a 3D movie at that. Actually it's a 4D movie because it includes smells and water as do most of the other 3D experiences at the parks.

Mickey's PhilharMagic opened at WDW in 2003. It replaced another attraction called The Legend of the Lion King which was a retelling of the famous movie on stage with life-size puppets. The current attraction is a 12 minute long film starring mainly Donald Duck and includes scenes from many favorite Disney movies. There are actually six Disney scenes and songs featured in the film. They are (in order) *Beauty and the Beast, Fantasia—Sorcerer's Apprentice, Little Mermaid, The Lion King, Peter Pan*, and *Aladdin*. The screen itself is one of the largest, seamless projection screens in the world. It is 150 feet long and 28 feet high. The theater and film itself includes many Hidden Mickeys as well. My personal favorite is right when the Aladdin scene starts. If you look to the lower left of the screen as Aladdin and Jasmine fly over all the buildings, you can see 3 golden domes that make a classic Mickey head. As I mentioned earlier, this ride also comes complete with wonderful smells and a surprise ending. Hint: be watching the back of the theater to the right of the projector when Donald flies through the air.

So what is the 3D film in this attraction all about? As I already mentioned, it stars mainly Donald Duck as he participates in several famous songs and scenes from our favorite Disney movies. At the beginning of the film, Donald is supposed to be unpacking instruments for a concert and is told not to touch Mickey's hat as he is supposed to be the conductor and wear the hat. Donald is of course tempted and puts on the hat anyways. Are you surprised? When he does, it turns into chaos and he spends the rest of the film trying to get control of the hat back. Only when Mickey, the true conductor, grabs the hat at the end do the instruments in the orchestra obey and follow his lead.

That leads me to our thought for today. Who is our conductor? Who do we follow? Do we look closely at who is wearing the "hat" to make sure it's the right conductor, or do we follow anyone and anything wearing the "hat" no matter what or who it is? The instruments in the film knew that it was Donald wearing the hat and refused to follow him correctly. I'm hoping we can do the same but it's not always easy. We are told in Matthew 7 to watch out for false prophets and teachers who will come in sheep's clothing but are really wolves. This means that in our lifetime, many people will claim to know God and teach us what is "right," but they will really be false teachers and won't be really following God's Word. We have to be very careful who we follow and listen to. We have to check God's Word in the Bible often to make sure that everyone we listen to is telling the truth. We are even told in I John 4:1 to test what we are told.

I hope you enjoy the Mickey's PhilharMagic attraction as much as I do. It's a creative film showcasing several great movies. It has great music and funny moments. Next time you watch it, pay attention to how the instruments in the orchestra respond to Donald and then to Mickey. Even though both are wearing the magic hat, they know who their true leader is. Think about who your true leader is. Who do you follow? Do you check Scripture to make sure what you are told is true? Do you test it as instructed? You should. We all should. Let's all make sure we are always following the true leader which is our Father in Heaven above!

DEVOTIONAL #18

"Splash Mountain"

So now that we are finally done with Fantasyland, where do we go next in the Magic Kingdom? There are many directions as there are so many different lands and attractions in the Magic Kingdom. Many people would probably head to Tomorrowland next which is a good choice, but we are going to keep this familiar and go where our family would probably go next. We're going to mosey on over to Frontierland! Why Frontierland you might ask? I guess it's because it contains two of the most popular attractions in the park. They are the two rides where lines can quickly get long, and so we want to go ahead and ride those before crowds get too crazy, right? Let's go ahead and ride one of those two rides right now. The first one is a ride that happens to be my personal favorite ride in all of the Magic Kingdom. I like it because it is a very long ride. It lasts nearly 11 minutes (10:41 to be exact). I also like the music, the story, the creativity and the mix of thrills with peaceful moments as well. If you haven't already figured it out, I'm talking about the famous Splash Mountain!

Splash Mountain is based on the 1946 film *Song of the South*, a somewhat controversial Disney film due to its handling of race relations. This is the first Disney film ever to feature live actors alongside animated segments. The film's famous song *Zip-A-Dee-Doo-Dah* won an Oscar for Best Song in 1947. The ride features an infamous 50 foot drop near the end that thrills (and sometimes scares) its riders. Lap bar restraints were added to the log-type boats in 2011. Before this, there were no restraints on this ride. They were mainly added due to a death in 2000 when a man tried to exit the ride in progress. He told fellow passengers he felt ill and had to leave. He tried to jump out and reach an exit, but was struck by another ride vehicle and later died at a local hospital.

So what can we learn from Splash Mountain besides the fact that you will definitely get wet! While that is a good lesson, I suggest that this ride also teaches us about Satan and how tricky he is. You may be wondering how in the world we can connect Satan to this fun attraction. Well, let me attempt to explain what I mean. Many people ride Splash Mountain having never seen the movie it's based on. Therefore, they really don't know the story behind the ride. Many just ride it and enjoy the fun characters and playful songs but don't realize there is a story going on. The whole ride focuses on Brer Fox and Brer Bear trying to capture Brer Rabbit. They go through many attempts to get him and do indeed capture him near the end of the ride. But Brer Rabbit is smart. He's cunning and tricky and he uses a little reverse psychology to escape. He tells Fox and Bear to "please don't throw me into that briar patch!" Being not too smart themselves, that's exactly what they do not knowing that's where Brer Rabbit wanted to go all along. That's his home. That's where he's comfortable. He wanted to go to the briar patch all along to escape their chase. So at the end of the ride, we see him smiling and laughing in the briar patch having fooled Brer Fox and Bear. And while we may root for Brer Rabbit and be happy he escaped, I suggest that the devil is very similar in how he fools us. Like Brer Rabbit, the devil is smart and knows our weaknesses. Brer Rabbit knew the weaknesses of Fox and Bear and used their stupidity, to put it bluntly, to get what he wanted. In the same way, Satan knows what tempts us. He knows what we are good at resisting and what we aren't so good at. He uses reverse psychology also to tell us it's okay to do something we really shouldn't do. I Peter 5:8 tells us that the devil prowls around like a lion seeking someone to devour. That someone is you and me. 2 Corinthians 11 even tells us that Satan disguises himself. He is sneaky and will trick all of us. He will make us think, say or do something that may seem fine at the time but really goes against God and His Word.

Splash Mountain is a great ride and a fun adventure that I could personally ride over and over. I love every part of it and I think you will too. But focus a little more on the story playing out next time. Watch how sneaky Brer Rabbit is at the end. And keep in mind how sneaky the devil is as well. Like Ephesians 4:27 says, "Give no opportunity to the devil." Don't let him trick you!

DEVOTIONAL #19

"Big Thunder Mountain Railroad"

If you know Frontierland at all, it's probably pretty obvious where we head next because it's right next door. We're going to ride Big Thunder Mountain Railroad! This is one of the famous three "mountains" in the Magic Kingdom along with Splash and Space. We'll get to Space later. For now, let's ride what is a favorite of many first-timers and veterans alike. While it is not my favorite, I definitely enjoy it and try to ride it each time I visit.

"Thunder Mountain," as many call it to make it a little easier, is an extremely fun and creative roller-coaster type thrill ride. It is pretty fast moving, especially for those riding in the back. It opened in 1980 after the first of its kind opened in Disneyland in 1979. One neat fact is that the sound of the ride was recorded and used in the 2nd Indiana Jones movie (*Indiana Jones and the Temple of Doom*) during the mine cart chase sequence. This actually took place over 10 years before Disney acquired the rights to the Indiana Jones franchise. It's also interesting that the same man who recorded the famous saying, "Hang onto your hats and glasses..." that you hear right before you take off also recorded the voice for Benjamin Franklin at the American Adventure in Epcot. There have been a couple of notable and unfortunate incidents on this ride. In 1998, a 5 year old boy at the Disneyland version was seriously injured when his foot became wedged right before the train pulled in to unload its passengers. He lost all the toes on his left foot to amputation at the hospital. In 2003, a 22 year old man died and ten others were injured when the locomotive in front became airborne after derailing and landed on the first passenger car. While I've never gotten to do it, I hear it's also a lot of fun to ride this at night as the fireworks from the nighttime show are going off. In 2012, it had a lengthy rehab which included a new interactive queue line. It also includes several famous hidden Mickeys and even a hidden Tinkerbell. The ride lasts about 3 minutes which is pretty long for a roller coaster. The WDW version is 25% larger in size to the Disneyland version.

Since this ride is called "Thunder" Mountain, let's talk about thunder for a minute. Can you think of a time when thunder was in the Bible? There are several. Thunder is mentioned in Exodus, Revelation, and I Samuel among others. You could also make the case for thunder during some of the storms of the Bible such as during Noah's ark, Jesus walking on the water, or Jonah. However, I want to talk about another "thunder story" that's maybe not quite as familiar to you. In John chapter 12, verses 20-36, Jesus talks to God in Heaven in front of the people. Jesus predicts His own death, admits He is troubled by it and asks that God's name be glorified because of it. God then speaks from Heaven and says, "I have glorified it and will glorify it again." The people hear the voice of God but most think it was an angel speaking or just thunder. They think God's voice was simply a rumble of thunder. Jesus immediately tells them that God's voice was for His benefit and not theirs. I don't think the people there that day realized what they heard. They just thought it was thunder, a simple storm, a low rumble you might hear if you saw some dark clouds on the horizon. But they got to hear the voice of God! And it sounded like thunder to them!

Have you ever heard the voice of God? Maybe when we hear thunder, that is God reminding us of His power. Maybe when we hear a bird chirping, that is God reminding us of His creation. Maybe the sound of the wind is God showing His presence all around us. In John 10:27, Jesus says that His sheep know His voice. We are those sheep and should know when He speaks to us whether it be through his Word, through others or even through a storm we hear in the distance. God speaks to all of us in one way or another. He tells us what we need to know to follow Him and be with Him one day.

The next time you ride Thunder Mountain or even hear the sound of thunder in the distance, think about God and his voice. Even better, take some time soon to just go outside into God's creation, away from man-made sounds and just listen to Him. However God chooses to communicate with you, just listen to what He is saying to you. Listen to Him and follow!

DEVOTIONAL #20

"Tom Sawyer Island"

Stepping off of Thunder Mountain, we might as well travel to the next closest attraction. It's a place our family doesn't travel to every trip. In fact, we've only set foot here a couple of times that I remember. This place is not really a ride, although you do have to ride something to get to it. Do you know now? We're hopping a raft over to Tom Sawyer Island!

Going to Tom Sawyer Island is something that our family only recently discovered. I guess we wanted to see what this island was all about. We actually ended up enjoying ourselves and stayed on the island for nearly an hour or so. There was a lot to see and explore, and I can see how some people would really enjoy this. I'd be more than willing to go back on our next trip if time allows or the request is made. I definitely think kids would especially enjoy the island with all its interactive play areas, caves and trails to explore. There is a Tom Sawyer Island at both Disneyland and WDW. Both are surrounded by what is called the "Rivers of America." At Disneyland, these waters are home to the Fantasmic show as well. To get to the island you must board a raft and travel across the river. There used to be a contest each day when the island opened about an hour after park opening. If you were one of the first on the island, you could search for a paintbrush that was hidden. If you found it and turned it in to a cast member, you would get a fastpass for either Splash or Thunder Mountain. This contest ended in 2013 however, probably because people would often run and even fight over the paintbrushes. In 1973, an 18 year old boy and his 10 year old brother managed to stay on Tom Sawyer Island at Disneyland past closing time. When they finally decided to leave, they chose to try to swim across the river. The younger boy did not know how to swim and so the older brother carried him on his back. Unfortunately, the older brother got tired and sank about halfway across the river. The younger one was able to stay afloat by dog paddling until a cast member rescued him but sadly his older brother did not make it.

Despite that horrible story, many people enjoy this island as a place to relax, especially in the middle of a hot or tiring day. Many older tourists will take the raft ride just to be able to sit on the island and enjoy the rest and people-watching. Many parents will visit the attraction to rest while their children play in the fun areas there. Nobody can deny that is a very creatively-designed island. I have no doubts that if I was able to visit WDW more often, and therefore had the time, it would personally be a great place to read a book or catch a nap. Have you ever been to an island? Many people choose vacations at various islands in the warm oceans. One of my favorite islands that I've been to is Disney's "Castaway Cay," their own private island that you get to visit while enjoying a Disney cruise. For many, going to an island is peaceful, relaxing and a chance to escape the cares of the world. For others, an island offers a sort of protection from the stress and business of everyday life. While there is nothing wrong with visiting an island for those very reasons, I suggest that God offers those same qualities to all of us, peace and protection from the world. Take the time to read Psalm 91 and see how God protects us. Also read 2 Thessalonians 3:16 and see how God gives us "peace at all times in every way." Sometimes the world is hard! We are going to have struggles, troubles and hard times. The Bible promises that. But luckily, we always have an "island" we can take a raft to so that we can escape the stress of the world. That island is God. If we go to Him in prayer, he promises us peace and protection. Always remember that our life here on Earth is just a short stop in our quest for eternal life in Heaven.

So if you have the time next trip, visit Tom Sawyer's Island. Find a chair there on the shore and just sit. Look out across the river and thank God for his beautiful creation. Thank Him that you have that moment to just relax and enjoy the peaceful water. Thank Him for His protection in hard times and not so hard times. I'm going to try and take the time to do the same. Our God is a loving God that watches over us and takes care of us despite our many faults. Praise Him for that!

DEVOTIONAL #21

"Country Bear Jamboree"

Today we head to our last Frontierland attraction. It didn't take us nearly as long to get through Frontierland as it did with Fantasyland, did it? That's because Frontierland technically only has four attractions. The last one is not a ride but another show of sorts. It has been around for a long time and involves some classic audio-animatronics. We're of course talking about the good ole' Country Bear Jamboree!

This is one of several attractions that was around on opening day at WDW in 1971. In fact, it is one of the few attractions at WDW first before it came to Disneyland. The bears inspired an $8 million expansion at Disneyland called "Bear Country" which has since been changed to "Critter Country." The Disneyland version opened in 1972 but was closed in 2001 and replaced with Winnie the Pooh. The original WDW version has not closed. This attraction is very special because it was a personal project of Walt Disney himself, which may be the reason it has remained opened despite sporadic popularity. Did you know that Walt Disney originally intended for this attraction to be a part of a ski resort he was trying to open in the mid-1960s? The ski resort never happened of course and Walt Disney died before the attraction ever came to existence making it one of his very last projects. When the ski resort fell through, Imagineers instead decided to at least put the bear show in the new Orlando park since Walt worked so hard on it. The attraction was very popular when it first opened which led to the counterpart at Disneyland. The Country Bear Jamboree attraction is one of several attractions that led to a Disney movie. In 2002, *The Country Bears* film was released and included several big name stars. Unfortunately, the movie was eaten alive by critics and didn't do well at the box office.

Personally, I enjoy this attraction, but maybe for the wrong reason. For me, it is a very nice and cool place to relax for the near 15 minutes of the show. It is also a good place to catch a quick nap, especially if you've seen the show as many times as I have. Now don't get me wrong, it's a good show and I try my best to stay awake. It is humorous and contains many classic songs. If you've never seen it, it's definitely something to check out. I like to watch it at least once per trip, but what lesson can we possibly get from these country bears?

Are there even any bears in the Bible? I suppose you could say there were probably bears on Noah's Ark although they aren't mentioned specifically, but there's actually another pretty well-known story with bears. Do you know it? Take a minute to read the story of Elisha in 2 Kings chapter 2. If you don't remember this story, it's one you won't soon forget because it is pretty unusual. Elisha has just given a new role as Elijah has been taken into Heaven. Elisha is God's new prophet and is traveling to Bethel when some children make fun of him. They basically call him "baldy" (which I take personal offense to being bald myself). After the young men call him names and tell him to go away, Elisha calls down a curse on them and two female bears come out of the woods and maul 42 of the youths to death. Yikes! After it happens, Elisha continues on his way. I don't know about you, but I think that would've been quite a sight to see. Actually I don't think I'd want to see forty-two children killed by bears. Thankfully the bears in Frontierland aren't quite that vicious. But this story, once again, shows the power of God and the dangers of getting in the way of His plan. Now I don't think God is going to send bears to attack you if you go against Him, but I do believe He punishes us today in other ways. I also believe He has a plan which will happen no matter what anyone, including the devil, may do to try and stop it.

Take a visit to see the Country Bears next time you're at Disney World. Enjoy the show and the air-conditioned theater. Try and stay awake and laugh at the subtle humor the bears provide. At the same time, give a thought to Elisha and the power and plan of God as well. Psalm 138:8 says that the Lord WILL fulfill His purpose for us. Hebrews 12:7-11 says that God does in fact discipline us. Knowing this, you can either choose to go against God's plan or accept and work for it. I suggest that we all choose to consent to God's power, plan and love and don't do anything to stand in His way. Let's all work hard to find out what God's plan for us is and make it our first priority to see it through!

DEVOTIONAL #22

"Haunted Mansion"

We are done with Frontierland so where do we go now? That's a toss-up! We could head over to Tomorrowland. That's a popular area with some big rides, but that's all the way across the park. Let's stay close just to keep things a little easier. Normally, in real life, we'd probably head to Adventureland next as it has several rides where lines can get long. However, for proximity's sake, we're going to quickly tackle the three attractions in Liberty Square before we go anywhere else. Liberty Square is an area somewhat between several other lands. It borders Fantasyland, Adventureland and Frontierland so it is a central hub of sorts that you walk through to get to these lands. However, it has a few important attractions itself. We're going to start with another one of my personal favorites...the Haunted Mansion!

You haven't really done Disney if you haven't ridden the Haunted Mansion. At least that's my philosophy! Haunted Mansion is one of those staple rides that everyone needs to do, and it is a favorite of many. It is definitely another classic, and I would feel very strange going to the Magic Kingdom and NOT riding it. I do understand that it scares some people, especially children. However, once you ride it, you realize it's really not that bad. You are pretty safely protected in your Doom Buggy, as it's called, the entire time. The Haunted Mansion has been around at WDW since day one. It was built in Disneyland a couple of years before in 1969. The Disneyland version actually lowers you down one level below ground in the "stretching room" so that you can walk under the railroad tracks, as the actual ride takes place outside of the tracks. The WDW version is not restricted by tracks so in the stretching room, the roof is actually stretching up and not the other way around.

There are way too many fun facts about this ride to list here so I will just name a few. First of all, at one point, this was slated to be a water ride where guests floated through a ruined plantation house, but that idea was scrapped. There is definitely a scary but intriguing story behind this ride that you may be able to get a cast member to tell if you ask. As you exit the ride, look for a wedding ring stuck in the pavement. It belongs to the bride inside who threw her ring from the attic. Also, if you stand in front of the invisible horse outside, you can hear him whinny. Finally, to many veterans, it's no secret that you actually "die" in this ride as part of the story. When you turn backwards in the ride, it symbolizes your death and fall from the attic window. After that, the ghosts acknowledge you and you begin to see them.

As I mentioned earlier, to some this is a scary ride, and I can understand why. There are many ghosts that pop out at you and some frightening scenes to be sure. Obviously it is all make believe and meant to simply give you a little thrill. Many people don't like haunted houses and scary places. Many people hate the thought of something or someone jumping out and scaring them. The unknown can definitely be scary. It is our natural reaction to want to know what is coming and so some people get frightened by what might or might not happen. The fact is that life can be scary in the same way. We truly don't know what each day holds. We can make plans and have expectations, but life often throws us some curve balls. We are even promised in Scripture that we will have suffering (John 16:33). However in that same verse, Jesus tells us to take heart because He has overcome the world. In I Peter 4, we are told that hard times will come upon us to test us. Verse 16 of that chapter tells us to not be ashamed of suffering but to rejoice with it and praise God for it. Do you rejoice when life surprises or even scares you? I realize that's easier said than done, but we have to remember that suffering in life is God's way of reminding us that there is something better coming.

I hope you like the Haunted Mansion. As I said, it is a personal favorite, and I enjoy it and tend to see or learn something new every time. I even enjoy being scared every once in a while. Next time you see that creepy mansion, be brave and enjoy the thrill. Don't be too scared. Remember that it's just a ride. In a way, life is just a ride too. It's a short scary ride on our way to eternal life where there will be no fear. God says that suffering is part of the ride, and it simply means that we are part of God's family.

DEVOTIONAL #23

"Liberty Square Riverboat"

The next attraction is also a part of Liberty Square, as its name implies, and you even board it in Liberty Square, but you actually travel through Frontierland as well on this ride. The entrance is right when you come off of Haunted Mansion. I'm talking about the Liberty Square Riverboat. I'll be honest in that I really don't know much about this attraction, and I'm not sure if I've ever ridden it. We always say we're going to do it, but we never seem to get around to it. I guess it doesn't really appeal to me as much as many other rides as I've ridden plenty of boats like it before, even here in my hometown of Nashville, TN. It's another one of those rides that I'd be glad to do if I had plenty of time or days at the Magic Kingdom, but that's not usually the case. I'm going to really try and give it a shot next time. With as many times as we've been to WDW, I need to be able to say I've tried every ride (except for those awful tea cups)!

There are actually not a whole lot of fun facts out there about this riverboat that I've been able to discover. It has been open since day one in WDW and Disneyland. Actually, it technically opened day TWO in Florida as it didn't sail on opening day. The Disneyland version is called the "Mark Twain Riverboat," but is pretty much the same thing. The WDW actual boat is called the "Liberty Belle" and has a maximum capacity of 450. Sometimes a lucky family is chosen to ride in the captain's quarters with the captain himself. Otherwise, there are three decks to choose from where you can sit, relax and enjoy the ride. It lasts around 17 minutes and takes a one loop, half-mile trip around Tom Sawyer Island. It is well-known that Walt Disney himself loved these river boats. When money for the original riverboat ride at Disneyland dried up, Walt finished the building project with his own money. The original ship at WDW was called the "Admiral Joe Fowler" but in late 1980 it suffered accidental damage while being moved by crane for routine maintenance and wasn't able to be repaired. The Liberty Belle replaced it and still sails today.

What kind of devotional thought can we get from a giant boat? Let's think about its name...Liberty. What does that word mean to you? Do you think of the Statue of Liberty? Maybe you think of the Declaration of Independence which mentions life, liberty and the pursuit of happiness? That word tends to make most people think of our country and the freedoms we enjoy. It makes me think of what this country was founded on and one of the greatest gifts we have which is freedom. For today, let's think about another freedom which is our freedom in Christ.

Romans 8:1-4 tells us that if we are in Christ Jesus, that is if we truly know Him and follow Him, then we will not be condemned. It goes on to say that the law of the Spirit has set us free in Christ Jesus. Galatians 5:1 tells us that Christ has set us free! In other words, because of what Jesus did for us on that cross, we have a very special type of freedom. We have freedom from death! We will of course still die physically one day, but spiritually we will live on forever in eternity with God which means we will never truly die. That's the freedom we are all given. In that same chapter of Galatians in verse 13, it tells us not to abuse our freedom. It says we should use it to serve others and share with them the freedom they can also enjoy through Jesus. Think about what a wonderful gift this freedom is. Freedom from death! Freedom from hell! Freedom from suffering or sadness or pain! Those freedoms are coming, and one day we can all enjoy them.

If you ever get to ride the giant Liberty Belle riverboat think about that word. Think about what that word "liberty" truly means to you. Take time during your 17 minute ride to thank God that for us as Christians, it means a whole lot more than just freedom in our country. While freedom on Earth is truly a great blessing from God that we enjoy, we also have a much more important freedom...eternal freedom through Christ! Praise God for that!

DEVOTIONAL #24

"Hall of Presidents"

Now we move to the only other real attraction in Liberty Square. I know it's your favorite and mine...The Hall of Presidents! Ok, so maybe there's a little sarcasm there. I honestly can't claim this one as one of my personal favorites. However, I'll admit that while I hated this attraction as a kid, it's starting to grow on me now as an adult. First of all, it is a nice, long, indoor, air-conditioned attraction. Secondly, it is a very patriotic and informational ride that can fill you with some good, old-fashioned American pride.

The Hall of Presidents attraction opened with the park in 1971. It is the only one of its kind meaning there is no attraction like it in any other Disney park around the world including Disneyland. Walt Disney actually wanted this attraction to be in Disneyland and called "One Nation Under God." Wouldn't that have been a nice name! However, the technology wasn't quite ready and had to wait. The attraction at WDW lasts 23 minutes making it one of the longest attractions in the park. The first 42 presidents were all sculpted by the same man, the well-known Disney personality Blaine Gibson. However, in 2009 when it came to sculpting President Obama, Gibson was 90 years old and handed over the reins to someone else. The lobby of this attraction features the official Presidential Seal and is the only place in the world, other than the White House, that is allowed to have this seal. It took an act of Congress to have it placed there!

The Hall of Presidents is a special attraction, not because it is necessarily a favorite of many or has some unique ride design. No, it is special because Walt Disney himself wanted it, and because it is about our great country of America. You may think our country isn't so great sometimes. I sometimes feel that way when I watch the news or see the latest round of political battles. While there are a lot of things wrong with our country, let's not forget what's right with it! America is still a great country! In spite of all the problems we may see on the news and in the papers, there are many blessings that God has given us through living here. First of all, we have so many freedoms here. Most importantly, we have the freedom to worship God when and where we want to. We have the freedom to talk about God to others. We have the freedom to pray to God, publicly if we want, and invite others to join us. Yes, there are some that want to take those freedoms away, and there are places where it might be difficult to do things publicly, but what we do at our own house and church is up to us. This is a blessing! The best thing about our country, and every country for that matter, is that God is in control. He is a part of our country whether certain people and leaders want Him to be or not. His name is still on our money. His name is still in our Presidential oath. His name is still in our courts and famous documents. A great majority of the people in this country still believe in God whether they act like it or not. The fact is that we are blessed here and need to remember that. The Hall of Presidents attraction, on some level, helps us to remember that.

We need to remember that we are instructed in Scripture to follow our government and adhere to the laws. Unless there are laws or instructions that go directly against God, we are instructed in Romans 13:1 to "...be subject to governing authorities." Peter also tells us in I Peter 2:13 to "be subject for the Lord's sake to every human institution." We may not always agree with our government or even like those in charge, but God commands us to follow the laws of the land and at least respect those in charge.

I plan to visit the Hall of Presidents next time I'm at the Magic Kingdom. I'll try hard to stay awake and actually listen to the words spoken and watch the action. I will also plan to say a quiet prayer and thank God for our freedoms, for our country and for our leaders. Please join me in continuously praying for our country and leaders. I also ask you to join me as I try to follow God and respect our leaders and follow the laws of the land. Most of all, let's all have pride in our country, always remember the great leaders that helped found it and how much God has blessed us. If more people would do those things and follow God's commands regarding government, it might just improve this country a little bit.

DEVOTIONAL #25

Pirates of the Caribbean"

It's time to move to a new land in the Magic Kingdom. This new land contains five rides or attractions that are all pretty enjoyable, some of which are quite popular among park guests. We're going to Adventureland! Can you name the five attractions here? I certainly enjoy this land. It's not quite my favorite land. That's Future World which is where we'll go next, but let's spend a few devotionals here in Adventureland since we are on this side of the park. We're going to start with what is a favorite of mine and, you guessed it, another classic! We're going to ride the Pirates of the Caribbean!

The Pirates of the Caribbean ride, or "Pirates" as we'll call it to make it easier, is another ride that would feel weird to not ride during a trip. I would survive without riding it, but I wouldn't like it. It's such a Disney staple and a ride I really look forward to. This ride is very special because it's the last ride that Walt Disney ever oversaw the construction of. It opened three months after his death in Disneyland. The WDW version opened a few years later in 1973. The attraction gave rise to the famous song "A Pirate's Life for Me" and even led to a popular film series starring Johnny Depp. The Disneyland version lasts 15 and ½ minutes while the WDW version only lasts 8 and ½ minutes. I will say that I enjoy the Disneyland version of this ride a lot better, not just because it's longer, but because a portion of it goes outside and through a restaurant there.

There are many other fun facts about Pirates. First of all, there is a long-standing urban legend that states that Walt Disney's body was cryogenically frozen and stored beneath this ride at Disneyland. Needless to say, that is not true. When the Disneyland version first opened, Imagineers were able to obtain REAL human skeleton remains from the UCLA Medical Center and used the bones in decorating the ride. These have all since been removed but to this day, some people insist that one remaining human skull is still being used. Several cast members have confirmed this but it's not known if they are just playing along or if it's true. The "fire effect" in the ride is very realistic. It uses cloth, fans and lights to make it look like flames and one fire chief threatened to shut down the ride until he realized the flames weren't real. Finally, there are two pirates playing chess in the queue of this ride and if you look closely, the game is said to be a stalemate meaning that neither will ever win. However, others claim that the pieces get moved from time to time meaning the game is not always in a stalemate. Check it out for yourself next time!

So on to our devotional thought for today. It's not exactly easy turning pirates into a lesson. To my knowledge, there aren't a lot of pirates in the Bible. That being said, there is one scene in this ride at WDW that does lead me to a very important lesson in Scripture. One of my favorite parts of the ride is when your boat enters a fairly large room right after going down the dark, steep hill. In this room, you are surrounded by a large ship on one side and a firing army on the other. In other words, you are caught in the middle as the two sets of pirates are firing on each other. Cannonballs and bullets seem to fly across your boat and splash in the water all around you. Many children who have never ridden before get a little nervous during this scene and bury their heads in fear.

Have you ever considered that that scene is how our life in sin is? We are constantly surrounded by sin and temptation. As I've mentioned before, Satan is very good at what he does. He is good at finding our weaknesses and filling our lives with temptation. Unfortunately, we often give in to temptation and participate in sin because like that scene in the ride, we are surrounded by it. It is "flying and splashing" all around us and our fear causes us to give in. Luckily, as always, there is a verse in the Bible to help us when all seems lost. I Corinthians 10:13 reads, "No temptation has overtaken you that is not common to man. God is faithful, and he will not let you be tempted beyond your ability, but with the temptation he will also provide the way of escape, that you may be able to endure it." Isn't that amazing?! Isn't God so good?! Despite the fact that we often give in to sin, let God down, stray from that path and continue to ask for forgiveness, God ALWAYS gives us a way out. He also tells us in Hebrews 2:18 that Jesus will help us out of temptation because he dealt with temptation first hand when Satan tempted Him in the wilderness. Just like our boat in that attraction, there is always a way out. We sail right through all that sin and scariness and come out the other side of the room. We aren't trapped! We don't have to give in and participate in that battle! We can just hold on to God, as many kids hold on to mom or dad, and eventually we will find our way out!

Pirates is a fun ride. Next time you ride, look for that scene. Remember when you are traveling through that room, and there is a battle all around you, that God is going to give you a way out. You don't have to be a part of all that sin. You aren't trapped. God gives you an out. Look for it! Find it! Get out of sin!

DEVOTIONAL #26

"Magic Carpets Of Aladdin"

Stepping out of Pirates, we head across the path to what I consider to be one of a few Dumbo copycats. There's another in Animal Kingdom that we'll get to later. For today, we're discussing the Magic Carpets of Aladdin! Honestly, this ride to me has always seemed a little out of place. It seems like they just stuck it there because it just barely fit. I recently heard a suggestion that it should be moved to the World Showcase at Epcot in Moracco, and I actually like that idea a lot. However, I'm guessing that won't ever happen so we'll just enjoy it right here in Adventureland.

The Magic Carpets ride was built in 2001 and has equals in Paris and Tokyo but not at Disneyland in California. The ride lasts 1½ minutes and is similar to Dumbo in that the riders inside can control the height of their ride vehicle. Guests in the other compartment can control the tilt of the carpet which is an added feature different from Dumbo's elephants. This was the first ever attraction based on the Aladdin film and features actual music from the film. Many Disney veterans know that the ride has a famous spitting camel as part of its decoration that will get you quite wet if you stand in the right spot just outside the line. Apparently the spitting is not on a timer but controlled by a nearby cast member watching guests walk by. There is another camel that will squirt you during the ride which has showered us many times. A couple of certain sons I know always try to steer our carpet so we purposely get wet.

If you've ever seen the *Aladdin* movie, you know that the magic carpet becomes a pretty important character. In fact, near the beginning and during the song *One Jump Ahead*, Aladdin and his monkey, Abu, actually ride a carpet to escape the bad guys as a foreshadow of getting the magic carpet later in the movie. Additionally, Aladdin takes Jasmine on a famous carpet ride during the song *A Whole New World* in his attempt to impress her. Of course at that point in the movie, she has no idea who he really is. She thinks he's some big-name prince with tons of money, servants and power. He has used one of his three wishes to make himself a prince when deep down, he's simply Aladdin, a poor "street-rat." Of course at the end, Aladdin finds out that he could've simply been himself and Jasmine would've liked him just the same, if not more. She was more interested on who he was inside, not what he had or looked like.

That point leads to our simple lesson for today. I Samuel 16:7 reminds us that God doesn't care what we look like on the outside. He doesn't care how much money we have. He doesn't care how strong or muscular we are. He doesn't care how powerful we are. This verse tells us that God looks at our heart. He looks at our inside to see who we truly are. In I Peter 4:10 we are told that everyone has been given a gift and should use it to serve others.

Think about Aladdin's story next time you ride his carpets. My advice to you, and to myself, is to appreciate who you are inside. Realize that God gave you talents and you are called to use those to serve others and to serve Him. Don't try to be someone or something that you aren't. Also, don't hide your talents as the man in the parable of the talents (Matthew 25) did out of fear. Thank God for who you are inside and take pride in that. We shouldn't have to pretend to be something we are not to impress others. The fact that God made us should be enough.

Finally, remember what Ephesians 2:10 says..."For we are his workmanship, created in Christ Jesus for good works, which God prepared beforehand, that we should walk in them."

DEVOTIONAL #27

"Jungle Cruise"

Exiting the carpets, we again head across the path to another famous attraction, the Jungle Cruise! I love this ride and always have. I remember riding this as a young boy. I hate that it typically has long lines as it is pretty slow loading. For that reason, we typically try to FastPass this one. The Jungle Cruise is a boat ride that has been around since day one at WDW as well as Disneyland. This is one of the originals that Walt Disney helped to plan. From 1955 to 1962 at Disneyland, the ride included standard narration describing what you were seeing on your jungle adventure, much like a nature documentary. Starting in 1962, the ride began introducing pun-type jokes into the spiel and hasn't changed since. If you've ever ridden this ride, you know the kind of puns I'm talking about. Yes, they are super corny, but that's one of the things that makes this ride great and leads to our devotional thought for today.

First of all, did you know that Walt Disney originally wanted real animals on this ride, but he was told that all of the animals would be nocturnal and asleep when guests were riding. Therefore Walt decided instead to incorporate animals he could control, also known as audio-animatronic. For a time, however, there were live alligators in the ride queue at Disneyland. This is also the ride that inspired Walt Disney to view his parks as never complete and always needing change. Apparently he overheard a young boy ask his mom to ride the Jungle Cruise and she replied, "no, we did that last time we were here!" (What a great mom.) Hearing that, Walt decided that his parks would always need to change to invite people to come back. The water of the Jungle Cruise is a lot cleaner than it looks. Brown dye is added to make the water look dirty and to conceal the fact that your boat is on a track. Another fun fact is that in 2004, one of the boats took on too much water and sank to the bottom. Luckily, the "bottom" wasn't too far and the boat was recovered and is still in use today. Finally, the Disneyland version features a famous tree just outside the entrance queue. That palm tree dates back to 1896. When the rancher who owned the land sold to Walt Disney, he requested that one tree be spared. Walt Disney obliged and had the 15 ton tree moved from the parking lot area to Adventureland and it survives today!

There are many more fun facts about this ride, but I just don't have the space to write them all. I do want to refer back to what has made this ride famous. The jokes. The puns. The traditional narration on this ride that makes you roll your eyes and groan with laughter, or at least fake laughter to be nice. Since 1962, the ride's tour guides have shown you around the jungle with a script that includes many quips and funny lines. Most of them are easy to get, but there are a few that you have to think about sometimes. Honestly, many of them are just so stupid that they are funny. As I mentioned, that's one of the main reasons I enjoy this ride so much. I've heard most of the jokes many times, but I always hope to hear a new one or two each time I ride.

What about in the Bible? Do you find jokes or humor there? What about humor similar to this ride where you have to think about it to see the humor in it. There's one particular story in the New Testament that comes to mind where the speaker didn't necessarily mean to be funny but it ended up being a funny moment. Do you have any idea what story I'm referring to? Take the time to read John chapter 13 to find the story. It's when Jesus humbly washed his disciples' feet. Jesus showed what it truly means to be a servant by getting up and washing each of his disciples' dirty feet. That's 24 feet in all! When he got to Peter, something very important happened. Peter refused saying, "you shall never wash my feet." Jesus basically replied telling Peter that unless He was allowed to wash his feet, he would have no part with Him." That's when Peter made what I think is a funny. He said, "Lord, not my feet only but also my hands and my head!" I've always thought that was funny, and I like to think that Jesus smiled or even chuckled at this line although the Bible doesn't mention it. Like the Jungle Cruise lines, it was subtle humor that you have to think about. Peter realized that to be with Christ and to truly follow Him, he had to humble himself like Christ and allow the Son of God to wash his feet. We also must do the same.

We have to be humble like Jesus was. We also have to wash feet, maybe not literally, but we do have to find ways to serve others. At the same time, we also have to allow our feet to be washed. How do we do this? We do this by accepting the words of Christ. We do this by following the words of Christ. We do this by living like Christ did. We are told in I John 2:6 that we are to walk in the same way in which He walked. Are we doing that? I'm asking myself, so ask yourself too! Let's all make sure we try to be imitators of Christ (I Cor. 11:1). Let's live like He did. When you ride Jungle Cruise next time, I hope you can enjoy the subtle humor. Maybe even give your tour guide an audible chuckle to make them feel good. Also take time to think about Peter. Think about how he made a funny too, and also how Christ showed him and all of us what it means to be humble and walk with Him.

DEVOTIONAL #28

"Swiss Family Treehouse"

As you step off of the Jungle Cruise, or even while you are riding it, you can probably see a large tree looming close by. This is where we are going next. This is definitely not a ride and to be honest, it's not too much of an attraction. It's the Swiss Family Robinson Treehouse! Yahoo. I'm not expecting a lot of applause here. Personally, and maybe this is just me, I wish they would replace this attraction. I've been through it several times, but unlike other attractions, I just don't get a lot out of it after seeing it once or twice. I'm not sure it will get replaced though. It's been around a long time, and it doesn't take up that much space so there really isn't room for anything else. Additionally, I'm sure some would argue with me that this is another classic attraction that has stood the test of time and needs to stay. I'm sure there are some that visit this tree every time they come to WDW and love it. However, with all due respect, I can easily pass this one by. I will admit that it is creative and fun to see the first time. I'll also say that the movie it's based on is a good one. However, I'm not sure many of today's generation have seen it. Nevertheless, let's talk about this tree because we can get a great lesson out of it and there are some interesting facts.

The Swiss Family Robinson treehouse was originally built in Disneyland in 1962, two years after the movie came out and seven years after that park opened. It has since closed in Disneyland but remains open in Florida, Paris and Tokyo. The Disneyland version has since been re-themed and is now "Tarzan's Treehouse." The tree in WDW is intended to look real but is actually made of concrete, steel and stucco. It is 60 feet tall and 90 feet wide. You climb 116 steps throughout the treehouse which has 1400 limbs and 300,000 plastic leaves which each cost $1 to produce. The star of the film playing the father was John Mills. He attended the grand opening of the tree in Disneyland in 1962 with his daughter Hayley. Hayley Mills would go on to star in several famous movies including the well-known Disney classic, "The Parent Trap." The tree's root system goes 42 feet into the ground which reinforces my earlier suspicion that this tree might be there for a while.

Have you ever seen the movie *Swiss Family Robinson*? Like I said, it is a pretty good movie. It is the story of a family which includes a father, mother and three sons who are shipwrecked on an island after being chased by pirates. There is a lot that happens to the family while on the island but an important part of the story is the treehouse. The family is very creative and salvages whatever materials they have to build themselves a home on the island. The treehouse comes complete with running water, various rooms and even an organ to play to keep the family entertained. It ends up being a pretty cool "house" that the family constructs since they are stuck on the island.

Imagine if you were stuck on an island. The popular TV show Survivor centralizes around that theory and forces its contestants to build their own shelter and fend for themselves (while surrounded by cameras and a production crew of course.) Do you think you could do it? Could you build yourself a shelter if you were alone? Could you build a treehouse like the Robinson family did? Would you be content and happy? Those are some hard questions to answer. What about this one...are you content and happy with what you have right now or are you always wanting more?

It seems as if there are a lot of people that are always wanting more. They want to be something better or have something more or change who they are. While it's ok to have goals and strive to be successful, we should all appreciate the talents and skills that God gave us and use those to His glory. The Robinson family did a great job on that island of making do with what they had, and they ended up turning just a few supplies into a pretty impressive home. At the end of the movie, three of the family members decide to stay on the island despite having the chance to leave. They are happy and content with what they have even though it's not much.

If you've never taken a walk through the treehouse, it's worth doing, at least once that is. Look around and enjoy the creativity. Think about how this family used what they had and turned it into something great. We need to do the same. We have all been given talents by God and we need to use them. Romans 12:6 says, "Having gifts that differ according to the grace given to us, let us use them!" God may have given you one talent or a dozen. It doesn't matter. What does matter is that we should be appreciative to God and happy with what we have. Paul says in Philippians 4:11 that he learned in every situation he was in to be content. If he could be content facing what he did, we certainly can. Do some exploring and figure out the talents God gave you. Whatever they are, use them for His glory. If you do so, you will be happy and content.

DEVOTIONAL #29

"Enchanted Tiki Room"

So now it's time for our last Adventureland attraction. It's one that you'll have to look up throughout the entire show to see. Today, we're headed to the Enchanted Tiki Room. This is definitely more of a show instead of a ride and is characterized by dozens of audio-animatronic birds talking and singing. This is an attraction that I enjoy but wouldn't be sad if I missed every other trip. I would be sad however if it disappeared because once again it is classic Disney and I like to catch it on occasion. This is also an attraction that's been around for a while.

When the Magic Kingdom opened in 1971, this attraction was present although it was called Tropical Serenade. The format of the show was virtually the same as it is today. From 1998 until 2011, the show was renamed The Enchanted Tiki Room (Under New Management) and featured Iago and Zazu from *Aladdin* and *Lion King* respectively. On January 12, 2011, a fire broke out in the attic of the attraction and the Iago bird was severely damaged in the blaze. This caused Disney to return the show to its original format where it remains today. Many might have been secretly happy about the fire as they found the Iago and Zazu addition to be too far of a stray from the original quality of the show. Many also found the two new birds annoying and unnecessary. A very interesting fact about this attraction is that it was the first ever in Disneyland to use audio-animatronics which has now become a staple to many beloved attractions. The Disneyland version was originally going to be a restaurant with the birds entertaining dining guests but that idea was scrapped. However, this is why the version there in California is the only attraction to have its own bathroom. The actor who supplied the voice for Lumiere in "Beauty and the Beast" is also the voice of one of the main speaking birds in the show which is Pierre, the French parrot.

So what is the theme of this attraction? That's pretty easy...birds! Lots and lots of birds! What about birds in the Bible? Can you think of a time when birds are mentioned in Scripture because there are several? I immediately think of Noah's ark and him sending the birds out to see if the flooding had subsided. I also think of the ravens feeding Elijah during the drought. For today, however, there is a very important passage featuring birds that I have personally used many times during my life that I'd like to focus on. Look at Matthew 6: 25-34. This is Jesus talking during the very important "Sermon on the Mount." This particular portion talks about worry. Jesus asks the people why they worry. He then asks them to think about birds of all creatures. He mentions how birds don't sow or reap. They don't work for food. However, they are always taken care of. There is always a worm, bug or other scrap for birds to find to feed themselves and their young. Jesus points out that if God takes care of birds, then surely He will take care of us, His chosen people.

I love this passage and as mentioned have read and used it many times. I think worry is a common weakness among humans in general. I know it is for me. I tend to think about all of life's struggles and problems and worry about what will happen. Jesus instructs us not to do that because God will take care of us. Peter reminds us in I Peter 5:7 to "cast all your anxieties upon Him (God) because He cares for you." It's human nature to worry. I think God knows we will worry, but it's when we let this worry consume us and affect us that it becomes a problem. We have to be disciplined and know when to "cast our cares" upon Him and let Him take control.

The next time you watch all those Tiki Birds sing, think about how God takes care of all His creatures, including the birds as well as you and me. We really don't have to worry. All that really matters is where we are headed when eternity comes. Everything else that happens in the meantime is minor compared to our future with God. So join me in letting God take control of our lives. It is only then that we can let all our worries fly out the window, and we can be just like the birds!

DEVOTIONAL #30

"Stitch's Great Escape"

It's now to time to begin our final land in the Magic Kingdom! Can you believe it? We are nearing the end of this phenomenal park. However, we still have three other parks to go of course. Lots of fun facts and great devotional thoughts ahead! For now, we are heading to Tomorrowland! We have several rides and attractions to do in this area which is my personal favorite of all the lands in the MK. However, even though this land is my favorite, it unfortunately includes my personal least favorite of all Disney attractions. According to other articles and information I've found, I think many would agree with me. So let's go see Stitch!

Stitch's Great Escape opened in 2004 and is arguably the most disliked attraction in the Magic Kingdom and possibly at WDW. In fact, there was recent talk of it closing down and being replaced. However, as of this writing it is still around with no definite plans for change, so I felt I had to include it. This attraction constantly gets bad reviews from kids and adults alike. There are a select few people that love this attraction (or maybe they just love to hate it) but it's definitely one or the other with most people with most falling into the hate category. This is more of an interactive show than a ride as you don't go anywhere but are forced to sit through 17 minutes and 30 seconds of Stitch and his annoying antics. This attraction is of course based on the 2002 movie *Lilo and Stitch*. The attraction tells the story of Stitch before he ever met Lilo. On the day it opened, Cinderella Castle had undergone an obvious change being covered in toilet paper with the words "Stitch is king" painted on the side, implying that Stitch had arrived at the Magic Kingdom and was immediately beginning his mischief. The attraction straps you in so if you are claustrophobic or scared of the dark, you are in trouble. Stitch is the first audio-animatronic to ever spit so prepare for that as well if you've never ridden. The Stitch experience replaced another dreaded attraction called Alien Encounter which was very similar except you were met by a scary alien instead of a scary Stitch. I have done this attraction twice. I did it when it first came out, thought it was pretty dumb and saw no need to repeat it. Then, on a fairly recent trip, my family retired early and went back to the resort so I decided to try it since I was alone. Once again, I decided that I had wasted 17½ minutes of my life. I don't see myself going back anytime soon and I do wish Disney would turn this into something else. I guess I see one problem they are facing as there is not a lot of space so possibilities are limited I'm sure. However, I'm sure that the Disney executives know the feelings of the majority here as they've no doubt seen the many reviews expressing hate towards this attraction.

So let's talk about hate. How's that for transition? Do you hate this attraction? If you haven't done it, don't judge yet and try it once. Why not? See what you think. Maybe you'll actually like it. (Not likely.) Maybe you'll tolerate it. However, the word "hate" might just be in your review of it as well. What else do you hate? Are there foods you hate? Places? People? Hopefully not! I was always told by my parents growing up that we were never to hate people. We can dislike them, but hate is a strong word! It's ok to hate things but according to Scripture, we shouldn't hate others. In fact the Bible talks about the word hate when it says, "Hatred stirs up strife, but love covers all offenses." (Prov. 10:12). It also says we are not to hate our brother calling us "murderers" if we do. (I John 3:15). Matthew 5 even tells us not to hate our enemies. We are told that the world will hate us (Matthew 10:22). We are also told what God hates in Proverbs 6:16-19. For today, though, I'd like to talk about something else that comes to mind when I think of hate. It's something we are not only allowed to hate but should definitely hate. Know what I'm talking about?

When I think of the word hate, I think of Satan. Hebrews 1:9 says that the Lord hates wickedness. Romans 12:9 tells us to hate what is evil. I think we can all agree that Satan is the definition of evil, so it is ok to hate him. I think we would all agree that we hate Satan. We hate what he does and who he is. We hate how difficult he sometimes makes it to live our life in accordance with God. However, do we really show our hatred for him? We should all show our hatred of the devil by not doing anything he puts in our way. We should flee from any temptation he throws at as. This will show the world how much we hate him. Sometimes we say we hate him but we gladly participate in the sin he throws at us which makes him happy.

It's ok to hate the Stitch ride, but give it a chance before you make that call. Stitch deserves that at least. Satan does not! We already know what Satan has done and will continue to do. The good news is that we also know that he will be defeated in the last days. God will win! The Bible makes this clear as well. Let's use this time in between to make sure Satan knows how much we hate him. Don't let him get to you. Don't let him win any battles in your life. Lean on God and His love will defeat the evil of Satan every time!

DEVOTIONAL #31

"Monsters, Inc. Laugh Floor"

Let's escape Stitch quickly and move on to the attraction directly across the path. It happens to be the other attraction in Tomorrowland that is more show-like as opposed to a ride. The rest of the attractions here will be rides or at least experiences where you get to move. I like today's attraction a lot more than I did Stitch, so get ready to laugh your socks off! Well, maybe it's not quite that hilarious, but it has definitely caused some laugh-out-loud moments for me in the past. Today we're visiting the Monsters, Inc. Laugh Floor!

For a long time, our family didn't visit this attraction. I'm not sure why. I suppose we really didn't know what it was, but knew it wasn't a ride per se, so we felt it okay to pass it by. However, I tried this one again when I was alone one time and loved it. I had no idea what to expect, but thought I should at least give it a chance. Every attraction deserves at least that, right? One thing I really liked about this attraction is that it involves audience participation, or forced contribution, which is even funnier. So my personal recommendation if you've never seen this is to give it a shot if you have the time.

This attraction was created and opened in 2007. It replaced the Timekeeper attraction which had been around for 12 years before. This is a very interactive 15 minute show where the monsters on the screen actually talk to and react to the guests in the audience very similar to Turtle Talk with Crush at Epcot. Live actors backstage work in front of a green screen to make the show come alive. During the pre-show when you are in line, you can actually text jokes to a certain number and your joke might just make it into the show. Before the show begins, the video screen shows random people sitting in the audience with funny captions attached. One of the audience members even is forced to dance during the show. I'm always secretly hoping my face won't appear on the screen for that part, although I enjoy laughing at others chosen for this honor. Basically, I really enjoy this show because of the laughter it typically causes.

I enjoy laughing. Who doesn't? I enjoy watching funny shows and videos. Can you think of someone or something that always makes you laugh? Is there a certain friend or family member that can always make you laugh? What about in the Bible? Can you think of times where people laughed in Scripture? We already talked recently about a time where Peter was inadvertently funny, but there wasn't necessarily laughter. What about times in the Bible when there was actual out-loud laughter? I can think of two stories that pop into my mind. One is in the Old Testament and one in the New. However, they both have something very important in common. In the Old Testament, we go to Genesis 18:12 where Sarah laughed when God told her and Abraham they would have a child at ages 90 and 100 respectively. In the New Testament, we look at Luke 8:53 where the people laughed at Jesus when he told them a little girl wasn't dead but only sleeping. So what do these stories of laughter have in common? They both involve people doubting and the power of God. Both involve God's children actually laughing at Him because they don't think He can do what He claims. What about you? Do you doubt God's power? Would you ever laugh at Him or any claims that He can do something amazing?

I'm so glad God gave us laughter. It's one of my favorite parts of life. Life would be pretty boring and sad without it. It's good and even healthy to have fun and to laugh. I believe it's a true blessing from God and He likes when we laugh. However, we should never laugh at the power of God. We should never doubt Him. The Bible clearly teaches that "with God, all things are possible." (Matt. 19:26) There is nothing God cannot do. Jeremiah 32:17 even says that nothing is too hard for God. Our minds cannot even comprehend His power and what He can make happen. So why would anyone ever doubt and especially laugh at Him?

Check out the Monsters' Inc. Laugh Floor, especially if you've never seen it. See if you laugh too. I think you just might. At the same time, think about God's power and how mighty He really is. Think about all the miracles and wonders He has done Himself and through His Son, Jesus Christ. That same mighty and powerful God created you and me, and He loves us as His own children. That's nothing to laugh about!

DEVOTIONAL #32

"Space Mountain"

Now we head over to another one of my favorite attractions in Tomorrowland and in the Magic Kingdom for that matter. I already mentioned that Splash Mountain is my favorite ride in the MK, but this is up there in the top five for sure. It is another ride that has been around for a long time, is loved by many, and feared by some. Today, we're riding the infamous Space Mountain!

Space Mountain is that big white thing you see when you first catch a glimpse of the Magic Kingdom. It's easily visible even from the air as I've seen it many times flying over either on the way to or from Orlando. It is a roller coaster and thrill ride that has become a staple of all the Disney parks around the world. It takes place completely in the dark making it seem much faster than the 30mph that it tops out at. My youngest son had the pleasure of riding it recently with the lights turned on, and I admit I was jealous! He got to do it as part of a school trip where they compared the ride with and without lights. Space Mountain actually began as a dream of Walt Disney himself. He planned a roller coaster called Space Port that would've had four separate tracks. This plan was shelved due to lack of space and his death in 1966. Imagineers instead planned Space Mountain, and it was first opened in the Florida park in 1975. In late 1975, due to extreme popularity, the same ride was planned and built in Disneyland in California. Their version opened in 1977. This ride was only the 2nd attraction to be built in Florida first before it made its way to Disneyland. (The first was Country Bear Jamboree.) It features two tracks instead of Walt's original plan of four. The two tracks are almost identical, but one of the tracks is 10 feet longer because it has to go above the other at one point which adds to its length. This was the world's very first completely indoor roller coaster and was also the first roller coaster to be controlled by computer. Finally, this is the only attraction in Florida where you load outside the perimeter of the train. You actually travel down underground and under the tracks during the lengthy queue for this ride. I think this fact might change with the addition of the Tron ride coming soon to MK, but I'm not 100% sure on that. Now there are a couple of other rides at the MK where you travel under the tracks during your ride and after you've already loaded. Know what they are? I'll let you know at the end of this devotional.

I do love this ride. This is one of the few I can remember riding as a child. I can actually remember riding it the first time, absolutely loving it, and thinking how cool it was to be in the dark. I think the darkness makes it more thrilling and exciting. It puts a mystery factor into the ride as you never know which direction you are going to go or when you will travel up or down. There are some however that don't like this factor of the ride. They don't like not being able to see where you are going. They want the lights on. They want to know which direction they'll be heading next. It's an understandable fear and reason why some choose not to ride this classic attraction.

What about you? Are you in the dark? Can you see where you are going? I don't mean on Space Mountain, and I don't even mean when you walk down the street. I mean in your spiritual life. Can you see which direction you are going with God in mind? Are you heading toward God or are you traveling away from Him? The fact is that sometimes it's difficult in life to know which direction we are going. Sometimes we are traveling in completely dark surroundings and we don't know what is the correct direction. Sometimes we all get confused and may think we are going the right way when we really aren't. Our lives can often become a dark ride that's difficult to navigate. The good news, no the great news, is that we have a guide. One of my favorite verses in all of Scripture is Proverbs 3:5-6 which says "Trust in the Lord with all your heart and do not lean on your own understanding. In all your ways, acknowledge Him and He will make straight your paths." Isn't that a wonderful gift from God? We don't have to lead ourselves. God will lead us if we just trust in Him. He will make our paths straight. There is also a famous passage in Psalms 119:105 saying that God's Word is a lamp to our feet and a light to our path meaning that if we read and study the Bible, it will guide us to Him. We have a map or a guidebook to lead us. It doesn't matter if the way is dark or confusing.

I hope you like Space Mountain as much as I do. I know it can be scary but if you can conquer the darkness, it can also be a very fun ride. Next time you enjoy it, see if you can see anything. Put your hand in front of your face during the ride. Can you even see your hand? It doesn't matter. The track will lead you back to the start of the ride and you'll be fine. In the same way, God will always guide you back home even when you can't see the way yourself. Thank you God for showing us the way and for always being our guide! (The other two rides that secretly travel outside the train tracks after loading are Pirates of the Caribbean and Splash Mountain.)

DEVOTIONAL #33

"Tomorrowland Transit Authority Peoplemover"

Let's switch gears and go from a thrilling and slightly scary roller coaster to a much more peaceful and relaxing experience. It's another one of my favorites and a favorite of my entire family. Have you noticed that I have a lot of favorites?! This one I like not because it's anything particularly special, but simply because it has to be the most tranquil and comfortable ride in the park. Let's go ride the Tomorrowland Transit Authority PeopleMover, famously known as the "TTA" for short.

The TTA, formerly known as the WEDWay PeopleMover (WED for Walter Elias Disney) until 1994, is simply that...a people mover that transports you slowly around Tomorrowland in and out of several of the attractions. In fact, some Disney traditionalists still may call it the "PeopleMover." It is a constantly moving ride which makes for generally short waits on this nearly exact 10 minute experience. The length of the track is just over a mile and can hold up to 320 guests at a time. It was built at WDW in 1975 based on the similar attraction in Disneyland. The original attraction used covered cars with open track while the newer WDW version uses open cars with a covered track. The Disneyland version closed in 1995 and no longer exists while the WDW version is still going strong. I hope it stays that way! The WDW version uses magnets unlike the original which used tires. Up to 20% of the magnets can fail and the ride will still work properly. This ride famously runs through Space Mountain where you can view the loading zone and actual dark part of the ride. If Space Mountain breaks down, the TTA doesn't so this is one way you may catch a very rare glimpse of Space Mountain with the lights on. Finally, while riding the TTA you get to catch a glimpse of the original model for EPCOT that Walt Disney himself envisioned.

As I mentioned earlier, this is a peaceful and slow-moving ride that tops out at around 6 miles per hour. It's not super exciting. It doesn't go fast. It has no hills. It just moves, but that's what I love about it. It moves for 10 minutes and you get a nice, relaxing rest as you ride it. If you time it just right like we try to do, you may have a car all to yourself which makes the ride even more enjoyable. To me this ride just screams the word "peace" which is what I want to talk about today. How much peace do you have in your life? How much quiet time do you get? Do you ever get to just sit, relax and think about God without something of the world invading your mind or time? If you're like me, these peaceful times are few and far between. There is always something I need to do or a deadline I have to get to. I long for some quiet time where I don't have anything to worry about. The good news is that God promises us this peace.

In II Thessalonians 3:16 we read, "Now may the Lord of peace Himself give you peace at all times in every way." Jesus even says in John 16:33 that the purpose of His message was so that we can have peace. He also says that peacemakers are blessed in His famous Sermon on the Mount in Matthew chapter 5. Finally, the famous passage from Psalm 23 talks about God having us lie down in green pastures and leading us beside quiet waters. God gives us peace. He gives us a peace that "surpasses all understanding" (Php. 4:7). There have been times in my life where I was way too stressed, worried or sad about something. I have prayed specifically for peace and I can honestly say that God has answered. I have experienced this peace that passes understanding. I have had a calm and relaxing sense about me that I couldn't explain. In a time where I should've been upset or worried, I was not. I know without a doubt that God answered my prayer and gave me peace. He offers it to you as well.

I love the TTA. I would ride it two, three or even four times every time we go to WDW. There have even been a couple of times where the cast members graciously let us just stay on and keep going around and around. It's just the most relaxing ride there ever was. If I could move one ride to my own neighborhood, it just might be the TTA. I need a daily ride on it to just stop, forget about life's worries and cares and focus on God. Try and do that when you ride it next. Close your eyes. Feel the breeze. Take a deep breath and focus on God. Thank Him for the peace and quiet you are experiencing. Thank Him for the peace He offers us that we can't even understand. Thank Him that one day we can all experience this peace every day and all day as we celebrate eternity with Him and His Son.

DEVOTIONAL #34

"Buzz Lightyear's Space Ranger Spin"

So where should we go next here in Tomorrowland? I'm thinking we disembark from the TTA and head straight to the ride right across from its exit. This is another one of my personal favorites and was a first of its kind. In fact, this is one of the few rides that Magic Kingdom in Florida had first and has since spread to all the Disney parks around the world including Disneyland in CA. It's a ride based on a certain flying, popular, greenish, space ranger. Let's go ride Buzz!

Buzz Lightyear's Space Ranger Spin was opened at WDW in 1998. Other attractions that have been in this building have been If You Had Wings, If You Could Fly, Delta Dreamflight and Take Flight. The current experience is a 4-5 minute interactive ride where you are instructed to shoot as many of the targets with your laser gun as possible. The more difficult the target, the more points you receive. For Disney fanatics, like yours truly, there are some hidden and special targets worth major points. You can find these by searching the internet. The highest score you can receive is 999,999 which can pretty much only be achieved by finding these special targets. If you can manage this highest score and the rank of "Galactic Hero," talk to a cast member and they will give you something special (usually a button or sticker). While your laser gun produces a red dot across the room, the laser itself isn't harmful so you need not worry about getting a shot to the eye. Disney has confirmed that they are similar to the bar code scanners at grocery stores and have even been certified by the FDA. This is one of the few rides you can see while riding the TTA as well. There used to be more windows available to look down on this ride, but some were covered due to the ride's configuration. Remember the hair salon scene on the TTA? That used to be a window looking down.

One of the reasons I love this ride is because you have something to do. You have a mission. You are competing with yourself to score big points by finding and hitting important targets. One of those special and high-scoring targets is at the bottom of Emperor Zurg's ship. As you most likely know if you've seen the "Toy Story" movies, Zurg is

Buzz Lightyear's archenemy. In the movies, Buzz is always trying to defeat Zurg. As you ride this attraction, you have taken on Buzz's role to defeat Zurg by shooting at him and the targets around his ship to score big points. This leads to our devotional thought today.

We as Christians have been given a role in life similar to Buzz Lightyear. We don't have to fight Zurg, but we do have to battle Satan every day. Satan is our mortal enemy who is always trying to defeat us. We have been given a "laser gun" of sorts to shoot and defeat him with, and we have the responsibility each day to fire on him. Our laser gun is the Word of God, the Bible. It is the best tool we have to know Satan's strategy and plan our battle against him. The more we study and learn how best to do that, the more points we will receive. Maybe we won't get literal points, but we will score points with God in the fact that we will grow closer to Him and keep Satan from ruining our spiritual lives. James 4:7 tells us to submit to God and resist the devil. If we do, it says Satan will flee from us. We can submit to God by knowing Him, listening to Him and following Him. This will give us the power we need to resist and defeat Satan just like Buzz defeats Zurg. Don't you want to defeat Satan and disappoint him in his attempt to control your life? I know I do!

The next time you ride along with Buzz and shoot your laser blaster at those targets, maybe pretend that you are shooting at Satan for one round. See how many points you can score against the devil. Do the same in your Christian walk each and every day. Keep firing at the devil by focusing on God and knowing His plan for your life. In that way, you will get the highest score with God and will be rewarded... not with a "Galactic Hero" button, but with eternity in Heaven. That's a much better reward!

DEVOTIONAL #35

"Tomorrowland Speedway"

We have three Tomorrowland attractions to go. Can you name them? For today, let's add a little speed to our adventure! Know what I mean? Let's go ride the Tomorrowland Speedway! This is a ride I enjoy, and I especially like watching my sons' happiness when they get to drive. At the same time, I don't get too sad if we have to pass this one by due to lines or lack of time. This is a rare Disney ride that is not too unique to Disney. What I mean is that many theme parks around the world have a similar ride so maybe that's another reason I don't mind missing this one. Additionally, it is typically a long, hot and exhausting queue line, and I don't mean tiring. I mean exhaust...like from the cars. The smell of and heat from the cars exhaust is often overwhelming. Nevertheless, this can be a fun ride so let's discuss it briefly.

The speedway has been around since day one in the Magic Kingdom. It's also been around since the beginning at Disneyland, but there it is known as Autopia. It was also known to be one of Walt Disney's favorite attractions. This ride was even opened in Marceline, Missouri, Walt Disney's hometown in Walt Disney Municipal Park there in 1966. It unfortunately closed 11 years later in 1977. Over the years, in Disney World, the ride length has been shortened due to the construction of Space Mountain and Mickey's Birthdayland which later became Toontown Fair and then an extension of Fantasyland. It has lost over 32% of its original length due to these construction projects. The ride features 146 race cars with a top speed of 7.5 mph. It takes an average of 5 minutes to make the one loop on the track.

You may be able to guess the message here as it's a pretty easy one. This ride is a race, right? They don't tell you it's an official race when you get in the car to drive and sometimes the car in front of you can make it pretty difficult to win. However, you are in a race car and if you've ever driven them before, you know you want to go as fast as you can. You also know you want to get to the finish line before the drivers beside you do, especially if they are family members. This is true of any kind of race. I mean, that's what a race is, right? Have you ever been in a race? Maybe you haven't driven in an official car race, but what about a running race? Have you ever raced your friends or family for fun?

"First one to get there wins!" Have you ever heard that shouted? Why do we race? Maybe because it's fun. It's a competition. It's interesting to see who's fastest and who wins. It's even enjoyable to watch other people race. Some of my favorite Olympic events are the track races. Do you like to race? Did you know that you are in a race right now? Even if you are sitting or lying down reading this, you are in a race right now. Did you know that?

I was a running coach for many years coaching middle and high school Cross Country for 16 years. During that time, I Corinthians 9:24-27 became one of my favorite passages. It reads, "Do you not know that in a race all the runners run, but only one receives the prize? So run that you may obtain it. Every athlete exercises self-control in all things. They do it to receive a perishable wreath, but we an imperishable. So I do not run aimlessly; I do not box as one beating the air. But I discipline my body and keep it under control, lest after preaching to others I myself should be disqualified." So what does this passage mean? It basically means that life is a race. We are all running this race called "life" to get the prize. What is the prize? It's better than any medal or money you might win at an earthly race. The prize is Jesus. The prize is eternity with Him. Paul makes a famous quote in 2 Timothy 4:7 when he says, "I have fought the good fight. I have finished the race. I have kept the faith." Philippians chapter 3 also talks about pressing on toward our goal and obtaining the prize. We are in a life-long race and if we keep working hard and pressing on, the prize will be unimaginable. It will be so worth the fact that the race itself will be difficult. As challenging as it may be, I urge you to work hard to stay in the race because Satan tries to make you quit, give up or get disqualified.

Next time you visit WDW, check the line and try a spin on the Speedway. Race those cars! Have fun! Beat the other guys! Win! But remember the more important race of life and win that one too! It's much more important, so don't give up no matter what happens!

DEVOTIONAL #36

"Astro Orbitor"

Two more attractions to go, not just in Tomorrowland, but in the entire Magic Kingdom. Today we are heading in a new direction. Not left. Not right. Not even straight forward. We're heading up! We're getting on an elevator to ride this ride. I think this is the only ride where you have to ride a ride to get to the ride. (Was that confusing or what?) Ok, so you just have to ride an elevator to get to this ride, but today we're going to ride those spinning planes that you see hovering above Tomorrowland. Let's go take on the Astro Orbiter!

The Astro Orbiter used to be known as Star Jets when it first opened in Disneyland and WDW. It opened at WDW in 1974, three years after the park opened. It is a rotating ride similar to Dumbo and Aladdin's Magic Carpets, however this ride has a unique advantage. Because it is directly above the TTA, and you have to ride an elevator to get to it, it provides a wonderful view of Tomorrowland and the entire park for that matter. The ride does 11 rotations per minute and averages 1.2 million miles a year! Wow! The ride itself is based on drawings by Leonardo DaVinci made almost 5 centuries ago. While the ride may seem like it's hundreds of feet in the air, it's actually only about 60 feet or six stories high. The ride is not for those who may be afraid of heights or get motion sickness easily. This is a ride our family typically doesn't do just because the line is nearly always long. That being said, if I ever see it with a short line, which is rare, I'll do it. It's a great view if nothing else and I enjoy it. That is, I enjoy it as long as I keep my head straight. The first time I rode this a few years ago, I remember turning around and looking back several times. When I did that, the motion started to get to me.

So what's today's lesson with the Astro Orbiter? Boarding this ride, you'll notice that you are actually not in a plane as I mentioned earlier. You are in a rocket. I've always said that I would actually enjoy getting into a real rocket and traveling into space. I'm not sure my stomach would like it, but I think that would be an adventure of a lifetime to be able to soar high above the Earth. When you get in one of the rockets of Astro Orbitor, you expect to go fast, and you do. You expect to have a thrilling ride, and you do. You expect to feel the wind as you travel, and you do. Maybe you also expect to go somewhere, but you don't. I mean you're in a rocket for crying out loud! Rockets are supposed to go fast and travel great distances, right? Unfortunately, these rockets are an exception to that rule. They just keep going in circles. When the ride is over, you realize that you are right back where you began. I mentioned earlier that those rockets travel over a million miles a year, but they don't really go anywhere. Isn't that amazing? Isn't that like life sometimes?

Sometimes on our spiritual journey, we have really good intentions. We have goals, dreams and aspirations that we are going to go far. We have an aim of doing great works, making a real spiritual difference and pleasing God. We're going to get in our spiritual rocket and travel straight to God. No stops. No detours. Unfortunately, even with these good intentions, we sometimes end up right where we started, no closer to God or maybe even further away. Something gets us off track or stands in our way and we just travel right back where we started. Consider these verses from Colossians 3:1-5, "If then you have been raised with Christ, seek the things that are above, where Christ is, seated at the right hand of God. Set your minds on things that are above, not on things that are on earth. For you have died, and your life is hidden with Christ in God. When Christ who is your life appears, then you also will appear with him in glory. Put to death therefore what is earthly in you: sexual immorality, impurity, passion, evil desire, and covetousness, which is idolatry."

If we truly want our spiritual rockets to make it to God one day so we can be with Him forever, we have to set our minds on Him like these verses say. We can't let any idols cause us to just go in circles and not get anywhere. What a waste of our time and lives! Please believe when I say that God strongly desires for us to come to Him. He loves us so much and His desire is that we follow His ways and spend eternity with Him, but if we only have good intentions, it's not enough. God is not going to just give it to us. He makes that pretty clear. He can't make it that easy or nobody would try and this world would be an even scarier place. We have to work hard for our spiritual reward. We have to work hard to follow His ways throughout our lives. When (not if) we make a mistake and start heading in circles, we have to quickly correct it, accept God's grace and forgiveness and get back in a straight line to Him.

If you can catch a short line or are willing to wait, I hope you get to ride the rockets of Astro Orbiter. I think you'll enjoy the ride. I know you'll enjoy the view, but keep in mind that you won't really go anywhere except around and around. As you ride, consider where your life's rocket is going? Is it going in circles also or is it traveling towards something? I hope that answer is towards God. Keep it heading that way! Don't let it veer off course! You'll be very happy in the end when you finally step out and see you've arrived at the ultimate destination!

DEVOTIONAL #37

"Carousel of Progress"

It's time to head to the last attraction in Tomorrowland and in the Magic Kingdom. As you can guess, the MK has the most attractions among the four parks so we will have spent the most time here. For today, we're going to make some progress. Know what I mean? We're going to ride the infamous Carousel of Progress! I saved this one for last on purpose because it is a very special ride. This unique ride and show combination has quite a famous claim to fame. It holds the world record for the longest running stage show with the most performances in the history of American theater. They'll tell you that fact right after you board and before you start moving. It is also one of the only attractions at WDW to be touched by Walt Disney himself. Most attractions can't make that claim since Walt died before WDW even opened, but this attraction is actually older than WDW itself.

The Carousel of Progress was built for the 1964 New York World's Fair. Walt Disney loved this attraction. It is estimated that he rode it 14 times during his life which ended just 2 years after it was built. General Electric approached Walt Disney to develop a show for the company's pavilion at the World's Fair and Disney was happy to comply. The attraction was then moved to Disneyland for six years until it was moved to WDW where it has remained ever since. It has seen some updates over the years but remains generally the same as Walt left it. When it moved to WDW, GE which still sponsored the attraction asked the famous Sherman brothers to write a new song for the attraction and so "Now Is the Time" was written and stayed in the show until 1993. It was then that the attraction was no longer sponsored by GE and decided to bring back its original song to many veterans' (including the Sherman brothers') delight. The new version of the original song, "There's a Great Big Beautiful Tomorrow," had a more contemporary feel and remains in place today. The nearly 21 minute show has six stages, can hold up to 240 guests, and has 8 characters in 4 scenes. The other 2 stages are used for loading and unloading.

There are many more fun facts about this attraction, but let's talk about the point of it all. The reason Walt Disney loved this attraction so much was that it defined him and what he was all about...progress. Walt

Disney's life theme was progress, and he worked hard to improve and better the world around him. The Sherman Brothers even noted that the song "There's a Great Big Beautiful Tomorrow" and its lyrics defined Walt. If you've ever ridden this attraction, you know that as you go from scene to scene, more progress is made throughout the 1900's and beyond. Progress is a good thing. Like Walt, we should always seek to make progress and to make things better. It's a good idea to set goals to better ourselves, our families, and our work so that we don't remain stale in what we do. So what about you? Have you made progress in your life?

Isaiah 43:18-19 tells us to not remember the former things, nor consider the things of old. It then says, "Behold, I am doing a new thing." In 2 Corinthians 5:17 we read "if anyone is in Christ, he is a new creation. The old has passed away, behold, the new has come." If we are truly following God and have become a new creature in Christ through baptism and by following Him, we are making progress. We are putting away the old and becoming new. That's what progress is! So I ask again...are you making progress? Some people, including myself, have trouble with progress or change. We tend to like things the way they are and are hesitant to make changes. However, when it comes to our relationship with God, change and progress can be a good thing if we are trying to better ourselves. Are you trying daily to grow closer to God? You can always improve your relationship with Him. Are you trying to study His Word to learn more about Him and His plan for your life? You can always learn more about Him and His plan. Are you sharing the good news with others so they can also become new? There is always someone that needs help, encouragement, or just to hear about God. God calls us to make progress and change ourselves and others for the better. We can't become stale in our spiritual lives. We can't remain lukewarm. Read Revelation 3 starting with verse 15 to see what God says about that. We have to constantly work hard to make ourselves better and improve ourselves. All of us, me included, have something (and probably many things) we can do better.

I do love the Carousel of Progress. It's another one of the classics that I love to do each time. There have been rumors of this ride shutting down in the past, but I sincerely hope they just remain rumors. This ride is too special, and just the fact that Walt loved it so much and had a hand in it makes it worth keeping. It's nothing spectacular. It's quite simple, but it's Walt Disney wrapped up in a 20 minute stage show. It sums up the message he taught. That message is that progress in this world is important. I choose to take that message further and say that it's not just important to make progress with the things of this world, but definitely in our own spiritual lives. So have you made progress today? How can you make progress tomorrow? Think about that!

DEVOTIONAL 38

"Happily Ever After"

We've now done all the Magic Kingdom attractions, rides, and shows, but hang on for one more entry. The Magic Kingdom needs 38 devotionals because there's one more thing we need to talk about. It happens every single night in fact at the MK. It puts a perfect exclamation point on my day in the park every time I visit. Happily Ever After!

Happily Ever After is the spectacular show complete with music and fireworks that takes place every night at Cinderella Castle. It is a popular show that draws in massive crowds. This show debuted in May of 2017 replacing Wishes that had been the nightly show since 2003. Wishes had replaced Fantasy in the Sky, another nightly show that began when the park opened. Happily Ever After runs 18 minutes and includes projection directly on the castle as well as lasers, lights and many pyrotechnics. It also includes a wide range of characters and music from numerous Disney films. One of the most impressive parts of this show is the projection mapping on the castle. Disney promised (and delivered) that it would be the most advanced projection ever seen. While they had projected video on the castle before like a giant movie screen, the projections now seem to fit architecturally to the castle making for a stunning and awe-inspiring visual display. Just like its predecessor show Wishes, this show is highlighted by Tinkerbell flying from the castle across the park toward Tomorrowland. Tinkerbell has actually been flying across the park in the nighttime show for over 30 years. She made her debut in 1985. Currently, she flies 850 feet for less than 30 seconds. She is typically played by a woman, but there is one case where a petite male played the role. There are a total of 3 Tinkerbells available just in case something happens to the first one. Each one cannot weigh more than 95 pounds (there goes my chances!) in order to make the flight as her battery pack and costume increase her weight to 140 pounds on average. Tinkerbell is required to take the elevator to the castle suite each night and then climb a ladder to the appropriate window. A Disney cast member meets her and gets her in the harness. At the proper time, the cast member gives her a good push to try and get her to fly all the way to the landing pad behind Main Street. If Tinkerbell doesn't make it with one push, she turns off her battery pack to go dark and must pull herself the rest of the way. It is estimated that the nightly show costs around $50,000 each night in fireworks making Disney the largest consumer of fireworks in the world.

So why is this show called Happily Ever After? Disney is all about happiness. It is often called the "happiest place on Earth." Disney is also known for being a "magical" place where all your dreams can come true. In the same way, this show was designed to bring people together, to have families stand together and enjoy a fantastic show, as well as to end the night with a very happy experience. That's the dream of Disney...to bring people together to have a magical time and experience their "happily ever after." That's what makes them come back, right?

So what would make you truly be able to live happily ever after? Disney claims that it can make all your dreams can come true. Can all your dreams and wishes actually come true? I could ask the old classic question made famous in Disney's Aladdin film...if you had three wishes, what would you wish for? What if you just had one wish? Would it be money, fame, a giant mansion, long life? Mark 8:36 says, "For what does it profit a man to gain the whole world and forfeit his soul?" In other words, there is no point in wishing for anything of this world like money or fame because those things are all just temporary. It's not worth giving up your soul! If you truly had one wish, I hope you would share the same wish I do. I would wish for my soul to be with God forever and have my family with me. Well guess what? That wish can come true. It won't be granted by Disney but it can be by God. The Bible tells us several times that we can know we have salvation with God. The Bible also talks about our wishes. In John 15:7 we are told that if we abide in Christ and let His words abide in us, we can ask for whatever we wish and it will happen. A chapter earlier in John 14:14, Christ tells us that we can ask for anything and He will do it. While on Earth, God will give us what we ask for at His discretion. Sometimes He says no, but we have to trust that He knows best, listens and considers every request we make. Best of all, He will give us our true happily ever after of Heaven in the end if we follow the steps He's laid out for us.

I love the show Happily Ever After. There have been a couple of times that due to exhaustion, we chose to skip it, but I don't like missing it. It is a wonderful way to end the night at the Magic Kingdom. It is a memorable experience that makes you feel a sense of excitement and euphoria. In addition, it reminds you of all the wonderful Disney films with happy endings. Let's keep in mind that all we really need to be happy is eternity with God. Everything else will pass away eventually. The next time you see the show and enjoy the fireworks, thank God that He is forgiving and has promised us eternity through His grace and love. With that assurance, how could we not be happily ever after?

DEVOTIONAL #39

"The Monorail"

Now we're officially done with the Magic Kingdom! It took us 38 devotionals which is over 1/3 of this book. The MK is truly an attraction-filled park. However, there are other great parks a-waitin'! So now where should we go to? Epcot? Animal Kingdom? Hollywood Studios? Well, before we go anywhere, we have to get there, right? So let's consider how we should travel to our next park? I think we should take another very important "ride" at WDW. We can't just skip over this very important part of WDW. Technically, it's an attraction too! We have to talk about it, discuss it, learn about it and yes, make a devotional thought from it. So I'm sorry, but the next park will have to wait one more entry. Today, we are going to talk about the infamous Monorail!

The Walt Disney World Monorail was built in 1971 along with the Magic Kingdom. When it was first built, there were two lines: a resort line and a line directly to the MK. In 1982, the Monorail was expanded and added a line to Epcot. Today, there are still the three lines with six stations and twelve trains. It is estimated that 150,000 Disney guests ride the Monorail daily with 50 million riders each year. The total length of all the tracks is 14.7 miles. The average speed of the Monorail is 40 mph with the top speed at 55 mph. Each Monorail train still has a pilot in the front cab, but they are fully automated and the pilot doesn't control the train anymore like they used to. There has only been one fatality on the Monorail taking place in 2009. One of the pilots was killed when the pink and purple monorails collided. Since that day, families are no longer allowed to ride in the front car. The pink and purple trains were retired and have not returned. Starbucks even had to change its Disney mug which showed the purple monorail moving through Epcot. The phrase you hear each time the doors close, "Please stand clear of the doors. Por favor, manténgase alejado de las puertas," has become somewhat of a famous saying for Disney fans.

I love the Monorail. To me, riding it means I'm truly there at Disney World, and I feel so happy when I'm on it. Depending on where we stay, we don't always get to ride it. However, I'm always up for leaving the park or making a special restaurant reservation just to get a chance to take a trip on the Monorail. It just one of those unique Disney things that everyone has to do! What lesson can we learn from this iconic "train?" The lesson I thought of is based on the whole purpose of the Monorail. Why was it built in the first place? What purpose does it serve? I think it was built to get people from one place to another much faster. Let's face it…if you do want to leave the Magic Kingdom and travel to Epcot, depending on the time of day and the crowds, it is probably faster to take the Monorail; especially as opposed to finding your car, driving, parking and traveling to Epcot that way. While it doesn't always work out, it was definitely built to be a faster form of transportation and typically tends to be. What about our life journey? What is our purpose here on Earth? Where are we trying to get to? What's the fastest way? Think about that.

I hope we could all agree that our purpose in life is to get to God. We are to use the blessing and time of our earthly lives to prepare ourselves for Heaven and take as many others with us as possible. So how do we get there? What's the fastest way? Have you ever heard what John 14:6 says? This is a verse we should all know and share with others. In it Jesus says, "I am the way, and the truth and the life. No one comes to the Father except through me." Another famous verse, John 3:16, reminds us that if we believe in Jesus, we will have eternal life. So according to the Bible, the fastest way which is the only way to get to our Father in Heaven is through His Son, Jesus. We have to know Jesus, follow Jesus, love Jesus and live like Jesus. If we do those things consistently throughout our lives, then we'll be on the Monorail to Heaven.

Take a ride on the Monorail if you have the time. Listen for the famous saying when the doors are about to close. I think I can finally say it right. Enjoy the smooth and quick ride as you view Disney World out the windows. At the same time think about our quick journey. Life on Earth is so short compared to our future in eternity. The question to ask is…where are you going? Are you on the fastest route? Are you truly going through Jesus to get to God? Make sure you are. Thank you Jesus for giving us and showing us the Way!

DEVOTIONAL #40

"Epcot"

Exiting the monorail, we are now at my favorite of the four parks... the Experimental Prototype Community of Tomorrow, or EPCOT. Just like we did with the Magic Kingdom, let's spend some time today talking about Epcot in general before we actually explore inside.

Epcot opened on October 1, 1982, exactly 11 years to the day after the Magic Kingdom opened. This new park was opened on 300 acres making it more than double the size of the Magic Kingdom. It is currently the third most visited theme park in North America and the sixth in the world. It is sometimes referred to as a permanent "World's Fair" as it celebrates culture with interactive exhibits often showcased. The main icon of this park is hard to miss. It looks like a giant golf ball and sits front and center as you enter the park. It's actually called Spaceship Earth and we'll talk more about it later. This park was actually called Epcot Center until 1994. At that time, the name was changed to Epcot 94. For the next several years, the year would follow the name until they dropped that idea and just called it Epcot. As I mentioned earlier, Walt Disney envisioned Epcot as a city, a home to 20,000 people complete with businesses at the center and neighborhoods on the perimeter. He saw the main form of transportation to be monorails and people movers. There would be cars allowed but only below ground so as to keep all pedestrians safe. This was a real dream of his, and he tried very hard to get the project going. He was told he had to get the Magic Kingdom up and running first before he could secure permission and funding for Epcot. Unfortunately, as you know, he died before the Magic Kingdom was opened so his dream of Epcot never really became a reality. Disney executives did not want to go through with his exact project without his guidance and expertise. Therefore, they adapted and came up with an alternate Epcot that would hopefully be a little more practical for Orlando guests and honor Walt's vision at the same time. It took an estimated one billion dollars to build Epcot and at the time was the largest construction project in the world. On the day it opened, a family was surprised and presented with a lifetime pass to Epcot and the Magic Kingdom. What a gift! On that day the park was dedicated and water from all the major rivers of the world was poured into the fountain found behind Spaceship Earth. The park is divided into two main sections: Future World which contains most of the rides and attractions and The World Showcase which contains pavilions for 11 different countries around the world. It is said that there is currently space for 9 more although it is unsure if Disney will ever add additional pavilions. There have been rumors from time to time of adding Puerto Rico, Russia, Switzerland, Costa Rica, Spain, Venezuela, United Arab Emirates and Israel.

As you head into Epcot, you can find a plaque that was placed at the dedication. It reads: "To all who come to this place of joy, hope and friendship, welcome. Epcot Center is inspired by Walt Disney's creative genius. Here, human achievements are celebrated through imagination, the wonders of enterprise, and concepts of a future that promises new and exciting benefits for all. May Epcot Center entertain, inform and inspire. And, above all, may it instill a new sense of belief and pride in man's ability to shape a world that offers hope to people everywhere."

Notice that it says Epcot is a place of joy, hope and friendship...three qualities that are very welcoming and Disney can take pride in. For today, let's talk about those words in relation to our spirituality and what we find about those words in Scripture. The Bible speaks of joy as one of the fruits of the Spirit in Galatians 5 meaning that the Holy Spirit fills us with joy when we become his child. Scripture speaks of hope in Romans 12:12 when it tells us to rejoice in the hope we have through Christ Jesus. Finally, Jesus himself talks of friendship in John 15 when He says we are His friends if we follow His commands. He also says He no longer calls us servants but friends. What a wonderful blessing to be called a friend of Christ! However my favorite verse regarding these qualities is found in Romans 15:13 when Paul says "May the God of hope fill you with all joy and peace in believing." It has two of the qualities in just that one verse: hope and joy. Our God is a God of hope, and He fills us with joy. He sent His Son to us to be a friend and show us the way to reach Him. There are many other verses in the Word about all three of these qualities. Can you name any others?

Epcot is an outstanding park. As I mentioned, it is my favorite, although it is a very close race. One thing I love about Epcot is I tend to discover something new every time I visit. Having visited there many times, I can say that it truly is a place of joy, hope and friendship. I also know that our God is a God of those qualities too, as well as many others. We are so blessed to be His children. We are so blessed to have these qualities as a part of our lives. Make sure to thank God today for giving us these things.

DEVOTIONAL #41

"Leave a Legacy"

Now that we've entered Epcot, where are we heading first? While it may seem obvious to Disney veterans (most likely heading to one of three very popular attractions), we're going to continue to wait on any rides because there is actually something else you come to first when walking into Epcot. If you've been to Epcot, you probably know what I'm talking about. It's all those silver metallic-looking things sticking up with thousands and thousands of pictures and faces on them. Just what are those things? Have you ever wondered? It's called Leave a Legacy, and I think they are worth a devotional thought today.

Leave a Legacy began in the fall of 1999 as part of the millennium celebration and gave guests the opportunity to purchase a small square on one of 30 granite megaliths. The megaliths range in height from 3 to 19 feet, and the heaviest ways more than 50,000 pounds. The same man who designed the Epcot icon Spaceship Earth also designed this display right in front of it. The Leave a Legacy program continued until 2007 when it was ended for an unknown reason. Altogether 500,000 of the possible 700,000 spaces were sold meaning there are many blank spaces on the display. Guests could purchase a photo with one person for $35 or two people for $38. Guests were assured that the photos would be on display for at least 20 years which means the monoliths will be there until at least 2027. Many guests would like them to disappear sooner as they don't like the look and wish Disney would replace it with something more eye-appealing. Personally, I don't mind the display and like the idea but just wish you could still participate. I would love to be a part of this monument at what is a relatively reasonable price.

So what's the message from this Leave a Legacy display? You can probably guess the lesson from this one. It's right in the title. I think this is the only devotional where the name of the attraction is also the spiritual message. What does it mean to "leave a legacy?" What's your definition of legacy? A legacy is what people remember you by. It's the impression you leave behind on others. What is your legacy? Nobody wants to think about this, but what if you left this Earth today? How would you be remembered? What would your legacy be? In Psalm 78:4, we read that we are to tell the coming generations of the glorious deeds of the Lord. In another Psalm (145), we are told that one generation shall commend God's works to another. In many verses of the New Testament, we are told to teach and preach to others. In other verses, such as I Timothy 4:12, we are told to set a good example and live like Jesus. If we do these things, we will leave an impacting legacy for others to remember. Helping others to know God and His Son because of our example and teaching is a great legacy to leave behind!

Next time you walk speedily (no running! Ugh!) into Epcot, don't stop at Leave a Legacy. It's too important to get to that first ride, especially if you are there at park opening. Instead take some time later in the day, maybe as you are leaving the park to check it out. Look at how many people paid to get their faces on those monuments. Disney made some pretty good money there! Those people wanted to leave just a small part of themselves at Disney World. I understand that because I'd love to do the same. More importantly, I want to leave an impression on others that I come in contact with...and not a small one, but a very large and important one. I want them to know the fact that I follow God and try to live like His Son, Jesus, every day. That's the best way to leave a legacy!

DEVOTIONAL #42

"Spaceship Earth"

Unless you are staring at your shoes as you walk, which I strongly advise against, you have no choice but to stare at one of the largest icons at WDW. That big ball! What is that thing? The "Epcot Ball" as some affectionately call it, is actually called Spaceship Earth. It does look like a giant golf ball, right? It's visible from far away, even from your plane to and from Orlando if you look closely. A lot of people just assume it's just an icon or a fancy decoration. In fact, we have some friends that just passed it by for the longest time because they thought it was nothing, but it's definitely so much more than that. It's an amazing attraction and one of the most creative ever done by Disney in my humble opinion. It also happens to be one of my favorites. I know you're shocked since I say that quite a bit. Normally I probably wouldn't ride it first because there are some very popular rides we would need to get to before the lines get crazy. However, since we are right here and this is a virtual walk through the park, let's go ride Spaceship Earth!

Spaceship Earth was built as the Epcot park was built and opened with the park on October 1, 1982. Contrary to many first-timers' beliefs, it IS a ride and a pretty long one at that. The ride lasts 15 minutes and is a walk through history with a look at the future as well. The entire attraction is narrated and has been hosted by such famous voices as Walter Cronkite, Jeremy Irons and currently Judy Dench. The entire structure is 180 feet high and its foundation pylons are sunk into the ground up to 120 feet. Spaceship Earth is the largest free-standing sphere in the world and weighs 16 million pounds. Even at that size, it's not the largest thing at Epcot. Any idea what that is? The fact is that the entire sphere of Spaceship Earth could fit inside the main tank at The Seas pavilion! More about that later. At one point during the ride, your car turns around backwards and you can see the planet Earth up above. It's at that point that you are at the very top of the sphere, nearly 180 feet in the air. Think about that next time you ride. This giant ball took more than 2 years to build and was designed so that rain never runs off of it and falls on anyone. Instead, rain is channeled into a drainage system that actually directs the water into the Showcase Lagoon in the park. From 2000-2007, there was a giant Mickey hand holding a wand put on top of the sphere to celebrate the millennium. A lot of Disney veterans didn't like this addition and were happy when it was taken away.

As I mentioned, when you ride this attraction, you are taken on a ride through history. You start with thousands of years into the past and are slowly taken all the way up to the present. As your ride vehicle turns around and goes backwards back to the start, you are also shown a short video about what your future might hold, complete with your actual face in the video (one of our family's favorite parts). So here's a question for you to think about today...what if Spaceship Earth was a ride about you? What if everyone got to see your history as they rode, starting with your birth up to the present. Then as they rode back down, they got to see a video of your future. Wouldn't that be a fun ride? You might be thinking that would be scary instead.

Think about your past. Would you want others to see it? The truth is that there's nothing you can do now to change that part. Your past is done. There may be some things in it that you don't like or wouldn't want others to see, but it's there and luckily no such ride exists for others to see your past mistakes. Disney's technology isn't quite that advanced, at least not yet. However, what about the future part? That's the part we need to focus on. What will your future hold? When you ride Spaceship Earth, they give you a guess of what your future might be. The truth is that nobody, but God, really knows what's in your future. The great part is that you get to decide. You will determine what your future holds. Jeremiah 29:11 is a great verse in Scripture. God says, "I know the plans I have for you...to give you a future and a hope." God gives us hope for the future. He gives us free reign to determine our earthly future and what it will look like. Philippians 3:20 also tells us that our citizenship is in Heaven. We are only here on Earth for a very short time and are to be preparing for Heaven every single day. Therefore as we plan and determine our future here on Earth, it should also include preparation for our eternity.

Would you want to ride Spaceship Earth if it really showed your true future? When you ride it next time, think about what your future might look like? Have you thought about it? At this very moment as you are reading this, you still have the chance to make your future a great one. You have the opportunity to plan a future that includes staying on the path with God, telling others about Him and making sure you are destined for eternity with Him. Don't make your future, which will soon be your past, a ride that you wouldn't want others to see. Make it a story that you would be proud to display. Make it a journey that will influence others and cause them to want to follow you to God. That will be a history and future worth seeing and one that you and God will be proud of!

DEVOTIONAL #43

"Test Track"

Now that we've ridden the "big ball," which way do we go? Disney veterans know that we basically have a three-way choice here. There are three very popular attractions at Epcot that most people flock towards. One requires a left turn into Future World, one a right turn, and the final means we head straight towards the World Showcase. It's debatable which way is best, but our family typically chooses to make the left turn into what is called Future World East, so that's where we're headed today. Let's go ride Test Track!

Test Track is an amazing ride and a one of a kind to be sure. At the same time, its line can get very long, very fast. It also tends to break down more often than some of the other rides. For these reasons, we typically try to get to this one early in the day or even first. Why is Test Track so popular? Like I said, it's very unique as well as an adventurous thrill ride that can be enjoyed by just about anyone of any age. Test Track opened in Epcot in 1998 and was sponsored by General Motors. When it first opened, the premise was that you were basically a test dummy and were testing out new cars for brakes, weather conditions, speed, etc. In 2012, the ride went down for an 8 month long refurbishment. The whole concept and back story of the ride was changed, however the actual track did not. I'll admit that I wasn't happy about the changes at first, and it took some getting used to. As time has passed however, I have come to the conclusion that I definitely like the new version better. In the new version, sponsored by Chevrolet, you get to design your own car and see how it scores during the tough road conditions. It's become a sort of competition to see who can design the best vehicle. Our family always enjoys the friendly contest to see who's car can rank the highest.

Test Track holds some records at Disney World. It is the fastest attraction on property with a top speed of 65 mph. It is also the most expensive attraction ever with a whopping $300 million spent in all including refurbishments. In case you're curious, second place goes to Radiator Springs Racers in Disneyland at a $200 million price tag. The final record for Test Track is that it is the longest attraction in terms of track length at 5246 feet, only 34 feet short of a mile. Each Test Track car is designed to last one million miles. Wouldn't it be nice if our cars would do that? Every year, the cars travel an average of 50,000 miles. Originally, Test Track was intended to go 95 mph but was revamped for safety. This ride does shut down if lightning is detected within 5 miles due to the outside portion of the track. The cars reach their top speed of 65 mph in 8.8 seconds.

Many Disney guests would say that this is their favorite ride at Epcot and maybe in all of WDW. It is actually my second favorite at Epcot. If you know Epcot, you can probably guess my first. (More on that later!) One of the reasons I personally enjoy this ride so much is what the ride changed to in 2012. I do think it is very clever to be able to design your own car and see how it does. It's a challenge and makes you really think, strategize and plan in the short 3 minutes or so that you have to construct it. It's also a lot of fun to compete against others to see who can build the best car. The more we ride it and try out new things, the better our cars become. Over the years, we have learned some tricks and secrets to make our cars perform even better. You can also search online for some great tips.

What would be a good lesson from this attraction? It's fun to try and build the best and highest scoring car, but luckily we don't have to do that in life. We don't have to build the best car to do well with God, right? However, we do have to build something else in our spiritual lives. We have to build the best Christian! Part of living a Christian life and following the plan of God is to spend time each day building ourselves. We have to build our moral character. We have to build our influence on others. We have to build our reputation, mission and purpose. We have to spend actual time and thought making sure our lives are following the steps that God and His Son, Jesus laid out for us. We will never be able to build a Christian that is perfect, but if we keep working and learning ways to improve, we can acquire some secrets and strategies to make ourselves even better. Read Romans 5:1-5. In these verses, Paul gives us a list of how to build ourselves into a proper Christian. He gives us some vital components we need such as perseverance, character, and hope and explains how gaining those things make it easier to obtain the next quality. Galatians 5:22 adds some other assets we need in the infamous list of the "Fruits of the Spirit."

Most people I know enjoy Test Track. The next time you ride, you may find it difficult to build the perfect car, and you may be disappointed with your score. Keep in mind though that it's just a ride. What you should be more concerned about is the kind of person you are building right now in yourself. How does that perform? What score would God give your design? Do you need to get rid of or replace some components? Work hard to build the perfect Christian. You won't ever reach perfection but that's what we should strive for (Hebrews 6:1). You can always improve so don't ever stop trying!

DEVOTIONAL #44

"Mission: SPACE"

In reality, coming out of Test Track, we would most likely run all the way across Future World to ride one of the two other very popular attractions. However, since we are already over on this side of the park, let's go ahead and ride the other attraction over here. This one happens to be right next door and is called Mission: SPACE. Personally, I have mixed feelings about this ride. When it first came out, I tried it, and you can probably guess what happened if you've read the "tea cups" devotional back at the Magic Kingdom. My body just doesn't like to spin and does this ride ever spin! However, a few years later, they made a major adjustment on this ride and made it more tolerable for wimps like me.

Mission Space opened in 2003 at Epcot replacing a beloved attraction, Horizons that many still miss and talk about to this day. There are actually some hidden tributes to Horizons throughout this attraction. It took 650 Imagineers the equivalent of 40 years of time to develop the ride having to invent a lot of the technology. The LRV (Lunar Rover) suspended from the ceiling inside is on loan from the Smithsonian in Washington DC. According to Disney, it is the only LRV built by NASA that isn't on the moon. While riding Mission Space, you experience 2.5G of force which means your body is feeling more than twice the force of gravity. There is a little controversy surrounding this ride as two people have died after riding it, although both had pre-existing conditions. One was a 4 year old boy with an undiagnosed heart condition. The other was a 49 year old woman who had high blood pressure and suffered a stroke. Because of the controversy and the number of people reporting nausea and sickness, Disney made a change in 2006 and began offering two options. There is now the orange team which is the original ride with intense spinning, but there is also a green team option that offers no spinning. Your enclosed vehicle still moves and sways, but doesn't spin providing a less intense experience. I'm all about the green team! I typically don't do simulators well spinning or not, but I decided to give it a try a few years ago. I actually enjoyed it and was able to tolerate the ride. However, I don't think I could do it more than once a day. It is quite claustrophobic, and the vomit bags sitting in the compartment in front of you don't exactly provide much comfort.

As I mentioned, there are now two versions of the ride. There is the orange intense version and now the green less intense version. This gives more people the option of trying the ride even if they tend to get motion sickness like myself. That leads me to our thought for today. This orange vs green choice you have to make when entering the queue of Mission: SPACE has a similarity to our lives. We have choices in life that ultimately lead to our eternity. We can choose the green team and take the easy route. A lot of people choose this simply because it's easier and less intense. It's not as difficult to deal with and is more comfortable. This is called the wide road in Matthew 7:14, a verse we have talked about before. However, we are told to stay on the narrow way in that same verse. This is the orange team. Yes, it's more intense and challenging. Yes, you are going to have to work hard to accomplish it, but if we want our Heavenly reward, we must do what we are told and follow God's ways at all times. If we mess up, we must get right back on the narrow way. It's the way we must take to win the prize that God has promised us. Like I mentioned, unfortunately a lot of people choose the easy way. They let life's pleasures rule their lives and choose to spend a majority of their time indulging in things that move them further and further away from God. Proverbs 14:12 talks about this when it says, "There is a way that seems right to a man, but its end is the way to death." Additionally, I Corinthians 10:31 tells us that whatever we do, we should do it all to the glory of God. So are you doing that with each choice you make? Do you consider God and ask His help in every decision you make, especially the big ones in life. Or do you take the easy way out, doing what's fun or what you see others doing even though it may be leading away from God?

If you're brave next time, try out Mission: SPACE. Maybe you don't even have to be brave. Maybe you live for the intense spinning simulation. However, it's also okay to choose the green team if you want. I'll be proudly in the green line. It may be the wiser choice for your health after all. When it comes to life, however, and the decisions you make, don't choose the easy way out. Choose to follow God at whatever cost. You'll be so much happier in the end if you do.

DEVOTIONAL #45

"Soarin' Around the World"

There is a third ride coming to this side of the park where we currently stand. Disney has announced it will be one of the longest, enclosed roller coasters in the world and will be based on the hit films from the *Guardians of the Galaxy* series. However, as of this writing, construction has barely broken ground so we don't quite know enough about it yet to make a complete entry. Therefore, we'll move on and head over across the park to Future World West! There are a few notable attractions here that we need to discuss. We're going to start today with my very favorite attraction in all of Epcot. That's not an easy decision to make. I like Test Track a lot, and I'm pretty sure my family puts it in first place. However, I give the nod to this incredibly creative attraction we are discussing today. Let's go ride Soarin' Around the World!

Soarin' is a very creative attraction that has many positive elements including the music, the video, the smells, and the height. It opened in 2005 replacing an attraction called "Food Rocks," an animatronic stage show that ran from 1994-2004. Soarin' opened first at Disneyland but was so popular they decided to bring it to Florida even though the original film was made all in California. It enjoyed even more success in Orlando upon its opening. In June of 2016, a new version of the film opened with an improved quality film and a new soundtrack. This new version is now officially known as Soarin' Around the World because the film now has scenes all around the Earth as opposed to just California. The Imagineer who conceived this ride used his child's erector set to build a model of what the ride would look like. It was the first of its kind and used a unique but creative system to raise people between 40-45 feet into the air. If you listen carefully, you will hear references to flight 5505 during the pre-show. This is a nod to May 5, 2005 (5/5/05), the date that Soarin' first opened. There are a couple of notable hidden Mickeys during the film. The first is during the hot-air balloon scene. Watch carefully for three balloons coming together at just the right time. The other one is near the very end of the film and uses fireworks and the infamous Spaceship Earth to form a classic hidden Mickey. This is the most popular attraction at Epcot and recently added a third theater to accommodate more guests per hour.

If you've ever ridden Soarin', you know the classic ending of the film. After 5 minutes of scenes from all over the world, where do you end up? Back at Epcot! Back home! The film takes you all over the globe but ends up back home in the park where you are. I enjoy traveling all over the world on our "flight" but I love that you end up back in the Disney parks at the end. The old California only version of the film did the same ending at Disneyland. It's a great ending. It's familiar. It's home, and that is where our devotional thought centers today.

Our lives here on Earth are like that great film in Soarin'. We travel to so many places in life. While we may or may not end up living in different places throughout our lives, our lives inevitably have so many paths. We meet new people. We form new relationships. Each person's life brings new jobs, new houses, new experiences and new adventures. The film about our lives would include many different scenes as well. Even though we each travel so many different paths throughout our lives, the amazing part of our film is that the endings can all be the same. At the end of our films, we can all end up in the same place, home!

Once again, the message is Heaven. According to Scripture, we are all heading in that direction if we stay on the path that God has directed us. Matthew 25:46 tells us that the righteous will go on to eternal life. Read II Corinthians 5:1-10 as well. It talks about how life on earth is temporary like a tent. I remember when I used to coach Cross Country that one time I set up our team tent only to have it totally bent and destroyed by a strong wind. It was frustrating, but I had to remind myself that all tents are temporary. God tells us our lives are the same. In James 4:14, it reminds us that our lives are just like a mist or vapor. They appear for a short time and then vanish. However, just like Soarin', we can all end up back home at the end and it will be permanent. Heaven cannot be destroyed like that tent. It will be forever. That's hard for us as humans to comprehend, but it's true!

I love Soarin' a lot! I think you will too. I recommend requesting a front row seat. The cast members will always accommodate your request. That way you don't have anybody's legs dangling in your view, and you get to go the highest of anyone. If you are like me, you will feel a "magical" and euphoric feeling up there as you get to experience amazing scenes, smells and music. It is a wonderful experience with a wonderful ending which is home. Make sure that your life has the same ending. Make sure that your ride is heading in the right direction and that the last scene will be God's house with the room He's got saved for you. What an incredibly happy ending that will be, and I want you to be there with me!

DEVOTIONAL #46

"Living with the Land"

We just rode the best ride at Epcot, in my opinion though some will disagree. Since we are here in the Land Pavilion getting off Soarin', we might as well ride the attraction right next to it. It's not quite as exciting as Soarin'. Actually some might think it quite boring, especially the kiddos. However, I have grown to really enjoy this attraction as well. It's called Living with the Land and is a very informative boat ride through several different rooms with numerous interesting sights.

Living with the Land was originally called Listen to the Land and opened with Epcot in 1982. As mentioned, it is a boat ride each of which can hold up to 40 people as each vehicle is technically two boats tied together. Up to 1600 people can ride this attraction per hour although it rarely has a crowd like that. Most of the time, you can get on this ride pretty quickly even if there is a decent line. As you begin the ride, you sail under the Garden Grille restaurant and see a farmhouse scene with several audio-animatronic animals. Notice the "82" on the mailbox. That is a nod to the opening year of Epcot. The animatronic dog in the farmhouse scene is the same type dog that you'll see in the Carousel of Progress and the jail cell scene in Pirates of the Caribbean at Magic Kingdom. Many agree that this is the same type of dog that Walt Disney himself had. This ride used to have live cast member guides that rode in the front of each boat and talked to you throughout similar to Jungle Cruise. However, in 2008, Disney got rid of the guides and provided recorded narration along the way. As you ride, you may see some park guests walking throughout the greenhouse. This is called "Behind the Seeds" and is a fairly cheap tour that you can do. We have done it twice now and it is well worth the price. We enjoyed it both times and learned a lot.

I like Living with the Land for several reasons. It is a nearly 15 minute ride that is very relaxing. It is also very informative, and I tend to learn something new each time I ride. It is quite fascinating to see the actual plants, foods and animals that Disney is growing through their research and study. Every time we go, there seems to be some new plant or crop that is being grown with very interesting results. It's also amazing to me that Disney uses most of these plants in their actual restaurants there on property. The attraction always makes me think about good, fresh-tasting food, fruits and vegetables. It makes me think about farming and people that work very hard every day to grow the foods we eat. It also makes me think about God.

Genesis 1:11-12 reads "And God said, 'Let the earth sprout vegetation, plants yielding seed, and fruit trees bearing fruit in which is their seed, each according to its kind, on the earth.' And it was so. The earth brought forth vegetation, plants yielding seed according to their own kinds, and trees bearing fruit in which is their seed, each according to its kind. And God saw that it was good." God planned farming from the beginning. He planned how we would grow our crops and produce food for ourselves. He even showed the first man, Adam how to tend to the garden and support himself and his wife. Farming was the original job you could say, and God planned it all. In Genesis 1:29, God says, "Behold, I have given you every plant yielding seed that is on the face of all the earth, and every tree with seed in its fruit. You shall have them for food." Farming is a gift from God. It is a responsibility and privilege that he provided for us. We need to remember that and be grateful for it.

I encourage you to ride Living with the Land and learn as much as you can. Listen to all the amazing facts about growing food, harvesting crops and raising fish. It's really pretty fascinating. Also remember that all of it is a gift from God. He has provided for us and always takes care of our physical needs. Remember Psalm 85:12 when we are told "Yes, the Lord will give what is good, and our land will yield its increase." Say a prayer of thanks to God for our blessings and for making our short time on Earth so enjoyable with the ability to provide for ourselves. It's all part of God's amazing and perfect plan!

DEVOTIONAL #47

"The Seas with Nemo and Friends"

Let's head out of the Land Pavilion and take a left. There are a couple of attractions in what is generally known as Seas Pavilion. This pavilion formerly known as The Living Seas housed the largest saltwater aquarium in the world when it first opened in 1986. It has since lost that record as bigger aquariums have been built, but it is still an amazing sight. The pavilion also houses two attractions and a restaurant. Today we are going to ride a very simple but popular attraction based on the movie *Finding Nemo* and officially known as The Living Seas with Nemo and Friends.

The Nemo ride as we'll call it to make it a little easier replaced the Living Seas ride that opened in 1986 with the pavilion. This pavilion was planned with the construction of Epcot in 1982 but wasn't fully completed and opened until four years later. At that time, guests could board what were known as "seacabs" and travel along the aquarium floor after riding down in fake elevators called "hydrolators." In 2007, Imagineers replaced the seacabs with clam-mobiles and re-themed the ride after the popularity of the movie *Finding Nemo*. It is said that Spaceship Earth, a.k.a. the "Epcot ball," could actually fit completely inside the aquarium. It remained the largest aquarium until the one in Atlanta, GA was built. The six million gallon aquarium houses 8500 creatures and guests can watch feedings twice a day. Only the sharks are fed after hours at night with a special light so they won't feed on the fish during the day. Guests can also pay extra to snorkel, scuba dive, or swim with the dolphins. There is a private room behind the aquarium that is used for cast members and private parties, such as weddings and special occasions. It has an amazing and spectacular view of the aquarium and even houses a glass piano. The Nemo ride itself is a trip through the famous movie and can accommodate 2200 guests per hour as it is on a continuous moving track.

Have you seen *Finding Nemo*, the movie? It's another Disney hit, a great movie and great story. In fact, the Finding Nemo show in Animal Kingdom, also based on the film, is one of my favorite shows in all of Disney. The movie is obviously about the clownfish Nemo and how he gets lost and separated from his father. The rest of the movie is about his journey to find his way back home to his dad. If you can't figure out the lesson from this story, you may need to go read Luke 15 and the famous Biblical parable. This movie, while probably not based on this well-known parable of Jesus', is very similar. In that chapter of Luke, we actually see three parables of Jesus based on something or someone being lost...a sheep, a coin and a son. Jesus' main point in all of these stories is that God rejoices when someone who is lost finds their way back to Him. It doesn't matter how lost we've gotten, how much we have sinned or how far away we've strayed, God is always there waiting with open arms to welcome us back. He is just like the father in the Lost Son parable as well as like Nemo's dad in the movie.

This is by far my favorite parable of Jesus because it represents so much hope. Isaiah 53:6 tells us that we are all lost. It says we are all like sheep that have gone astray. Jesus talked about lost sheep in one of the three parables and how God and Heaven rejoice when a lost sheep is found. The Nemo ride is simple. I actually wish there was a little more to it. It's still fun and a nice peaceful, entertaining ride through the story. When I ride it next time, I'm going to try to remember Nemo's story and how happy he and his dad are when he finds his way home. I'll also remember how happy God is when I come back to Him anytime I'm lost, and how He is always there waiting with open arms. Remember that you can never be too lost that you can't find your way back to God. Never! What an awesome God!

DEVOTIONAL #48

"Turtle Talk with Crush"

As I mentioned in our last devotional, there are actually two attractions in this Sea Pavilion. Some people may not realize this. It took a few years for my own family to visit the other one. We tended to skip this second attraction for whatever reason. I finally gave it a shot on a more recent trip and am glad I did. Yes, it's geared towards children and may not be an attraction you visit every trip, but it's worth doing at least once. It's called Turtle Talk with Crush.

This attraction first opened at Epcot in November of 2004 again after the popularity of *Finding Nemo* movie a year earlier. The attraction has since spread to several of the Disney parks, the Disney cruise ships and even a children's' hospital in California. I also had the pleasure of experiencing this on our Disney cruise a few years ago, and it was very creative and entertaining. In this attraction at Epcot, children typically sit up front while adults sit in the back. Once everyone is seated, Crush comes out on the screen and actually talks to the audience. Based on the kids' reactions and questions, different plots and endings can be triggered. This attraction can be very popular at times and a fastpass may actually be the best bet. In fact, just five days after it opened in 2004, it had to be shut down because of the crowds that would gather. The Imagineers had to move it to a bigger location within the pavilion and re-adjust the lines. The ride contains some scripted moments but also obviously contains some improvisation based on what the kids in the audience do. The hidden voice of Crush is backstage and can see the kids and their reactions at all times. The advanced technology used makes it look like Crush is saying whatever the actor backstage chooses to say. Crush has his own language and tends to pick the most energetic kids that raise their hand first to be a part of the show.

As I mentioned before, I had the pleasure of seeing a portion of this attraction on a Disney cruise a few years ago. While it wasn't the full show by any means, we did get to experience Crush coming to our table via a screen nearby and actually talking with our sons. He asked them what they did that day and when they told him they'd been to Atlantis, a waterpark in the Bahamas, he said, "Wow! You guys found Atlantis! They've been looking for that for years!" It made us laugh and was a pretty neat experience to have him interact with the boys and actually hear what they were saying.

Isn't it neat to have a projection on a screen actually hear you? I found it fascinating that Crush could actually talk with you and listen to you? Technology is pretty amazing. Want to hear something even more amazing? There is someone else who is also always listening to you and always hears you. He can always talk with you also. He's ready and waiting when you need Him. I'm talking about God of course. I John 5:14-15 tells us that God always hears us and will listen to whatever we ask for. John 9:31 tells us that God doesn't listen to sinners but only the godly that do His will. Proverbs 15:29 says that God is far from the wicked but hears the prayers of the righteous. You may be thinking, "But I'm a sinner!" Well, I am too. We all are, but if we are trying to do what is right and actively seeking God, I believe that He hears us when we are genuine in our prayers.

How often do you talk to God? I mean really talk to God! I don't mean just before a meal or in passing, but how often do you really spend time conversing with Him and listening to what He says back to you through His Word? How often do you just stop and thank Him for all that you have? I remind you that I Thessalonians 5:17 tells us to "pray without ceasing." He's ready, waiting, and listening to whatever you have to say. Just like Crush, he will respond to whatever you say. He will answer. It may not be immediate, and He may not always give you the exact answer you are hoping for, but He will answer! It's such a wonderful blessing to always have someone to talk to no matter where you are. It's even more of a blessing to know that He is listening to you even though you are just one of his many, many children. Take time right now to talk to God. Make it a daily habit and set aside some real, dedicated prayer time. Take advantage of that gift He's given us!

DEVOTIONAL #49

"Journey into Imagination with Figment"

We've done both attractions here in the Seas Pavilion, but take some time to just enjoy the aquarium as well. There's so much to see and learn. After that, let's head over across Future World West to what is called the Imagination Pavilion and visit the last two attractions in this area. Today we are going to do the one that is an actual ride. It's a pretty simple ride but a personal favorite of our family, especially my wife. She has been visiting Disney longer than I have and has pretty much been every year of her life and then some. She's got me beat with close to 60 visits throughout her life. She personally loves this ride and insists we ride it every time, which I don't mind obliging. It's called Journey into Imagination with Figment!

This is another basic ride where guests board a tram-like vehicle for transport into a Science Lab to study the body's five senses. Along the way, the tour is "interrupted" by Figment, a small, purplish dragon who keeps messing up the planned tour with his own agenda. This ride has had three names over the years but has always kept a similar format. From 1993 to 1998, it was known as simply Journey into Imagination. From 1999-2001, it was called Journey into your Imagination. Finally in 2002, it was changed to the current version which included Figment in the title. The current version includes the song *One Little Spark* which was written by the famous Sherman brothers. This is one of three Disney attractions to emit a foul odor, a skunk in this case. Can you think of the other two? One is the Bugs' Life film at Animal Kingdom. The other is Stitch's Great Escape in the Magic Kingdom. The first version of this ride included a human character named "Dreamfinder." When the ride was changed in 1999, many were sad to see this character go and still hold grudges to this day that he hasn't returned. The ride also uses a notable butterfly illusion that guests tend to remember. It used to be that the butterfly would appear from nothing when your car passed by. Now the butterfly disappears when you pass. This illusion is done with a mirror in the middle that is invisible to riders.

I do enjoy this attraction. It's simple but creative and fun. As I mentioned previously, it takes you through a science lab to study the five senses. You only get to experience three of the five before the tour is "cut short" by Figment, but let's think about all five of the senses for a second. Can you name them? They are sight, smell, taste, hearing and touch. How can we apply those five senses to our spiritual lives? Easy! The Bible actually talks about all five of our senses and how we should use each of them to worship the Lord our God. Consider the following verses:

Psalm 34:8—"Oh, TASTE and SEE that the Lord is good; blessed is the man who takes refuge in Him!"

I John 1:1—"That which was from the beginning, which we have HEARD, which we have SEEN with our eyes, which we LOOKED UPON and have TOUCHED with our hands, concerning the word of life."

Ephesians 5:2—"And walk in love, as Christ loved us and gave himself up for us, a FRAGRANT OFFERING and sacrifice to God."

There are many other verses we could look at, but the point is that we can worship and follow God using all five of our senses. Consider these questions:

Do you LOOK for God in all you do?

Do you LISTEN for God each day?

Do you USE YOUR HANDS to do the work of Christ and serve others?

Do you SMELL for danger and try your best to avoid sin?

Do you use your mouth to TASTE how sweet God is and tell others about Him?

The Figment ride is quite unique. It definitely has some surprises, some that are pleasant and some not so much. It also definitely makes you consider and use the five senses God gave you. We use these five senses every day repeatedly to survive and live a fulfilling life. Next time you ride, consider if you are using those same senses to their fullest extent to worship God. Make sure you are doing just that. Additionally, consider that even though our heart isn't one of the five, make sure you are also giving your full heart to God. That's where He belongs and that's where He will be if we use all five senses to truly know God and invite Him into our lives!

DEVOTIONAL #50

"Disney and Pixar Short Film Festival"

Let's stay put in the Imagination Pavilion because there's another attraction we can tackle here. Actually, after you ride Figment, it's fun to stay and play with the variety of exhibits in the pavilion. Our boys have always enjoyed this creative and interactive area. Once you've done that, you can take just a short walk to the theater that's in this pavilion and enjoy a fantastic film. Actually, it's a group of three films. Today we're going to view the Disney and Pixar Short Film Festival.

This attraction takes place in what is called the Magic Eye Theater. I had to dig deep to find that name as I've never heard anyone call it that. This theater has hosted several notable 3D and 4D films (which includes smells, water sprays or the like) throughout the years. The theater opened with the park in 1982 with a film called *Magic Journeys*, a piece that looked at the world through the eyes of a child and featured music by the Sherman brothers. In 1986, this film was replaced with the well-known *Captain EO*, a film starring Michael Jackson and directed by Star Wars creator George Lucas. This film, although not the best production ever created (actually it was pretty bad) was very popular among certain audiences and had what many would call a cult following. In 1994, the film was once again changed to *Honey I Shrunk the Audience* after the movie of a similar name did so well. Over time, this theater was visited less and less as the movie popularity gradually wore off. In July of 2010, after Michael Jackson had died unexpectedly, Imagineers brought back *Captain EO*. Recently, in December of 2015, the film was once again changed to what it is today, a film festival featuring three of Pixar's best short films now produced in 3D. The three films periodically change so return guests can see new ones.

While I enjoyed the *Honey I Shrunk the Audience* film back in its day, I was quite glad that *Captain EO* had finally finished its run. While I'm a Michael Jackson fan, that production was less than stellar and I don't miss it. However, I really enjoy Pixar's short films. I have seen many of Pixar's short films, and there really hasn't been one I didn't like. I also like how this theater brings them more to live with 3D effects that are well done. While I'm not sure they are showing it currently because they rotate the short films here, at one point they showed what is my favorite short film that Pixar has done. It's the one called "For the Birds" and I strongly suggest you go on YouTube or a similar site and check it out if you've never seen it. It's short and sweet, but a funny and meaningful story. It is also the subject of our devotional thought today.

Again, go watch it first if you haven't seen it. This devotional will be a lot more meaningful. Plus I'm about to give away the story (spoiler alert!) In the film, there are many little birds sitting on a power line minding their own business when a giant, loud and fairly unattractive bird squeezes his way in between them. The little birds are annoyed and begin to make fun of the big bird. They try desperately to get rid of him because he's different. I guess I won't spoil the ending, but I'll just remind you of the old phrase "what goes around comes around." We are all different. God made us that way and what a blessing it is! As I've mentioned before, it would be quite a boring world if we were all exactly the same. Take some time to read I Corinthians 12. That passage reminds us that we all have different gifts. We were all given different qualities and talents by God, but we are to use what God's given us and work together to form one body which is the spiritual body of Christ. Romans 12:3-6 also reminds us of this. Everyone has something to bring to the table. We should appreciate that and thank each other for each person's specific gifts. The body of Christ, His church, can't survive with just one person. It takes many of us to form that one body.

Many of the Pixar shorts have good messages. I encourage you to watch them all, and I hope Disney continues to rotate through them in this attraction. For now, my favorite is about a bunch of birds and how they learn about being different. Being different is all a part of God's plan. Work hard to see and appreciate the differences in those around you.

DEVOTIONAL #51

"Mexico Pavilion"

We've now completed the Future World half of Epcot so now we need to venture over to the other half of the park. When I was a kid, this was the boring half. It just seemed too educational with no excitement or thrills, and I was happy to avoid it. Well, I guess I'm becoming one of the old people now because I really enjoy this half which is known as World Showcase. Additionally, to Disney's credit, they have gradually over the years made this area of the park into an appealing journey through various cultures with a variety of activities and options for all ages. I feel like it's a lot more alluring to even children now than it was during the decade it first opened. We're going to use the next series of devotionals to travel "around the world" and talk about each land or country represented. The entire journey is a 1.2 mile walk through eleven different countries. One may choose to go either direction around the world but we are going to go clockwise for our studies. We'll start in Mexico!

The Mexico pavilion is unique in that it is all encompassed in one building. It is not quite as spread out as the other World Showcase pavilions tend to be, although there is a lot packed into that one building. This pavilion was built with the park and opened in 1982. It resembles a Mesoamerican pyramid with the many steps that you may have seen in pictures or several locations throughout Mexico. Luckily, you do not have to climb all those steps to get inside as most of them are fake and not for guests use, despite what at least one guests thought (more about that later). At the top of the pavilion, there is a hidden room that is one of the major control areas for Illuminations, the nighttime closing show of Epcot. Inside the pavilion you will find the San Angel Inn, a restaurant that is based on another restaurant that has been operating in Mexico City for over 100 years. This is one of only two pavilions in World Showcase that includes a ride, although at the time of this writing, there is another ride planned in the France pavilion in the near future. Currently, the Gran Fiesta Tour is a simple boat ride that takes guests through Mexican culture as you follow the adventures of the Three Caballeros, Panchito, Jose and the star of the show, Donald Duck. This version of the ride with the three ducks replaced El Rio de Tiempo (which means the River of Time). This was the original ride that lasted until 2007 when it was updated. It was pretty much the same ride but did not include the animations of the Three Caballeros. This ride was originally going to have an outdoor portion but did not get completed on time. Because they wanted to open this pavilion with the park in 1982, they had to cut up to 40% of the planned ride.

As I mentioned earlier, the outside of this pavilion resembles a Mesoamerican pyramid with many steps. In November of 2015, a man decided to try and climb the pyramid. He was quickly detained and escorted from the park. If you look at the design of the building, it bears a slight resemblance to a structure in one of the famous stories of the Old Testament. Do you know which story I'm referring to? In ancient Mesopotamia, the people used to build what were called ziggurats, huge step-like buildings used as temples to their gods. The Mexico pavilion resembles this design. There actually is one of these ziggurats in the Bible. Check out Genesis chapter 11 if you need a reminder of the story. In that chapter, the people attempt to build a giant step-like building all the way to God. They want to be equal with God and build this structure for all the wrong reasons. God foils their plan by creating languages and making it impossible for them to communicate. In Philippians 2:6, we read that even Jesus himself did not consider equality with God something to be grasped. Even Jesus knew He could never be equal with God. We should remember the same and respect the authority and holiness of God. God is to be esteemed, feared and loved. We are not His equal. We are His children, His servants and His creation. The Bible makes that quite clear.

Take some time to explore the Mexican pavilion. Eat in the restaurant where you can sit by the water and watch the boats peacefully go by. It's a beautiful setting. Enjoy the fun boat ride with the Three Caballeros. Take some time to appreciate this unique and important country and learn about their culture. As you enter, note the design with the steep steps and pyramid shape. Don't try and climb them. It won't end well. It didn't end well in Genesis for the people trying to build a similar structure to God. Don't try to be God's equal or "climb those steps" to Him. Don't boast in your relationship with God and appear to others as anything but a humble servant. Respect that God is our Father and He is in charge. Have an attitude of humility towards Him as His Son, Jesus did. That is the best way to grow closer to Him and to rightfully be one of His children.

DEVOTIONAL #52

"Norway Pavilion"

Continuing around the circle of the World Showcase, we come next to the Norway pavilion. If there was someone who had no idea what countries were represented at Epcot and you asked them to guess, I'm assuming that Norway most likely wouldn't be in their top choices. I don't know about you, but I don't typically think of Norway when listing popular or well-known countries or those most visited by tourists. However, once you spend some time exploring this pavilion and the history behind it, Norway just might become an interest of yours. It's a fascinating country that I wouldn't mind visiting for real after experiencing this pavilion.

Norway's pavilion did not exist when Epcot opened in 1982. It was added later in 1988. In fact, it was the last pavilion added and one of only two funded by the government of the home country. (Morocco is the other.) Disney actually wanted all of the pavilions to be funded by their own governments when Epcot was originally being designed and planned. However, most countries were not interested in funding their pavilion not knowing how popular these pavilions, and quite frankly the whole park, would be. Therefore Disney decided to instead get sponsors for each pavilion. However, when Norway was later added, the Norwegian government agreed to fund part of the construction with Disney's assistance. In fact, the day it opened and was dedicated, the crown prince (now king) of Norway came to the opening and the dedication was broadcast on national TV in his home country. The pavilion is staffed by 130 cast members from Norway who each sign a contract to work between 6 and 12 months. This is similar to what most of the World Showcase pavilions do. The pavilion itself is designed to look like a Norwegian village. The main restaurant there, Akershus, is named after a restaurant in the capital city of Oslo. Norway is the other pavilion besides Mexico that currently has a ride. The original ride, Malestrom, was a boat ride through the history of Norway. In 2016, it was replaced with Frozen Ever After, based on the movie *Frozen* which took place in Norway. The huge success of that film led Disney to make this fairly quick change. The new ride used the same track as the old ride but was refurbished to include scenes and music from the famous movie. There also used to be a large Viking ship in front of the pavilion which was used as a playground for children. This however was removed in 2008.

While I enjoyed the original ride in this pavilion, Malestrom, I would agree that it needed updating, and I didn't mind them throwing a little Frozen into it. Some people strongly disagree and miss the old ride. I understand that, but I enjoyed the movie *Frozen*. Did you see it? I guess a better question would be did anyone NOT see it? I felt it was a good story with good messages. Did you know that the Bible talks about being frozen? Well, not exactly, but it does talk about ice and snow. I've never been to Norway, but I know that much of the country is above the Arctic Circle. Take a look at Norway on a map and you can see that it can get very cold there. I don't like being cold. I would much rather be too hot than too cold. What about you? I enjoy winter for a short time and then I'm ready for spring very quickly. However, we are to be reminded that winter, ice and snow is a gift from God. In Job 37:6-10, we are told that God makes ice and snow and we are told of His power. Do you remember Queen Elsa in the movie? She was terrified of her power to change things to ice. She tried to hide it. However, once she "let it go," she created much beauty with it. In the end, she learned that her power was a gift and a blessing. That's how God is. He can turn something that we might see as scary or harsh into something beautiful. Just a couple of years ago, we got nearly a foot of snow and ice and many were complaining and worried about it. However, once it all settled and we really took some time to view the frozen world, it was extremely beautiful and a blessing.

Ecclesiastes 3:11 reminds us that God has made everything beautiful in its time. You may not like the cold and snow like me, but you have to admit that the frozen world can be beautiful. The next time you visit the Norway pavilion, think about the beauty of God's creation and thank Him for all the seasons. Even though winter may not be your favorite, it can be a welcome and picturesque change from the hot summer. Once again, it would be a boring world without the changes He provides. His creation is truly a blessing!

DEVOTIONAL #53

“China Pavilion

So now that we've explored Norway, let's head to a slightly warmer climate all the way across to a different continent. Well, actually at Epcot, it's right next door to Norway. That's what makes the World Showcase so amazing! You can travel from one country to another and virtually around the world in just a few steps. Next on our journey is China! China is a place I have always wanted to visit. It's on my bucket list you might say. When I used to teach World History to sixth graders, we would end the curriculum each year talking about China, and I remember so much interesting history from this most populous country. The China pavilion at Epcot is no different. I have explored the pavilion some, but I know that there is so much more I could see and learn here. I look forward to doing just that on our next trip. In researching the pavilion for this devotional, I found many reviews stating that China is the most beautiful and has the best recreations of any of the other pavilions.

China was one of the original pavilions created with the opening of the park. While there is no ride, there is a movie in a large 360 degree theater. The film shown is called “Reflections of China” and contains images collected over a 25 year period. Those viewing this film get to see some of the more familiar Chinese sites such as the Great Wall, but also get to see some lesser known areas of China. You do have to stand during this film and some have been known to get motion sickness because of the movie being all around you. Apparently the trick is that if this happens to you, just look down at the ground for a few seconds and you will be ok. The China pavilion contains some great restaurants, exhibits and even the performance of Chinese acrobats from time to time which is an amazing act. There is a cart nearby called “The Joy of Tea” that sells more than just tea. They also serve ice cream and frozen slushies of various flavors that come highly recommended. I haven't had those yet and definitely need to try them! You can meet Mulan at this pavilion, the star of the popular movie of the same name. That's another great Disney movie with a great story.

Today, I want to focus on one of the more beautiful parts of this pavilion. There is an exquisite and peaceful Chinese garden on the property with a large structure at the center. The structure is called the Temple of Heaven. If you go inside this temple, the acoustics are very impressive. You can stand in the center and hear whispers from all around the room. Try it next time! There are also great reviews of these gardens and temple saying how peaceful they are. It is a great place to explore for some quiet in the midst of what can be a hectic park with many visitors. It may just be what you need in the midst of your crazy day at Disney.

Isn't this just like what we are promised in our eternal future? The kingdom of Heaven in the middle of peace! This world is a blessing and God gives us many gifts in it. However, it can be loud. It can be chaotic. It can be scary and troublesome. We are actually told that in Scripture. However, keep in mind what we have to look forward to. We are promised the Kingdom of Heaven one day because of the sacrifice of our Lord and Savior Jesus Christ. That being said, Psalm 4:8 reminds us that while on Earth, God gives us peace and safety when it says, "In peace I will both lie down and sleep; for you alone, O Lord, make me dwell in safety." However, we are also told in John 16:33 that trouble in this world is inevitable but that Jesus has overcome the world. That is our promise and hope of peace for eternity in Heaven. Romans 14:17 actually tells us that Heaven is a place of peace. Because of Jesus, we will one day have that garden of peace with the Kingdom of Heaven all around us forever! Won't that be incredible! I can't wait!

If you have time on your next visit to Epcot, give a few minutes to explore China. Visit the garden. Take a deep breath. Close your eyes. Thank God for the quiet, beauty and peace you are experiencing. Visit the Temple of Heaven and imagine what your eternity will be like one day in the real Kingdom of Heaven. Listen to the whispers and hear the voice of God promising eternal life to us if we follow His plan. Thank Him for the hope we have through His Son. Yes, you will no doubt have troubles as long as you are living, but you will also have the knowledge of what is to come. Thanks God that the best is yet to be!

DEVOTIONAL #54

"Germany Pavilion"

Continuing our clockwise trek around the world, we come to Germany next. What do you know about Germany? If you're like me, the answer is "not much." Germany is a European country that I'm just not as familiar with as compared to some of the others. As always, however, you can definitely learn a lot by visiting the German pavilion at Epcot. So let's do that today!

The Germany pavilion was opened with the park in 1982. The original design of this pavilion called for another boat ride. This ride would take guests on a tour of the famous Rhine river that runs through Germany. This ride would've been similar to Malestrom, the old boat ride in the Norway pavilion. There would've been detailed miniatures of famous landmarks in Germany. The ride was part of what was called "phase 2," but unfortunately, due to time constraints, phase 2 never happened. The building where the ride would've been was built and is now used as a workshop, for float storage, and for cast member rehearsals. The pavilion itself is designed to look like a German town. Germany is known for being home to the Brothers Grimm who wrote many famous fairy tales including Snow White. For this reason, you can often find the famous princess greeting guests at her wishing well there. There are no attractions at this pavilion, only a couple of restaurants and shops. There is however a very large miniature train that was built for the flower and garden festival several years ago. The train was intended to be temporary, but was kept due to its popularity. I do enjoy just sitting and watching the train. It's an elaborate set with much detail included. The next time you visit this pavilion, pay attention to the clock tower. On the hour, two figures will come out and ring the bell. Many guests don't know about this and don't even notice this interesting touch. One of the restaurants at this pavilion, Biergarten, is known to have very good food and also daily celebrates Oktoberfest, a famous German festival. If guests are in the restaurant at the right time, they can enjoy music and participate in dancing there.

It sounds to me like Germany is yet another pavilion that I need to spend some additional time exploring. I have visited it just briefly and tasted a pretzel from there, but that's about it. I would like to eat at some point at the Biergarten restaurant because I've heard many good things about it. Like so many of the other pavilions, I do wish it had an attraction. Most of the countries in World Showcase at least have a show or film. This is one of the few that has nothing at all. I wish they had gone ahead with their original plan to have a boat ride along the pretend Rhine River of Germany. I realize they were trying to get these pavilions up and running for the park's grand opening, but I wonder why they didn't add the ride later. I assume funding was probably another issue. It just seems to be that there was so much potential here that never got realized. This brings me to my thought for today.

What kind of potential do you have? Are you living up to and realizing your full potential? Galatians 6:9 says "And let us not grow weary of doing good, for in due season we will reap, if we do not give up." When I hear people talk about the various pavilions at Epcot, what they did on their vacations, and what they enjoyed, Germany rarely comes up. Think about what it could've been. If they had built this ride there, Germany would most likely be one of the more popular and visited pavilions. Instead, they gave up on the plans. While I guess there may be more to it than that, don't let yourself fall into the same category. Don't ever give up on your potential to do good and serve others like Jesus did. Another great verse along these lines is found in 2 Chronicles 15:7 where it reads "But you, take courage! Do not let your hands be weak, for your work shall be rewarded." While we shouldn't do good things just to be rewarded, this is a great reminder to not give up on what we can do. We (myself included) often make the mistake of underestimating ourselves. We get lazy and tell ourselves or others that we are doing our best when we really could do more.

Don't get me wrong. Germany is still a fine pavilion that is well done. I truly do want to explore it more next trip. I just can't help but think of the potential it had to be more. Think about your potential. What are you truly able to do? A better questions...what has God called you to do? Are you doing all that you can? Are you living up to your full potential? Evaluate yourself daily and try to add to what you are doing or do something new to serve God and others. Remember the words of Joshua from the first chapter of his Bible book, "...Be strong and courageous. Do not be frightened, and do not be dismayed, for the Lord your God is with you wherever you go."

DEVOTIONAL #55

Italy Pavilion"

Moving on from Germany, we continue on to the next pavilion. We are almost to the very back of the park and have walked over half a mile to get here. We next come to a country that I am particularly fond of. During the summer before my senior year in high school, I had the opportunity to travel to Europe for the first time in my life when we visited Italy. It was my first time overseas. It ended up being the trip of a lifetime, one I will never forget, and one that I thoroughly enjoyed. I'll always remember my trip to Italy which happens to be the pavilion we are talking about today.

Italy of course is a very popular country in Europe and gets many tourists each year. Italy has so many wonderful cities, monuments and famous landmarks to visit. I remember fondly visiting Venice, Milan, Florence, Pisa and of course Rome among many other amazing places. Traveling into the Italian pavilion at Epcot may not be exactly like visiting the real thing, but you can certainly get a taste of Italy from this beautiful attraction. The Italian pavilion opened with the park and just like Germany, was originally designed to be much bigger and include a ride. Phase 2 of this pavilion also called for a boat ride. It was to be a gondola dark ride as if you were in Venice. You would have traveled through Roman ruins during your ride. However, again due to money and time constraints, the ride never happened. For a long time, there was a wall at the back of the pavilion where the ride would've been with nothing behind it but empty space. However in 2010, the pavilion did add a restaurant called Via Napoli in this space that has become quite popular. This restaurant is famous for its amazing pizza, even though pizza technically didn't originate in Italy. This is a common misconception. Via Napoli actually imports special water from Pennsylvania to simulate authentic Italian pizza dough. There are three main ovens in the restaurant that represent the 3 active volcanoes in Italy. Check out the ovens next time you are there. You will notice that each one represents the face of a god that their volcano is named after. There are no real attractions in this pavilion, but you can meet Pinocchio from time to time as his movie was set in Italy. This pavilion is known for its great food including the gelato, a much-loved Italian treat. You can even purchase a gelato sandwich that is said to be very good. There is a famous juggler, Sergio, who is also a comedian. He performs daily and uses audience participation in his show. Outside and in front of the pavilion, there are authentic gondolas in the water. These gondolas are not for use and the public can't board them, but the bridge over them makes for what is probably the best view of the water and the Illuminations show in the park.

One of my favorite parts of my trip to Italy back in high school was visiting the city of Venice. This is one of the most beautiful cities I've ever seen. What I remember most about this city was that the streets are made of water! You don't really need a car to get around. You take boats, gondolas to be exact, to get to wherever you want to go. I'll never forget my first gondola ride. I remember being amazed traveling down the "streets" in this boat. It was truly an amazing sight. It reminds me of some other streets that will be amazing. While streets of water are impressive and different, imagine traveling down streets of gold. One day you can! In Revelation 21:21, John is describing Heaven and tells us that he saw the great street of the city and it was a street of gold. He describes it as "pure gold, like transparent glass." Take some time to also read Revelation 22:1-5. It continues to describe how beautiful Heaven will be and even says we will get to see the face of God! Don't you want to see this glorious place? I know I do very badly.

Italy is beautiful. Many other cities there, such as Florence, are described by many as some of the most beautiful cities in the world. The Italian pavilion at Epcot is also beautiful. It is a good reminder of the real thing. However, all of that pales in comparison to what Heaven will be. I'm going to Heaven, not just to see how beautiful it is, although that is certainly something I'm looking forward to. More importantly, I'm going to see my Father and His Son who saved me by giving up His life on that cross. Please join me there! Make sure your life is on track to be there one day. We can all walk down those beautiful streets of gold for the rest of eternity!

DEVOTIONAL #56

"American Adventure"

So now we come to the very back of the park and to the center pavilion. We've made it to America, the best pavilion in the whole park and the whole world for that matter! Ok, so maybe I'm biased. Maybe I have too much pride in my country. Maybe I'm actually lying because unfortunately, I don't think this is the best pavilion. I think it's good, and some may consider it the best, but I think it could be so much better. Let's explore the American pavilion today and see what it does have to offer.

The American pavilion is a colonial style building that does stand out among the other pavilions in the fact that it is a fairly large building. It's actually a 5 story building but forced perspective and the way it was designed make it look like it's actually just 2½ stories. There were 110,000 bricks used to create this structure. There was much debate among designers just how this building would look and where it would be. Originally, the American pavilion was going to be a grand structure at the front of the World Showcase sitting between it and Future World. It was going to be a two story building. The actual pavilion would've been mostly on the 2nd story while the 1st story would've been a huge gateway into the World Showcase. After much thought and discussion, it was decided that this might make America look too showy by overshadowing the other pavilions. Therefore, it was decided instead to put it at the very back but in the center of all the pavilions and built on higher ground than the others. The American pavilion has no ride, but it does have a well-known and popular show called The American Adventure. As you walk to the show, you ascend stairs in the back hallway of the pavilion. This hallway contains all 44 flags that the USA has ever used. The show lasts 28 minutes and uses around 35 animatronics. There is a computer controlled device called the "war wagon" that runs the whole show and holds all the sets and scene changes. The animatronics actually travel under the audience seats when not in use.

As I mentioned, while I like this pavilion and do have a sense of pride in it, I do think it could be better. I wish there was a ride or even a notable, well-loved restaurant. I wish that it was obviously the best pavilion being that America is the host country and home of WDW in the first place. I do think there are some good things and the show is done well, but I just think it could be better. Being America, our pavilion should be the host and be a little more prominent, not in a bragging way of course, but in a leadership way. This brings me to my devotional thought.

We are all called to be leaders for God. What kind of leader are you? Do you stand a little higher than others? Again, we don't want to lead in a bragging, holier-than-thou way, but there is nothing wrong with being a strong, Christian leader. There is nothing wrong with letting others know who you are and what you stand for through your words and actions. There is nothing wrong with being the "host nation" of Christianity to show others what it means to be a Christian. Jesus certainly did that while He was here on Earth. He led by example. He told it like it is and wasn't afraid to stand up to his critics and enemies. At the same time, He was humble, compassionate and didn't boast about his greatness. I Timothy 4:12 tells us to set an example for others. Jesus showed us what it meant to be a leader when in John 13:13-17, He talked about the fact that to be a leader, you have to serve. Matthew 20:26 also tells us that if we want to be great, we have to be a servant first.

I'm glad America has a pavilion. I think it could be better, but there are some definite good things. I do have pride in our country and am proud to be an American. I'm glad the pavilion attempts to serve as a host and leader for the other nations with its height and central location. I am trying my best to do the same in my own life. I'm trying to be a good example. I'm trying to lead others to God by being a good example and through my actions and words. I'm also trying to become a good leader by serving others as Jesus instructed and did. I can always do better of course, and I invite you to join me in trying to daily lead others to God. It's the mission we were all given.

DEVOTIONAL #57

"Japan Pavilion"

We are more than halfway around the world and are now making our way around the opposite side of the path through the remaining 5 countries. We are now ready for Japan! Japan is another country that I don't claim to know a whole lot about, especially in regards to its history and culture. I do know that Japan is a country with a large population and huge economy. It does have an interesting pavilion at Epcot with several interesting facts I can share. So let's explore this unique pavilion.

The Japan pavilion opened with the park in 1982. While there was never a planned ride originally, there was a show proposed for this pavilion called Meet the World showing the history of Japan. Unfortunately the show never opened. A similar show did open at Disneyland in Tokyo, however one key element was missing. There were some key parts of World War 2 omitted from the show. There is speculation that this is what kept the show from opening at Epcot. Disney feared the omission might upset some WW2 veterans and for that reason, the show was never approved. The show building and rotating platform were built, but never used. At one point, Disney did consider adding a ride at this pavilion. It would've been a ride similar to the Matterhorn attraction at Disneyland in California. However, it would've featured Mt. Fuji, the well-known tallest mountain in Japan. Once again, this ride never came to light. The speculation here is that Kodak, a major sponsor of Disney, didn't want the ride because the Fuji company is a major competitor of theirs. Fuji of course did want to sponsor this ride but was never successful. At one point, there was even talk of Godzilla or a lizard-like creature being featured here. Another consideration was a "bullet-train" attraction where guests would walk through a train and see the Japanese countryside out the widows. The train would then shake and make the guests feel as if they were riding these trains through Japan. The Japanese pavilion features a pagoda that is 85 feet high with five levels. The five levels represent earth, water, fire, wind and sky. For many years, there was a female at this pavilion named Miyuki. She was the only female candy artist in the world and would create animals, flowers and other items out of very hot soft dough that would harden when cooled. She worked at the pavilion from 1996-2013 until her retirement. There is a distinct part of this pavilion that is actually a slight distance away at the waterfront. You'll notice it easily if you look for it. It's called a Torii gate. You can get a great picture of Spaceship Earth through the Torii gate. A Torii gate is a Japanese religious symbol that represents transition from the profane and evil of the world to the holy and sacred. Many Buddhist temples in Japan feature these gateways as you enter. It's a very well-known religious symbol in Japan and is held sacred to many in that country.

So what about Christians? What symbol do we hold sacred? You might say the cross and you'd be right. Many Christians use the cross as their religious symbol having crosses in their homes, churches or around their necks. Whether you have a cross displayed or not, think about the cross for a second. What does the cross mean to you? How much do you focus on it? How much do you talk about it with others? Is it something as sacred and holy to you as the Torii gate is to many in Japan? I Corinthians 1:18 tells us that the message of the cross is the power of God to those being saved. Colossians 2:14 tells us that the cross is so powerful that it has cancelled any debt we owe. Finally, I Peter 2:24 reminds us that Jesus bore our sins on that cross and this means we die to our own sin and are healed of any "wounds" we may have. What a gift the cross is to all people!

The Japan pavilion is another beautiful one. I am happy they can display and showcase their culture including the Torii gate. At the same time, if we are true Christians, we should be proud to show and highlight our most famous symbol. The cross should be a very powerful symbol to us. I personally wish there were more crosses displayed, even at Epcot. Sometimes I am saddened that Christians as a whole aren't bold in their faith and fail to display their beliefs publically. I think a lot of people worry about offending others who maybe aren't Christian, but is that really a good reason to hide the symbolism of the cross? Let's not be a part of the norm. Let's show how much the cross means to us by showing it and telling others about it. Let us never forget what Jesus did for us on that cross. Let us never forget what it means for us and how we now have the hope of eternal life with our Father because of it. That makes it the most important symbol in the world!

DEVOTIONAL #58

"Morocco Pavilion"

Moving on past Japan, we now come to what I would suspect is the most unfamiliar country to most people. It is also the only representation from the African continent. It's the pavilion representing the nation of Morocco. I could ask what you know about this country, but I'm afraid I might just get a blank stare in return. If I'm being honest, I would probably return the stare myself. I really don't know much about Morocco. Ok, I'll be honest. I don't know squat about Morocco. I am glad that Africa gets at least one pavilion. Personally, I would love another, possibly Egypt or South Africa. What do you think? For today, let's focus and learn a little about Morocco.

Morocco was another one of the two pavilions that didn't open with the park. Norway was the other if you remember. Morocco was actually the first expansion pavilion and opened on September 7, 1984, two years after Epcot opened. This is the only pavilion in Epcot where the country's government aided in the design. The King of Morocco actually sent royal craftsmen to aid in the building of the pavilion. It is actually still sponsored by the government of Morocco making it the only pavilion that can make that claim. All others are sponsored by a company. The design of this pavilion is set up to look like a Moroccan city. The lights on this pavilion have religious significance and for that reason this pavilion does not light up during the Illuminations show as do the others. This pavilion has no attractions, but there is a native belly-dancing show that is said to be entertaining. If you view this pavilion from across the water, say from Mexico or Norway, you can actually see the Tower of Terror from Hollywood Studios behind the Moroccan pavilion. Imagineers didn't want this structure to spoil the look of Morocco. Therefore, they had that side of the Tower of Terror made up to look Moroccan as well. At certain times, you can meet Aladdin and Jasmine at this pavilion as their movie was based in Northern Africa. Morocco and the United States are said to have a good relationship, and Morocco was actually the first country to recognize America as an independent country back in the 1700's. If you visit the restaurant called Marrakesh in Morocco, you can see letters from George Washington and the King of Morocco from that time showing this relationship.

Even though this pavilion has many unique features and is a beautiful representation of its home nation, this pavilion is often skipped by park guests. One source even said it may be the least visited attraction at WDW. While I'm not sure if that's literally true or not, it makes sense to an extent. Perhaps the reason is that people simply do not know much about this place. They are unfamiliar with Morocco and for that reason often choose not to visit. They don't get to see that it's beautifully designed with many interesting shops and wonderful places to eat. People might find they actually enjoy this pavilion if they'd just give it a chance. They might just see it as a hidden treasure. Let's talk about treasure today.

Have you ever seen the 80's movie *The Goonies* about a group of kids that find hidden treasure? It's a great film with an entertaining story. The Disney film *Aladdin* also has a large portion about finding hidden treasure. This is what leads Aladdin to the genie in the first place. What about you? Have you ever found hidden treasure? Have you ever seen people on the beach with metal detectors? I always wonder what kind of treasure they actually find. Maybe you've never found a real treasure, but let me suggest that you have access to a real treasure right now! What am I talking about? I'm talking about the Bible of course! God's Word! Hopefully you have a copy. If you don't, please get in touch with me, and I will get you a copy. I'm sure any church can get you a copy as well. It truly is a treasure. After all, it is the guidebook or map that leads us to God. It is the set of instructions for us to know how God wants us to live our lives. Yes, it was written by a bunch of men, but they were very important men, and they were all inspired by God. 2 Timothy 3:16 tells us that all Scripture was "breathed-out" by God. In other words, God literally spoke and approved every word in there. The Bible is the best-selling book of all time by far and will never fade away. The Bible even says that itself in Isaiah 40:8 which reads "The grass withers, the flower fades, but the word of our God will stand forever." Hebrews 4:12 reminds us that the Bible is living and active. I have no doubts that it always will be. It is so valuable and God will never let it be anything other than a true treasure. So do we treat it like the treasure it is? Do we read it often, study it, follow it, live it, and share it?

Morocco is an interesting pavilion to visit. While I have visited, I know there is much more I can learn and see there. I'd like to discover the hidden treasure that this pavilion is. I'd like to see what most people don't and realize the importance of this culture. At the same time and more importantly, I want to demonstrate to others how important the Bible is. God does have a plan that includes eternal life with Him and the Bible shows us the way to obtain that. That is a fact and that makes it very important. Do others around you know about your hidden treasure? It's definitely worth sharing and there is plenty to go around!

DEVOTIONAL #59

France Pavilion"

Heading out of Morocco, we next come to France, the most visited country in the world. It stands to reason that the France pavilion is also visited by a lot of park guests. Let's go explore this pavilion today and learn about some interesting facts.

The France pavilion opened with the park in 1982 and was designed to look like a village in Paris, the capital and most popular city. Obviously the most well-known icon in Paris is the Eiffel Tower so Imagineers decided to put the same icon in Epcot, on a slightly smaller scale of course. The Eiffel Tower at Epcot is a $1/10^{th}$ size replica of the famous tower. The color of the tower matches the color it was when it was first built in the 1800's, not the color it is today. While you aren't able to climb this smaller version as you can in Paris or really even get very close, there is one report that says there is a door at the back of the pavilion marked "Keep Closed." However, if you choose to disobey that rule and open it, you find yourself underneath the tower with a great view. I think I found this door on our last visit but was too chicken to "break the law." Maybe next time I'll live dangerously! While there is no ride in this pavilion as of this writing, there is a ride coming! A ride based on the film *Ratatouille,* which was set in France, is planned to be coming soon. This pavilion does currently have an 18 minute film called *Impressions De France*. This film ranks a little better than the others because you do get to sit down. It is a panoramic style film on five screens showing the landscape and history of France. Of course the famous Disney film *Beauty and the Beast* is also set in France and you used to be able to meet Belle here. However, she has since been moved to the Be Our Guest restaurant at the Magic Kingdom. Now you can meet Aurora from *Sleeping Beauty* instead. There is also a well-loved comedic chair-climbing and balancing show that takes place at this pavilion. In 1990, a very special addition was added between this pavilion and the United Kingdom pavilion which we'll talk about next. In that year, Disney added what is called the International Gateway. This was a new entrance gate into Epcot that is kind of hidden between these two pavilions. It also serves as a waterway into the park much like the English Channel flows between France and the U.K. in Europe. It is this International Gateway that brings us our devotional thought for today.

This new entrance into Epcot opened the doors for a whole new section of Disney. They began building hotels outside this gate along what is today called the Boardwalk. Many of Disney's most loved hotels are now along the water in this circle which eventually leads to another park, Hollywood Studios. Guests can now walk from the Studios to Epcot along this boardwalk, passing many beautiful hotels and enter Epcot in a somewhat secret manner. This park gate is much less used compared with the front gate and serves as a huge advantage to guests of these hotels. This is the only park at WDW that has two entrances. The DCA park in California has a similar situation with a "secret" entrance for guests of the Grand Californian hotel there. This entrance at Epcot is said to have many special things about it. There are special decorations there, especially around holiday times. The lines are always shorter, and the cast members who work this gate often do special things with special traditions. In short, it is another one of Disney's secrets that many don't know about. Check it out next time you are walking around the France pavilion.

Secrets are sometimes very important and often cause problems when they are broken. On the other hand, sometimes secrets cause problems when they are kept. Whether you have secrets or not, there is one thing I hope you realize. God knows any secret you may think you have. Ecclesiastes 12:14 says "For God will bring every deed into judgment, with every secret thing, whether good or evil." God knows everything you do or have ever done. We are told He will bring these into judgment. Psalm 44:1 also says that God knows the secrets of our heart. Romans 2:16 even says God will judge our secret lives. Is that scary? It shouldn't be, but I think all of us have gone through times in our lives where we wouldn't want God to judge us on what we did. I know I have. The good news is that God also promises forgiveness if we are sincere in our asking. The Bible says that God will remember our sins no more in Hebrews 8:12. We have to be really careful about what we are doing behind closed doors when we think we are acting in secret. God always knows. We have to live our lives as if God is always standing right beside us because in reality He is!

Secrets can be good. Disney secrets can be really good and beneficial for those who know them. There are many secrets that you can learn about Disney the more you visit and research. The International Gateway at Epcot is just one of those many secrets. We all have secrets whether they are known or not. If you think you have secrets from God, think again! Trust me when I tell you He knows. If you do have secrets that you know He wouldn't approve of, ask for His forgiveness because He'll give it to you. Additionally, work hard to keep those things out of your life. In the end, you'll be glad you did.

DEVOTIONAL #60

"United Kingdom Pavilion"

We have only two more pavilions in this expedition around the World Showcase. Talking about each of these pavilions and traveling figuratively around the world is really making me want to go back and explore these pavilions with more time and detail. I think there are so many visitors that just don't realize what a treasure this part of Epcot really is and how well done and detailed each of these places are. Today we are visiting the next to last pavilion going clockwise around the lagoon. Get your British accent ready because we are going to spend some time in the United Kingdom today!

This pavilion opened with the park and was designed to look like a traditional British village. Sometimes this pavilion is called the most authentic to the real thing as many natives say they really feel like they are in Great Britain here. While there is no ride or film included with this pavilion, there are some interesting things to see. For example, there is a great hedge maze that kids tend to especially enjoy. There are some beautiful gardens and buildings including a replica of Anne Hathaway's (William Shakespeare's wife) cottage. There is great detail on the buildings here including smoke stains on the chimneys that were hand painted. Another popular inclusion are the realistic looking red phone booths that you will see in the UK. Guests love getting their picture taken inside these booths. You can sometimes see characters here from *Mary Poppins, Alice in Wonderland* and *Winnie the Pooh*. Also, the fish and chips available is among the most popular foods around the World Showcase. Lines for this yummy treat sometimes mirror some of the longest lines for food in Epcot. (I personally love the fish and chips!) There used to be a British Revolution band that mirrored the Beatles but this unfortunately ended in 2011. Now there is a performing group called the World Showcase Players that do comedy sketches and acoustic songs. The cast members that work here are well-known for being some of the friendliest in all of Epcot and even WDW as a whole. There are several documented cases online where they are said to be very kind at carrying on long conversations with tourists. This brings me to my thought for today.

Are you known for being friendly? Do others see you as kind and willing to listen and carry on a conversation? Do you go out of your way to be encouraging and welcoming to others, especially visitors or those who need help or just need a friend? Mark 12:31 reminds us that the second greatest command ever according to the Bible is for us to love our neighbor as ourselves. In other words, we are to love other people just as much, if not more, than we love ourselves. We are to make it a goal in life to love others second only to loving God. Psalm 133:1 tells us that it is good when brothers dwell in unity. And in John 15:13, Jesus says that there is no greater love than friendship, even being willing to lay down our lives for our friends.

How honorable and commendable for the UK cast members to have the reputation for being so friendly. Next time you are there, see if that reputation stands true. Strike up a conversation with one of them and I'll bet you'll get great eye contact, a genuine smile and a great chat. In the meantime, check yourself to see if you are being the best friend you can to others. Make sure others see you as a friend and someone they can go to for a helping hand or a willing ear to whatever their needs are. Jesus certainly gave us a great example of how to be a friend to all, even those who are against us or believe differently than we do. Jesus was a friend to sinners and saints alike. We should try our best to do the same.

DEVOTIONAL #61

"Canada Pavilion"

It's time for our last pavilion of the World Showcase at Epcot. I'm really going to miss talking about these 11 countries. I had actually considered skipping the World Showcase or just doing one devotional for them as a group as I wasn't sure there would be enough information about them. I'm sincerely glad I didn't. I've learned so much and hope you have as well. We started in Mexico, America's neighbor to the south so it's only appropriate that we end in Canada, our neighbor to the north.

The Canadian pavilion also opened with the park in 1982. This pavilion was designed a little differently than the others. It was planned to look like Canada's outdoors as opposed to the other pavilions which tend to focus on the buildings and architecture of their native lands. The Canada pavilion is decorated with beautiful gardens, a giant waterfall, a pool with fountains and totem poles. There are actually three 30-foot totem poles featured. Two are made of fiberglass and one is authentic wood. There is a 14 minute film associated with this pavilion called *O Canada*. Guests do have to stand through this circle vision 360 style film that uses 9 cameras to display a panorama of the Canadian landscape. The film was updated in 2007 and added actor Martin Short as the host and narrator. The Canadian tourism commission wanted this update particularly to remove the stereotypes in the film. Stereotypes also played a role in the building of this pavilion. Disney really wanted the Canadian government to fund the building of this pavilion. However, when the government heard about the stereotypes planned that showed Canadians as lumberjacks, they refused to help with funding. Disney then threatened to pull the pavilion but ultimately didn't and sought out corporate funding instead. At times, you can see characters here from the *Brother Bear* and *Pocahontas* movies. The Le` Cellier restaurant at the pavilion is a popular eatery and is considered one of the best steakhouses at Disney. It was originally just a cafeteria style restaurant and was designed to look like a wine cellar. One really cool fact about this pavilion is that lights for the Illuminations show actually rise and appear out of the rocks at this pavilion. In fact, many guests try to sit on these rock walls and are constantly told to move before the show so they won't be injured by these rising lights. Additionally, there is a hidden hinged rock on the side of the pavilion across from the waterfall. If you lift this rock, you find a valve that when turned will shut off the entire waterfall. I believe I found this valve on our last trip. I didn't turn it, and I wouldn't advise trying it. You may just win yourself a one-way ticket out of Epcot.

I mentioned stereotypes. What is a stereotype? It means to have a fixed idea about something or someone and to only think of them one way. The Canadian government was adamant in the beginning and recently with the film that they didn't want the Canadian people portrayed in just one certain way. They wanted to show that their people are more than just lumberjacks. It's a valid argument and one I'm glad Disney seemed to have eventually listened to. Did you know that there are several Bible passages about stereotypes? In John 7:24, we are commanded to stop judging others by mere appearances or just by the way others look. Matthew 7 verses 1-2 tell us not to judge others or we will be judged in the same way. An Old Testament verse, Malachi 2:10 reminds us that we all have one Father and were created by the same God. Finally keep in mind the story of David in the Old Testament. When God chose him to be the next king, it was clear that He looked at David's heart and not his outer appearance when the choice was made.

Unfortunately, we sometimes tend to make snap judgments about people using only what we see. We tend to think that we know others before really getting to know them. This is wrong and strictly forbidden in the Bible. We need to work hard to get to know others and what is in their heart before we pass any kind of judgment or stereotype someone. Surely we want others to do the same for us. We were all created by God and all have something to offer. Take a hard look at those around you and make sure you know them completely, on the inside and out. See what all they have to offer and don't be too quick to judge. It would be a much better world if everyone did the same.

DEVOTIONAL #62

"IllumiNations"

So that's it with Epcot, right? We've done all the rides and attractions in Future World, and now we've gone all the way around World Showcase visiting each pavilion. So we can move on to the next park, correct? Not quite. There's one more thing we need to discuss here at Epcot before moving on. If you've visited Epcot and stayed through park closing, you certainly know what I'm talking about. We can't leave Epcot without talking about its infamous night time show. So let's discuss IllumiNations!

Officially called IllumiNations, Reflections of Earth, this show debuted in Epcot on October 1, 1999. At that point it was called IllumiNations 2000 Reflections of Earth and was to be a temporary show. However, it was so popular that it stayed put, they removed the 2000 from the name, and the show has remained ever since. The show has received several awards including eleven straight "Best Outdoor Night Production Show" awards. There are three main acts in the show. The first is called Chaos and represents the creation of Earth. The second is called Order and this is when the giant Earth globe appears with different scenes as the Earth "cools." The final scene is called Meaning and is when the globe opens up revealing the torch representing unity. As I mentioned earlier when discussing Morocco, this pavilion doesn't light up during the show for religious reasons. Norway across the water also doesn't light up to create balance with Morocco. Otherwise, the other nine pavilions light up to the music and provide a wonderful addition to the show. The giant Earth globe was the world's first spherical display system and is the most complicated piece of show equipment in Disney history. The globe is 28 feet in diameter and sits on a 10-foot pedestal. The globe is seated on the only barge in the show with an actual driver. On September 19, 2005, another barge, the inferno barge, caught fire when a firework on board prematurely exploded during the day. There was extensive damage. The narrator at the beginning of the 12½ minute show is the same voice of the man who provided the voice of Tigger and Pooh. Some have said if you stand near the Mexico pavilion at just the right time, you can look across the water behind Morocco and see another nighttime show, Fantasmic at Hollywood Studios near the Tower of Terror while watching IllumiNations at the same time. Mexico is also a great place to stand to see the show getting ready. A large bridge opens up near the Mexican pavilion to allow the barges to come through for the show.

The IllumiNations show is quite a sight! If you've never seen it, it's definitely worth sticking around for if you can get a good seat. Sometimes, these are hard to come by. The amount of fireworks, spotlights, lasers and lighted displays is pretty fantastic. In fact, the luminosity of the searchlights in the show equal one billion flashlight bulbs. You can also feel the heat from the fire in the show from pretty much anywhere around the lagoon. Needless to say, the light from the show is visible from miles away. Let's discuss what the Bible says about light? The fact is that the word "light" is mentioned nearly 300 times in God's Word, including over 100 New Testament references. Most of these verses instruct us to be a light or describe how God or Jesus are lights. In John 8:12, Jesus told us that He was a light and if we followed Him, we would never walk in darkness. I John 1:5 tells us that God is light and there is no darkness in Him. As mentioned, we are also told to be lights. In Luke 8, Jesus uses the example of someone lighting a lamp. They don't hide the lamp or lantern. They put it on a table or stand so all can use its light. In the same way, everyone should be able to see us as an example and light for God and His Son, Jesus Christ.

IllumiNations is a great show, and its name is certainly appropriate. There is no way to hide the immense light that illuminates from this show. The whole lagoon, and park for that matter, is greatly brightened by the light. Let us all take that as an example of how we should be as well. Even though we are each just one person, we can easily be seen by those around us by showing what it truly means to live as a Christian. Let your light shine!

DEVOTIONAL #63

"Disney Boats"

Now that we've officially finished Epcot, it's time to head to our third park which will be Hollywood Studios (HS). Why the Studios? Epcot and HS are practically right next door with only the BoardWalk in between as I mentioned a few devotionals back. Just like before when we traveled to Epcot by monorail, we have to get to HS first. Unfortunately, there's no monorail that goes here. You will soon be able to travel by sky bucket in a roundabout way, but those aren't quite finished yet as of this writing so we'll have to wait. We could travel by car or taxi or bus, but since this is all hypothetical, let's do something different. Let's travel by boat! There is actually a boat service that goes from Epcot to Hollywood Studios and back. Actually, there are several places throughout Walt Disney World where you can travel by boat. So let's take a lesson here and talk about Disney's boats!

Walt Disney World has a total of 37 boats at the parks. This of course does not count the cruise ships Disney owns or the boats inside the parks which make up several attractions. Today we are talking about the smaller passenger boats that take guests from parks, parking lots or resorts to various locations. The busiest boats on property travel from the TTC or Ticket and Transportation Center to the Magic Kingdom. There are 3 boats that make this trip back and forth. It is a five minute ride but they carry thousands daily. Each of these 3 boats are named for Disney executives and can carry up to 600 people. These 3 boats open a little later than the monorail does each day but can actually be a faster trip, especially if there is a line at the monorail. Disney also has boats that go from the Magic Kingdom to each of the surrounding resorts. In addition, there are boats from Disney Springs to several of the nearby resorts. One of the most scenic routes is the Green Route (each route has a color coded name). This is the boat from the Magic Kingdom to the Wilderness Lodge and on to the Fort Wilderness campground. If you are looking for something to kill time or just want something fun to do, you can ride this boat just to see the sights. It is said to be a very beautiful trip. On this route, you can see a bear face built into the Wilderness Lodge. You can also learn about Discovery Island and River Country which are now closed and abandoned but used to be integral parts of Disney World. Also, near River Country, an abandoned water park, you can spot a tree with white shoes in it. Supposedly the tradition is that when watercraft pilots retire, they throw their shoes in it as a final gesture. The best part of the Disney boats is that they are free for all, even non Disney resort guests. You can ride these boats just for fun if you have nothing else to do. Guests used to be allowed to sit in the pilot houses of certain ferry boats just like sitting in the front car of the monorail. However, as with the monorail, guests are no longer allowed to visit these areas for safety reasons. Disney boats always have at least 2 captains on board, sometimes 3. One pilot usually takes control for one direction while the other captain is in charge on the opposite way.

Riding the boats at WDW may not always be the fastest way to travel, but it just seems to be relaxing and fun. Boats also play an integral part in the Bible. Think about how many stories in Scripture deal with boats. From Noah's ark to Jesus walking on water to baby Moses and many more. Today I want to focus on another time Jesus was in a boat. There is only one miracle that is recorded in all four Gospels of Matthew, Mark, Luke and John. It is when Jesus fed the 5000. Just before that miracle, Jesus got into a boat with his apostles to try and obtain some peace and quiet time. He had been constantly bombarded by crowds and went into the boat in the Sea of Galilee to spend some time with his friends and with God. However, if you read this story in each of the Gospels, it's pretty easy to see that the people continued to follow Jesus anyway. The Sea of Galilee is not that big. In fact, you can walk around it and see boats in it the entire time. It seems like the people simply ran around the sea and met Jesus when he landed on the other side. If it was me, I know I would have been a little annoyed and may have even told them to leave me alone, but not Jesus of course. In Matthew 14:14, it says when Jesus saw the people, he had compassion on them. He taught them yet again and even fed them all with His famous miracle. What an amazing story that all began with Jesus on a boat crossing a small sea!

If you ever do choose a Disney boat for transport or even just for fun, think about Jesus on his little boat. Think about a crowd on the shore close by following you around. Would that be annoying to you if you were trying to rest? It's not easy to be kind to others, especially when we are tired, but there may just be someone that really needs a friend or to hear about God. In those times when you are exhausted, use Jesus as an example. Consider the fact that Jesus had a humble attitude and willingness to teach the people even when He was weary and really needed a break. Think about his compassion and his servant heart. What an amazing example He was and continues to be to all of us!

DEVOTIONAL #64

"Hollywood Studios"

Now that we've traveled across the water via the fun boats, let's get to our third park. It's finally time for Hollywood Studios! Before we get to any of the attractions here, let's once again talk about the whole park in general. Disney-MGM Studios opened on May 1, 1989 as WDW's third park. In 2016, it was the 5th most visited theme park in the USA and the 8th most in the world.

Hollywood Studios was conceived and created under pretty unique circumstances. The story goes that there were two Imagineers that were given the task to create two new attractions for Epcot in Future World. They came up with the Wonders of Life attraction which was actually created in Epcot. However, they also came up with a ride based on the history of film called The Great Movie Ride. This ride was to be placed between The Land Pavilion and The Imagination Pavilion in Future World West. However, when then CEO Michael Eisner heard about and saw the plans for the Great Movie Ride, he decided instead of building the attraction, they should instead turn the idea into a brand new park based on films and Hollywood. Thus a new park was born. Disney partnered with MGM Studios and called it Disney-MGM Studios, a name that stuck until 2008 when the partnership ended and the name changed to Hollywood Studios. Unless you've been living under a rock, you know that this park has been recently undergoing major changes. As of this writing, the new Toy Story Land has just opened (it actually opened the day I am editing this entry). The new Star Wars Land is scheduled to open in 2019. There is a rumor that the name of the park might also change. When the park first opened, the main icon of the park was the water tower there called the Earful Tower because of its Mickey Ears shape. In 2001, Disney added a giant sorcerer's hat from the Fantasia movie, and it became the new icon until it was torn down in 2015. The Earful Tower was torn down soon after that. Now this is the only park where there is no official icon although both the Chinese Theater and the Tower of Terror have both been unofficially named and used. When the park opened in 1989, the only two attractions were the Great Movie Ride and the Backlot Tour, both of which no longer exist. It was actually meant to only be a half-day park when built, but its popularity grew quickly and more attractions were added. This park is the 2nd smallest park at 135 acres although this number will change with the new additions. Only the Magic Kingdom is smaller in size, however it has many more attractions.

I enjoy Hollywood Studios a lot. I'll enjoy it a lot more when it's finished and all the new attractions and lands are added. Lately, it's been a point of discussion whether to even take the time to visit there or not due to the limit availability and several closures of attractions. I am hoping and sincerely believe that it will again become a great park in the coming years when everything is said and done. I can't wait to see what they do with it. It's pretty amazing to me how a simple but creative idea of a great attraction for another park became not just that one attraction, but a whole new theme park that has entertained millions for years.

What about you? Are you creative? Have you ever had a great idea? Have you ever invented something or thought of something that should be invented? Have you ever made a suggestion to someone that they hadn't thought of that turned out to be a great idea? I'd like to think I'm fairly creative and have come up with a few ideas in my life, like these devotionals for one thing. Of course I've never really created something huge, just some small things. It sure would be nice to be credited with some big idea though. It would be fun if something I thought of really caught on and a lot people benefitted from, like a whole theme park! That's what those two Imagineers did, right? They had one big idea of a film-based attraction and look what it turned into! My suggestion to you is to apply this concept to your spiritual life. We all need to start small and build our Christian lives gradually with God. Do you ever feel like you aren't doing enough in your spiritual life? Me too! Do you ever want to do something big and influence a lot of people? Me too! However, it's unrealistic to think that most people can start with something big. Instead, start with one person or one act of service and build from there. That's how to best build your Christianity. Colossians 3:23 reminds us that whatever we do needs to be done with our heart while Titus 3:14 tells us to just do good. Many verses tell us to do good and help others, but nowhere does it say we have to do something big. We can start small and build.

Don't get frustrated if you feel you aren't going anywhere spiritually. We all get stale from time to time and need a fresh start. If you are feeling that way, just start small. Come up with a small idea to help someone or serve in some way. Figure out a plan to gradually increase the time you spend with God daily. Then continue to add to your ideas and watch them grow. Who knows? You might just unintentionally end up with something huge, something of theme-park proportions that can bring many people to God!

DEVOTIONAL #65

"Slinky Dog Dash"

Now that we've left Epcot, ridden the boat over and discussed Hollywood Studios in general, let's enter the park already! Where do we go first? That's a good question with a lot of options. There are a few very good and popular rides here with more being added soon. Once Star Wars Land opens, our typical order of operations may change. For now, we're going to head first to what is most likely the most popular part of the park. Toy Story Land is brand new in 2018 and there are now three rides in this creatively themed area. We're going to start with what I'm guessing will be the most popular of the three. This is a rare entry in which I haven't ridden yet the ride I'm discussing. I have plans to visit in a couple of months to ride it, but it recently opened so let's discuss it. Let's go ride one of Disney's newest attractions, Slinky Dog Dash!

Slinky Dog Dash is a family-friendly roller coaster that officially opened in June 2018 with the grand opening of Toy Story Land. The story behind the ride is that Andy from the *Toy Story* movies has built a roller coaster using his toys and has decided to use Slink Dog as the ride vehicle. The vehicle can hold up to four trains and ends with a giant audio-animatronic of Wheezy, also from the films, singing to guests. The original Slinky toy was invented in the early 1940's by a man named Richard James. It was originally priced at $1 and was an immediate hit. In fact, James and his wife initially made 400 Slinkys and they sold out in 90 minutes. In the first 60 years of business, there were approximately 300 million Slinkys sold. It is now in the National Toy Hall of Fame in New York and is the official toy of the state of Pennsylvania. In 1952, the Slinky Dog toy debuted after a suggestion from a consumer named Helen Malsed. She received royalties of around $65,000 for the next 17 years. In 1995, the Slinky Dog toy was redesigned by Pixar for the *Toy Story* movie and was once again a huge hit. Slinkys are a very simple but fun toy. I remember having one as a kid and actually playing with it. As you probably know, Slinkys can do some interesting things. One of the neatest things I remember about a Slinky is that they can actually travel down stairs. The old advertising jingle even said "What walks down stairs, alone or in pairs, and makes a slinkity sound?" (No, I didn't know "slinkity" was a word either.) If you put a Slinky at the top of a flight of stairs and give one end a push, the Slinky will conform to the shape of the steps using gravity as it travels down. That leads me to a spiritual thought.

We are actually told in the Bible to not be like Slinkys. Ok, so maybe it doesn't actually mention Slinkys, but it does advise us concerning conforming. We are actually told not to conform to the world in Romans 12:2. We are not to follow the path of most in this world as the evil of the world can lead us away from God. I John 2:15 even tells us not to love the world. That being said, I'd rather focus on the positive verses concerning conforming. We are told a few chapters earlier in Romans 8:29, "For those whom he foreknew he also predestined to be conformed to the image of his Son." The verse before that says that God works for good for those who love Him. Isn't that a comforting verse? As long as we love God and show it, God will work for our lives to be good. We will still have rough times, but God will have a plan for us that will ultimately lead to good. All we have to do is conform to the image of Jesus. We have to live like Jesus did. We have to try and serve like Jesus did. We have to be a good example to others as Jesus was.

I cannot wait to ride Slinky Dog Dash. I am already counting down the days and watching videos of others riding it. By the time you are reading this book, I will have ridden it. I'm also looking forward to *Toy Story 4* coming out fairly soon where Slink Dog will once again have a role I'm sure. As you watch that character and ride his ride, remember how he can conform to many different shapes. We can too! We can choose the easy path and conform to the shape of the world, or we can work hard to conform to the shape of Jesus Christ. We can follow in His footsteps and love God accepting His plan for our lives. The first will only lead us to evil, but the second will eventually lead us to all things good. God promises that! We just have to be patient and wait for His plan to be complete. I promise it will be all worth it in the end.

DEVOTIONAL #66

"Alien Swirling Saucers"

Departing Slinky Dog Dash, we now head to the other newer ride in this area. It's another ride I've yet to do since I haven't visited this area yet. It's called Alien Swirling Saucers. It is on a smaller scale than the ride we just got off of. This ride was meant to be more of a ride for younger kids and is probably not quite as thrilling to most guests. However, Disney is known for having a good mix of attractions for young and old, enthusiastic and calm, brave and not-so-much. From what I've heard, this ride is one most people can do with no worries. Having not done it yet, I'm a little worried about the spin factor, but I've heard from friends who have done it that it's not bad. I'll be the judge of that soon on our next trip. I definitely want to give it a try. Let's go ride the Alien Swirling Saucers.

This ride also opened in June of 2018 with the new Toy Story Land. Many have said this ride is very similar to Mater's Junkyard Jamboree at Disneyland. If you know anything about the Alien characters in the *Toy Story* films, you will understand the premise of this attraction. You are basically at the restaurant Pizza Planet characterized by pizza decorations all around. 2-3 people board one of 22 available cars each being pulled by one of the Aliens in his spaceship. During the approximate 90 second ride, you are pulled around the arena as your car swings back and forth depending on which direction the Alien goes. During your trip, you are hoping to get chosen by the giant claw above you. As you go, you can push and play with the many different buttons and switches on the dash in front of you. You also get to hear 1 of 8 popular songs, all familiar but with a quirky new sound. There are lighting displays and sound effects as well throughout your trip. Outside the attraction, you can get your picture taken in front of many of the larger than life toys from Andy's room including a 10 foot Pixar ball or a 14 foot Buzz Lightyear.

The Aliens from the three and soon-to-be four *Toy Story* films are well-known and loved characters. They all look the same and speak simultaneously with the same voice. In the first film, they were first encountered by Buzz and Woody at Pizza Planet when they got stuck in the famous claw game. The Aliens appear to worship the claw hoping to be chosen and freed. In the same way, you are hoping to be chosen during your time on this ride. Since I haven't ridden, I'm not sure if someone actually gets chosen and what may happen if so. The Aliens actually played a pivotal role in the third film saving the entire group from incineration by using a giant claw to scoop them up just in the nick of time. I have no doubts that these cute little guys will reappear in the next film. As I mentioned, they see the claw as a sort of deity, constantly calling it their "master." They even state, "the claw chooses who will go and who will stay." Let's use that for our thought today.

I guess I could talk about worship and how we shouldn't worship claws from restaurant games, but I think I'll go a different direction. We are very similar to the Aliens in that we also have a master who chooses who will go and who will stay. As you might expect, I am talking about God. He is our one and only Master as it states in Colossians 4:1. He is also the only one who will decide whether we will be "chosen" for eternal life with Him in Heaven. Romans 14:10 says, "For we will all stand before the judgment seat of God." I Corinthians 4:5 says that we are not to pronounce judgment on anyone for that is God's job when the time comes. We are not to judge others and decide their eternity. That is God's job, and make no mistake, we will all be judged by God one day. We will all have to give an account of our life here on Earth and how we lived. God said that in the Bible many times, not to scare us, but to have us realize that we must take our lives seriously. We have a God-given mission while here to live faithfully to Him and one day we will have to explain to God the reason for our actions here while we live on Earth. Don't let that scare you but instead use it as motivation to work hard for your salvation. Do you best to be pleasing to God as it says in 2 Timothy 2:15.

I am looking forward to this Alien ride. I hope it doesn't make me queasy as some spinning rides do. I am cautiously optimistic that I'll be able to handle it. I hope you enjoy it too when you get a chance to ride it. As you ride and look up at the claw, remember who you look up to every day. Remember that God is your true Master and He will decide whether to reach down and grab you or not. Remember that He is a loving and forgiving God but He expects us to do our part. Salvation is a free gift, but we have to follow His plan and the steps He's laid out for us to obtain the gift. I hope and pray you will work really hard to be chosen by God. I pledge to you that I will be doing the same. Let's be chosen together!

DEVOTIONAL #67

"Toy Story Midway Mania"

Now that we've conquered the two newest rides here in Toy Story Land, let's quickly head to the veteran ride of this section. This is the ride that our family used to run to first. Before the others came along, this was typically the most popular ride in the park with very lengthy wait times. Therefore, we always tried to do this one first thing in the morning and hopefully score a fastpass for a repeat visit later. I claim this as my favorite ride in Hollywood Studios. Let's go ride Toy Story Midway Mania!

Toy Story Midway Mania opened in HS in May of 2008. This was the first ride ever to simultaneously be built in both the Florida and California parks although the Disneyland version opened two weeks after the WDW version. This attraction then opened in Tokyo Disney in 2012. At WDW, this ride replaced the Who Wants to be a Millionaire attraction which was a park version of the once popular game show. Toy Story has proven to be a very popular attraction, especially the Florida version, with wait times often exceeding two hours. It will be interesting to see if this has changed with the addition of two new rides in this land. In May of 2016, construction was finished on a third track so capacity increased by 50%. The opening of Toy Story Land also meant a new entrance and queue for this attraction. This ride is similar to Buzz Lightyear in the Magic Kingdom in that you have a role while riding. You are tasked with shooting as many targets as possible during six rounds lasting around 30 seconds each. There is then a bonus game at the end where you can earn extra points. One of the games includes breaking plates that are thrown into the air. It is estimated that guests break around a million plates every day. Each of the six games has a hidden "Easter egg" that if discovered opens more targets where you can really rack up points. You can find these secrets on several websites if you do the research. This is also a ride where you wear 3D glasses while riding although the ride is actually considered 4D because things might be "thrown" at you such as blasts of wind or a water mist. The Imagineers who created the ride actually wore 3D glasses while painting to add to the effect. The ride queue contains the most advanced Audio-animatronic ever in a giant Mr. Potato Head that can talk to you, say more lines than any other on property and can even remove and reattach his own ear.

As I mentioned, this is actually a 4D ride which makes it a little more difficult than say the Buzz Lightyear ride. Not only do you have to focus on the targets at which you are shooting, but you have to do so while having things thrown back at you. You have to constantly deal with distractions to conquer the games and score higher. If you'll remember, I likened the Buzz Lightyear attraction to shooting at Satan. This ride can have a similar message, but it has an added element that the other ride didn't have. This one shoots back! Doesn't Satan do the same? You can fight against Satan and his temptation but he will fight back, at least for a little while. 2 Corinthians 11:14 tells us that Satan disguises himself. He tries very hard to deceive you with his appearance and he'll try to trick you. Revelation 12:9 tells us that he deceives the whole world. He will work on you for a time and try to fight back. If you don't fight against him, he will eventually beat you. However, there is good news. If you stand strong and continue to fight, eventually he will leave you alone. I remind you of the verse I used with Buzz Lightyear in James 4:7 which tells us that if we resist the devil and all he has to throw at us, he will eventually flee from us. Isn't that something we should all work for? How awesome would it be to know that Satan has given up and run away from us! That should be a goal that we all strive for.

Toy Story Midway Mania is a ride I really look forward to. I get into it and really try and score a lot of points. I love to try to better my score each trip and find the hidden secrets and strategies. I love the 3D effects and even the 4D distractions. It's a very creative and fun experience. Fighting against Satan while he fights back is definitely not a fun experience. However, we can take comfort in the fact that it is possible to beat him and eventually make him flee from us. Once that happens, we will have no other option but to win this game of life and gain our eternal reward with God. Fight hard and score big against Satan!

DEVOTIONAL #68

"Tower of Terror"

We're done with Toy Story Land so where to next? In just a year or so, I'm sure we'll be quickly heading to Star Wars Land, but it's not quite open yet. Who knows? We may even be going there first depending on how the new attractions there turn out. Today, however, we're going to what is arguably the next most popular ride. It's a ride that some people won't do. It can be intimidating. It can make you feel queasy. It can terrify you to your very core. What is it? It's the Tower of Terror! (Insert scary music here). Yes, it can be scary, but it's another great ride that everyone needs to try at least once.

The Tower of Terror is an extremely unique and creative ride that represents Disney at its best. This attraction was built at the Studios in 1994. It was extremely popular when it opened as it still is today. In fact, it was so popular that Disney made a TV movie out of the attraction. Unfortunately the movie did not share in the ride's popularity. It flopped. I actually saw it and thought it wasn't terrible. Despite the film's lack of success, the ride has never lost its popularity. In 2004, the admiration for this attraction spread across the country and it was added to Disney's California Adventure park. It has also spread across the oceans to the Paris and Tokyo parks. The ride is 199 feet tall making it the 2nd tallest attraction. Only Expedition Everest at Animal Kingdom is taller at 199.5 feet. As previously mentioned, these attractions don't go over 200 feet because then they would have to add a light at the top for planes per aviation guidelines. When they were building the Tower of Terror, a sinkhole caused them to have to move the build site slightly. This ride is basically an entire story based on an episode of the *Twilight Zone* TV show. Imagineers actually viewed 156 episodes of the show while designing the ride. The story is set in a 1930's hotel that is struck by lightning. The strike causes the elevators to fail and fall. Lucky as you are, you get to board these "falling" elevators. You are raised 13 stories in the air and dropped several times at a top speed of 39 mph. What you may not know is that you are actually traveling faster than the speed of gravity because there are cables under your elevator that are pulling you down. What is most creative about this ride is that every ride is different. You never know how many times or how far you are going to drop. There are four different drop patterns and each ride is given a random pattern although all of them feature a fake drop as well as a full drop all 13 stories. When this ride first opened in 1994, each ride was only one drop. This was the first Disney attraction to offer video of your experience while the Seven Dwarfs Mine Train soon followed. When this ride was first suggested, CEO Michael Eisner wanted it to be not only a ride, but a real hotel as well, although that idea was quickly proven to be impractical. A final fun fact is that there actually is a real elevator inside this attraction but it is reserved for Cast Members as well as those with disabilities.

So I guess one of the main reasons some people don't like this ride or are too scared to ride it is simply the fall factor. They are scared to death of falling, especially multiple times, in that elevator. It is a scary feeling. Have you ever fallen? Have you ever gotten that queasy feeling in your knees when up in an airplane or high up on a ladder? The fear of falling is real and can be a real problem for people. The truth is we all fall. Maybe some will avoid literally falling, although that's rare, but what I mean is that we all fall spiritually. Romans 3:23 reminds us that we all sin and "fall" short of God's glory. However, there is good news too. God always helps us up when we fall. Psalm 118:13 says "I was pushed hard so that I was falling, but the Lord helped me." Proverbs 24:16 says that though we may fall even up to seven times, we will rise again. Isn't that a wonderful promise and assurance of God's grace and forgiveness? Do you want to know the real happy ending to this story? Even though we all fall spiritually at some point and maybe multiple times, in the end we will not fall but do quite the opposite. I Thessalonians 4:17 says that in end times, we will all be raised in the air to meet up with the Lord. Won't that be awesome! We won't be falling. We'll be rising, and I have a feeling that none of us will feel any fear of heights or falling at that point.

Are you scared of the Tower of Terror? It's ok if you are. It's a legitimate and understandable fear. You also need to understand that you will fall spiritually, and it may be scary too. Keep in mind that God is always there to pick you up no matter how far you fall. Also remember that if you keep your focus on God, one day he will pick you up big time...to rise up and meet Him in Heaven!

DEVOTIONAL #69

"Rock 'N' Roller Coaster Starring Aerosmith"

Yes, that's its official name, but we're going to shorten it for obvious reasons. The RNR Coaster opened in Hollywood Studios on July 29, 1999. It is the 2nd fastest ride in all of Walt Disney World trailing only Test Track at Epcot. This ride takes you from 0 to 57 mph in just 2.8 seconds with the most exciting start to a ride you can imagine. Riders experience between 4 and 5 times the force of gravity on the ride's first inversion which is more than the astronauts experience being launched into space. You can also find this ride in France at Disneyland Paris where it holds the record as the fastest roller coaster in all of France. While this completely indoor roller coaster only lasts 1 minute and 22 seconds, it is a thrilling ride where riders experience many twists, turns and loops during the over half-mile adventure. Riders also get to enjoy a selection of Aerosmith songs blasting in their ears during the ride. There are actually 125 speakers on each of the coasters including some in each headrest. There are 5 total coasters available although only 4 are in use at any one time. The other is kept as a backup if needed. The band Aerosmith has sponsored this ride since its beginning. The band even recorded several various versions of their songs especially for this ride. For example, instead of their classic "Love in an Elevator," you might hear "Love in a Roller Coaster" during your ride. On this ride's opening day, some guests were specially chosen to receive limo rides to the park as well as an all-you-can-eat buffet. They then got to ride the new coaster with a band member from Aerosmith. It was reported that the band all loved the ride and rode it multiple times that day.

If you've ever ridden this attraction, you know the most exciting, thrilling and scary part occurs at the very beginning of the ride. After boarding, you are taken slowly around a curve where your coaster stops and waits to launch. Luckily, you get a countdown from 5 so you know when you are about to take off, but the anticipation of what is about to happen is exhilarating. Once that countdown hits zero, you are zoomed into a 57 mph launch before you even realize it. It feels like your face is going to be left behind. As you wait in the queue for this ride, you can actually see people sitting and waiting to be launched. You can see and study their faces as they await their speedy departure, many of them knowing what is about to come. It is pretty interesting to watch people and the anticipation they are experiencing. Some look stressed. Some look scared. Some are calm. Some are fearless or so it appears. You can definitely see a wide range of emotions and reactions concerning what is about to happen. Do you enjoy that feeling of anticipation of what is about to come, even if it is scary? What else do you get emotional anticipating? I know I like to anticipate vacations. I love traveling. I love vacations. At the same time, I hate when they are over and sometimes I find myself thinking about that during the vacation. That's a bad habit I need to get out of. I need to enjoy the moments and not be sad about what is to come. Because of that bad habit, I sometimes enjoy the anticipation before the vacation more than the trip itself. I love having a trip to look forward to and plan for. In the same way, that short time before the roller coaster takes off is probably my favorite part of the ride. I really enjoy that scary and wonderful feeling of anticipation while waiting for that countdown to begin.

What does Scripture say about anticipation? What should we anticipate in our spiritual lives? In Joshua 3:5, Joshua himself tells the people to "Consecrate yourselves, for tomorrow the Lord will do wonders among you." What does that word "consecrate" mean? That word means to dedicate, devote or make holy. Joshua was telling the people that in anticipation of what God was going to do for them, they should prepare themselves by devoting their lives to Him. In James 1:12, we are promised the crown of life from God as long as we remain steadfast and dedicated to Him. If nothing else, you should definitely anticipate Heaven. I know I do. That is the ultimate "trip" that I am looking forward to. That anticipation never ends, at least not during our earthly lives.

Everyone needs to ride the RNR Coaster. It's a thrilling ride, and you can never go wrong with Aerosmith music, right? Ok, maybe that's my opinion, but I do think it is a fantastic ride. I will also admit it is a little intense, scary and nerve-wracking, especially the first time as you anticipate what is about to happen. The good news is that anticipation can be exciting and motivating, especially if we anticipate the right things. Make an effort to practice anticipating the greatest blessing we have in life, the hope of Heaven and eternity with our Father. In the meantime, practice what we are instructed in Scripture and devote yourself to God as you await that gift. Also, remain steadfast and completely dedicated to God not letting any temptation sway you away. You may have to wait a little longer than a 5 second countdown, but the "eternal ride" that is to come will be the most exciting journey you could ever imagine.

DEVOTIONAL #70

"Star Tours"

As far as rides go at Hollywood Studios, there's really only one more at this point. The rest of the attractions are considered shows or films. As you can see, HS just doesn't have the number of rides compared to the other parks. There are currently at least three more rides in the works, but for now, let's head to the last one currently available. Although this is technically a ride, you don't move very far, but you do definitely move. You move up and down and side to side and front to back and then repeat, and again and again...you get the point. Ugh! I'm almost getting sick just thinking about it. This is the other of the two rides at Disney, including the teacups at MK, that I simply can't do. I have done this one. I've done it a few times actually, but no more! It just makes me too queasy and nauseous. My family loves it, and more power to them. They can have it. Let's go ride Star Tours. Actually, you ride. I'll wait outside.

Star Tours is a simulator type ride where you get into an enclosed structure, strap in, and then are taken on a space journey with your favorite characters from Star Wars on the screen in front of you. Star Tours opened first in Disneyland in 1987. The Florida version followed a couple years later in 1989 just a few months after the park opened. The original Star Tours was altered in 2011 and became Star Tours—the Adventure Continues, which is now its official name. With that refurbishment, it added new characters and ride experiences. The old version of this ride took place just after episode 6 in the series which is *Return of the Jedi*. The new and current version supposedly takes place between episodes 3 and 4, just before the original *Star Wars—A New Hope* movie. When the original ride opened in the late eighties, both Bob Iger, head of Disney and George Lucas, creator of the epic Star Wars, were there. They both actually tried the ride as well. If you ever have to wait in line for this ride, listen carefully for the announcement overhead for a page of Egroeg Sacul. This is a nod to George Lucas which is his name backwards. You can also hear the Ewoks from *Return of the Jedi* having a party in the overhead speaker if you listen carefully. The ride takes 4½ minutes and can hold up to 40 riders per simulator. Most of the actual actors in the famous movies recorded their parts for the ride so you hear their actual voices. Each ride varies as there are 13 possible segments you can experience. You are always given a random 4 of those which makes for many possible ride combinations.

Did I mention that I don't like this ride? I've never done well with simulators of any kind. I wish I could enjoy them, but my body just doesn't like them for some reason. It has something to do with the simulator moving my body violently while I'm trying to concentrate on the screen in front of me. Those two things don't mix well for me. For this particular ride and many other simulators, you are essentially trapped inside a big box for the duration of the ride. Now I'm not generally too claustrophobic, but I know this scares some people. This "box" that you're in is big enough where it doesn't generally scare me, but extremely tight spaces can be quite nerve-wracking. I remember going caving or "spelunking" for you fancy people, as a kid and having to squeeze my body through some very small spaces for a good distance. This was a little frightening for me thinking about what might happen if I got stuck. How about you? Do you like small spaces? Are you claustrophobic? Let's think about that for our devotional thought today.

Sometimes we treat life like we are trapped in a box. Some of us, me included, get really comfortable in our own little box. We build up walls around us it's comfortable and feel fear when we have to travel outside that comfort zone. We like staying home in our own little circle of friends in familiar territory. However, to fulfill our real spiritual purpose and the plan God has for us, we have to come out of that box sometimes. We have to talk to others. We have to help those in need. We may even have to travel and be a missionary to those who don't hear the Bible regularly. 2 Timothy 1:7 says that the Spirit of God that we are given does not make us timid, but powerful. We need to embrace this gift of the Spirit and use it to courageously proclaim the name of God. In Joshua 1:9, he (and all of us) is told to be strong and courageous and unafraid for God will always be with us.

It's not always easy to step out of our box. Even though some of us are normally scared of small spaces, we feel fine in our own little world and get way too comfortable staying in our "box." Despite how you personally feel on Star Tours, examine your own world. Do you come out of your box? Do you step out of your comfort zone regularly to minister to others and tell them about your faith and the gifts you've been given? Do you ask God to give you courage to speak to others about Him? Give it a shot. What have you got to lose? The answers is nothing; but think about how much others have to gain if you step out and use the courage God will give you. It's so worth the step!

DEVOTIONAL #71

"Jedi Training Academy"

Ok, we're out of rides here at HS, so do we leave the park? No way! There are still plenty of amazing things to do here. While Hollywood Studios may currently be slightly short on rides, they are known for having many other great attractions. Actually we're going to try something that my family has never done, but I know a whole lot of other families have. Since we just enjoyed a Star Wars ride, let's try another Star Wars experience. It's only for children, but some people wait in very long lines to do it. While my boys liked the Star Wars films, they were never quite into it enough to really want to do this. However, this is something that has been and continues to be very popular at the Studios. We're going to give the Jedi Training Academy a try.

The Jedi Training Academy is a well-liked experience at this park and it would be irresponsible to just skip it. It's more of a show for those watching and from what I've seen, is quite entertaining. This experience is offered to children ages 4 through 12. If you are of that age, you can sign up for a time to go through this 20 minute encounter. Signups typically fill up very fast so this is why there is often a rush in the morning and a long line each day to secure a time. Each time slot takes only 16 participants who each receive a certificate upon completion. This training event was originally just a part of Star Wars Weekends when they began in 1997. The first Jedi Training Academy took place on October 9, 1997 and was an instant success. After a while with its popularity, Disney decided to make it a regular attraction and it has continued to this day. In 2015, it was updated to include new characters from the latest film. Each participant is given a light saber and robe to use while being trained with moves to fight the villains of the famous series. After their training, the children then have to use their new moves to fight the bad guys and use the "force" to get rid of them.

I've heard good things about this attraction and know that many enjoy doing it over and over. I think the biggest draw is that the kids love to fight evil and love to feel equipped to help the good guys defeat the bad. There is a sense of pride each child feels when the experience is over. They have benefitted from their training and have been successful in destroying evil. I think we all feel this pride at some point during our lives. We all have been trained and benefit from training. Whether at home, in grade school, college or specialized training, everyone is taught at some point in their lives. Being taught helps us all to become better equipped to face life and be able to make decisions. While we might not always enjoy certain types of training, we do better when we listen to our teachers and try to gain from what they tell us. 2 Timothy 3:16-17 reminds us that the Bible is given to us for training and for teaching others. In Psalm 144:1, David praises God for training him and preparing him for life. In addition, I Timothy 4:8 tells us that while physical training can benefit us some, spiritual training is best for us.

If you have some spare time while at Hollywood Studios, check out the Jedi Training Academy. You may be too old to participate, but it's a fun show to just watch. The look on the kids' faces says it all. They enjoy their training. We should all look to be trained. Scripture tells us how beneficial it is to be trained and we should take advantage anytime we can. Keep in mind that our ultimate trainer is Jesus Christ, our master Teacher. He has left us all with the training we need to face this world and be victorious over sin and Satan. Thank you God for that training and help us all to accept and work hard at it.

DEVOTIONAL #72

"Disney Junior, Live on Stage"

So now that we've worn ourselves out fighting the forces of evil, let's head to something a little less active and stressful. Let's go watch an entertaining show! There are several options of shows here in Hollywood Studios. That's something I personally enjoy about this park in addition to the fact that the many shows are all different and appeal to many different audiences. We're going to try a show today that tends to please a much younger audience. While it may be less stressful to sit and watch a show, this one isn't lacking on the excitement and, well, loudness. Think screaming and active kids for this one. It's a show that I've only been to once or maybe twice when our boys were much younger. However, if I had younger children today, I'm sure we would venture there more often. Let's go visit Disney Junior Live on Stage!

When the park first opened in 1989, this building was a restaurant called Soundstage Restaurant. It featured sets and decorations from the movies *Big Business, Beauty and the Beast* and *Aladdin*. This restaurant lasted until 1998 and closed due to lack of popularity. At that point, it was converted to a new show called Bear in the Big Blue House Live on Stage which just featured characters from the then popular TV show of the same name. In 2001, it was refurbished and added characters from the shows *Rollie Pollie Ollie, Stanley,* and *Book of Pooh* in addition to *Bear the Big Blue House* and renamed Playhouse Disney Live on Stage as Playhouse Disney was the name of the TV channel featuring these very popular kids' shows. Over time, new parts were added or taken away as the shows came and went. Other shows included over the years have been *Jojo's Circus, Mickey Mouse Clubhouse, Handy Manny, Little Einsteins, My Friends Tigger and Pooh, Jake and the Neverland Pirates, Sofia the First,* and *Doc McStuffins.* Just a few years ago, the name was changed to the current name of Disney Junior again to pattern the popular kids' TV channel. Currently Disney Junior is a 24-minute show that features the latest characters and one live host who is always named "Casey" despite what the cast member's real name might be. Guests sit on the floor and enjoy the show above them on stage. There is one row of benches in the back for those that get there early. It is advised that you sit in the middle of the floor as those right up front can't see the entire set. There are ten shows presented each day and similar versions featured in the California and Paris parks. This show is obviously mainly geared toward pre-school aged kids, and they tend to really enjoy it. Parents tend to enjoy it as well but mainly due to their own kids' smiles and laughter. Today's version features around 25 characters or puppets all controlled by 6 puppeteers or actors. The Disney Junior programming on TV is today available to over 75 million households world-wide and continues to attract big ratings and popularity among children of all ages. There are future plans to change this show to a dance party still featuring the Disney Junior characters.

So what is the lesson today? What can we learn from Disney Junior? Think about that word "Junior." Does that mean anything to you? It does to me. I am a "Junior." What I mean is that I have the same name as my father which means I technically have four names. I get to put a JR after my name on important documents. Honestly, I've always liked that about myself. Some might not enjoy not having a unique name, but I'm alright with it. I don't mind being a junior. There's a small sense of pride in getting to put those 2 letters after my name. Are you a junior? If you said no, think about it. Aren't we all juniors in some way?

Genesis 1:27 says that we were all created in the image of God. To me this means that God chose to put a little bit of Himself in all of us. What an honor! God loved us so much that He chose to use Himself in creating us! That's something we can all take pride in. We're all juniors when it comes to God. Jesus was also created in God's image. He actually was God in human form who came down to be an example to all of us. Jesus showed us what it meant to be the image of God and how to emulate and imitate Him. Our purpose and duty while we are here is to be like Christ and therefore God. We are to try our best to imitate Him and pattern our lives like His. Philippians 2 talks about this. It tells us to serve others as Jesus did. In I Corinthians 11:1, Paul says that he patterns his life after Jesus, and we should all do the same. And in 2 Corinthians 3:18, he reminds them that we are all to be transformed into the image of Christ.

So how are you doing? Are you wearing your "junior" name proudly? Do you take pride and share with others how God made you in His image? Do you respect that gift by wearing His name with honor and being a good example to others? Disney has made a fortune by appealing to kids all over the world with their characters, shows and entertainment. They have named their TV series Disney Junior in an effort to share their name to a younger generation. Remember today that God has done the same for us. He has shared His name and image with us. He has appointed us His "juniors." What a wonderful gift! Wear it proudly and don't tarnish that name. Instead, use it to bring as many people to God as you can!

DEVOTIONAL #73

"Indiana Jones Epic Stunt Spectacular"

On to another show we go! After all, I mentioned last time that Hollywood Studios has many shows to choose from. The one for today is definitely geared more toward adults although kids definitely enjoy it as well. I personally enjoy this show a lot and have actually had the pleasure of being a part of it twice, although that doesn't hold a candle to my lovely wife. She has been a part of this show many times. She knows the secret and has passed it on to me. If you've ever been to the studios, you probably know which show I'm talking about because I don't think there are any others that guests can regularly be a part of. Today we're going to watch the Indiana Jones Epic Stunt Spectacular!

The Indiana Jones show, as we'll call it, opened on August 25, 1989, just a few months after the park opened in May of the same year. The show is produced by George Lucas who produced and wrote the Indiana Jones movies. This show features stunts mainly featured and influenced by *Raiders of the Lost Ark,* the first Indiana Jones movie. The theater for this show holds over 2000 people, but it is often full at each of the several daily shows. If you want a good seat in the middle of the theater, you do have to arrive several minutes early or get a fastpass. Want to be in the show? Here's my wife's secret which always seems to work. You need to be sitting in the middle or near the middle of the theater. You need to be wearing a bright color (she wears pink) and be ready to jump up, scream and wave your arms right when the host asks for volunteers. It may sound crazy, but it works! There are some fun and not so fun facts about this show. First of all, the giant spikes that come up from the floor are triggered by the actor stepping on special pads and yes, they are dangerous and could hurt him if he made a wrong move. The giant ball that rolls after him weighs between 400-500 pounds. The small idol that he "steals" right before the ball rolls is an exact replica of the idol used in the film. The giant moving sets that you'll see being pushed halfway through the show are the largest moving sets in history and weigh approximately 100 tons. The not-so-fun-fact is that on August 17, 2009, one of the stunt performers in this show was practicing and suffered a head injury. He unfortunately died later due to his injury. I'll also mention that there is a well outside this attraction with a sign that says "Do NOT pull the rope." However, the "NOT" is crossed out. Make sure to look for this and pull the rope next time for a special surprise. I always worry that they may close this attraction one day due to its age. However, it is still very popular and they are planning a fifth Indiana Jones movie. So maybe these things will keep it going for a while. I certainly hope so as I like it a lot.

If you haven't seen the Indiana Jones movies, you should. They are great. Well, most of them. The fourth one is lacking a little, but the other three are exciting and action-packed. In all of the films, Indy is searching for something, trying to find a treasure of sorts. In at least two of the films, the main treasure he is looking for is Biblically related. In the first film, he's looking for the Ark of the Covenant and in the third film, the cup of Christ. While these are of course fictional movies, many people over the years have searched for Biblical treasure whether it be Noah's Ark, the Ten Commandments, or something else. Obviously, it would be amazing to find one of these Biblical treasures. While they may be really difficult or even impossible for us to find, there is a treasure we can all find. We've even been given the map!

God gave us His Word, the Bible that serves as our treasure map. It will lead us right to the treasure of Heaven. It tells us of the power of Christ and instructs us how to live so we can know Him and live with Him forever. The very important verse in John 14:6 says that Jesus is the only way to get to God. Through Jesus is the only way the map goes. There are no shortcuts or alternate paths. If you believe the Bible, you have to believe that we have to know Jesus and live like Him to get our treasure. John 17:3 even says, "And this is eternal life, that they know you, the only true God, and Jesus Christ whom you have sent." We must know Jesus, not just who He is, but have a relationship with Him. How else do we get to know Him? I John 2:3 says we will know Him when we follow His commands.

I'll say again that I really enjoy the Indiana Jones show. It's a nice, long, comfortable and cool attraction that has many moments of excitement. It's fun to watch Indiana Jones attempt to get his treasure and complete his mission. I also try to think about my own mission and I encourage you today to do the same. Are you seeking the treasure? Have you read the map so that you know how to get it? Do you really know Jesus and follow His commands? These are some questions to consider as you evaluate your relationship with God today.

DEVOTIONAL #74

"Muppet*Vision 3D"

Since we only have shows left at this park, let's move on to the next one. This is more of a movie as opposed to a show, but it definitely has some show qualities mixed in. It also happens to be one of my favorites. I love these guys! I hope they never get rid of it even though there has been the threat of just that. Let's head over to watch Muppet*Vision 3D!

Muppet*Vision opened on May 16, 1991, just two years after the park opened. This same show operated in California starting in 2001 but that one closed in 2014. With all the construction going on currently at Hollywood Studios, there is always talk and rumors of this one closing too, but like I said above, I hope that never happens. It just wouldn't quite be the same Disney without this classic attraction. This show takes place in a 550 seat theater and lasts around 15 minutes. The pre-show takes place in the lobby and involves an involved video which is almost as good as the actual show. If you get there late and miss the pre-show, you might want to stick around and watch it again. It has some very classic and funny moments. There are also many hidden treasures inside the pre-show lobby. For example, you can find a net full of Jell-O which represents Annette Funicello, probably the most well-known child mouseketeer. Another fun one to look for is right when you walk in. Look for a sign on an office door that says "key under mat." Go ahead and take a look under the mat and you'll find the key embedded into the floor. There are other fun things to find in the pre-show area as well. Take some time to explore. This attraction was one of the very last projects that Jim Henson worked on before his death in 1990. He actually died before the completed production ended. This is the only 3D attraction that actually calls the glasses "3D glasses." However, like most of its comparative shows, this show is actually 4D because it includes smells and water surprises. It also includes some actual characters making an appearance. This attraction was going to be part of a much larger Muppet area in the Studios, but when Jim Henson died, that idea was scrapped and only this film made the cut. Finally, the actual fire truck at the end of the film used to be stationed outside the theater but it was removed during a remodel.

For today's lesson, think about the following. I don't know how much you know about Jim Henson, the creator of the Muppets. What you need to know is that he was extremely creative, and much like Walt Disney created a whole new world of entertainment that continues to live strong today. Henson was the first person ever to give puppets more life and sensitivity by first using foam instead of wood to make them. He also was one of the first to move their hands and not just their bodies and heads. He spent countless hours creating character after character of these beloved creatures that have entertained the world with TV shows, movies, toys, etc.

In a similar but much greater way, God created us. He created our world and gave us life. He made us a lot more improved and complicated compared to the animals He created first. He allowed us to make our own choices. He allows us to show emotions. He gave us freedom to do what we want. Sure, he gave us instructions on how to live, but it's ultimately our choice. Proverbs 16:9 says that God establishes our steps but we make the plans. So what do we do with the life God gave us? John 15:16 tells us that we are to go and bear fruit by spreading God's message to others. Ecclesiastes 12:13 says that our whole duty in life is to fear God and keep His commandments. Are we really doing that daily?

I love the Muppets, especially their movies. They make me laugh, and I am in awe of the fact that one man ultimately created them. I am amazed and inspired by his creativity and genius. I need to make sure I have the same awe and respect for God who did the same but on a much larger scale. He created you and me and everyone around us. I need to be thankful for God's allowance to give us choices and freedom in life. I need to show my thanks to Him by making sure each day I am following His commands and making the right choices. That should be job number one for us. Make sure you are doing your job each day. Remember the reward that will come on the day when God says, "Well done my good and faithful servant!" (Matthew 25:23)

DEVOTIONAL #75

"Beauty and the Beast—Live on Stage"

Continuing our tour of the shows at Hollywood Studios, we move on to a wonderful one. It actually is my favorite at this park with the exception of the night-time show which we will get to later. This show is based on what has become a classic Disney movie. A few years ago, there were those pesky rumors about replacing this show. However, after the success of the recent live-action remake, I think it's safe for now. It would make me very sad if this show went away. It's always great even though I've seen it numerous times before. Let's discuss Beauty and the Beast—Live on Stage.

The Beauty and the Beast show opened in Hollywood Studios on November 22, 1991, on exactly the same day that the film made its box office debut. The show was supposed to be temporary lasting as long as the movie, but the show garnered immense popularity and was given the indefinite green light. The show takes place in a 1500 seat theater and lasts 25 minutes. It is a mini-version of the movie highlighting the best songs and action from the film. The Beauty and the Beast film that the show is based on was the first ever animated film nominated for a best picture Oscar. It was also the first Disney film to become a Broadway musical in 1994. Walt Disney actually considered making this famous story into a film way back in the 1930's, but it never materialized. The first run of this show at the Studios featured 5 of the popular movie songs but they were in no particular order. It was a sort of random showcasing of the music. In 2001, the show was tweaked and changed to reflect more the order of the film. The show was even featured on an episode of the Oprah Winfrey show. 3 of the 5 songs featured in the show and movie were actually nominated for a best song Oscar. They are "Belle," "Be Our Guest," and "Beauty and the Beast," the last of which won the award. The film also won an Oscar for best musical score. A fun fact from the original film...when Maurice gets lost near the beginning of the film, there is a sign in the woods pointing in several different directions. If you look close and squint, one of the signs says "Anaheim," a nod to the home of Disneyland.

Another fun movie fact is that the chief animator wanted the Beast to stay the Beast and didn't really like the idea of him turning back into a man. They even recorded Belle saying the line "Can you grow a beard?" for the end of the film but it wasn't used. The line however was used in the live-action remake.

Beauty and the Beast is arguably one of the greatest Disney films of all time. Even the remake did exceptionally well at the box office and was loved by many. It is a great story and comes complete with wonderful music, singing and humor. If you've never seen it, you definitely have a movie to watch. In the film, the Beast has the goal of getting Belle to love him even though he is hideous and scary on the outside. This leads to our spiritual thought for today which is one we've alluded to before. We are all different on the outside. God made us that way. We all look different. We all have features about ourselves that we like and some that we might not like. The world unfortunately often judges people based on their outward appearance. Some people are judged to be beautiful and others might be given an ugly label. This is an unfortunate part of the world we live in. The good news is that we as Christians know for a fact that God cares nothing about our outward appearance. Of course He wants us to take care of our bodies and be a good influence to others. However, look what God says in Jeremiah 17:10. It reads, "I the Lord search the heart and test the mind, to give every man according to his ways, according to the fruit of his deeds." Additionally, Jesus reminds us in Matthew 5:8 that those that are pure in heart are blessed and shall see God. David even asks God in Psalm 51:10 to create in him a clean heart and renew his spirit. These are both inner qualities.

The *Beauty and the Beast* movies and show are wonderful. I could watch them over and over as I love the story and music. I also love the message. In the end (spoiler alert!), Belle does learn to love the Beast and sees that even though he may not be attractive on the outside, he is beautiful within. She loves him for who he truly is. God does the same with us. So don't worry too much about your outer appearance. Make it a priority instead to make sure your heart and mind are pure and clean. That's what matters to God!

DEVOTIONAL #76

"Voyage of the Little Mermaid"

Going to amusement parks growing up, it was all about the rides for me. I never really enjoyed shows nearly as much. However, as time goes by, I am getting to where I actually prefer to sit, rest, and enjoy a good show. Maybe that's why I enjoy this park so much. Disney just does shows right. They know how to make them really entertaining, interactive and full of surprises. This show certainly has all those things. Today, we're going to watch the Voyage of the Little Mermaid.

This show, based on *The Little Mermaid* movie, began at the park in January of 1992. It replaced a show that had been there from day one called Here Comes the Muppets. The current show is 17 minutes long and features songs and reenactment of famous scenes from the movie. In that short time, it can only include highlights, but it does a good job showcasing the best ones. The show features puppets and audio-animatronics for many of the characters, but also includes live performers for the two main characters, Ariel and Prince Eric. The famous song "Under the Sea" features 100 puppets displayed in black light. The cast member puppeteers wear all black so you only see the puppets. This is one of the main reasons that you hear the request for "no flash photography" during the show. Doing so would illuminate the cast members and ruin the effects of the song. The show does become somewhat interactive by spraying you with a light mist at times and shining lasers throughout the audience. One of the highlights of the show is a giant audio-animatronic of Ursula that is 12 feet tall and 10 feet wide. This show has been delighting audiences for many years even though it was originally supposed to be a temporary, 18 month attraction. It's also interesting to note that one of the early "Ariel's" went on to win Miss America in 1993.

We have already talked a little about this movie when we rode Under the Sea back in Magic Kingdom. If you'll recall, during that devotional we talked about the fact that Ariel was willing to give up her life "under the sea" to fulfill her dreams of living as a human. We made a reference asking what you would give up for God. Today, I'd like to look at another aspect of the movie. This thought shines a different light on Ariel and looks at what is possibly a negative characteristic she had. The early part of the movie focuses on Ariel's disobedience of her father. She disagrees with his thoughts on humans and continually goes against his wishes. She wants to explore the surface of the water, watch the humans and interact with them. Despite her father's stern warnings, she does just that and ends up in big trouble. That leads to this question to consider today. How often do we do the same?

Part of being a Christian is learning how to trust in God's plan for our lives. We often feel that we want or even need things to go a certain way in life. We may pray earnestly for God to do something or change something. When we receive a "no" or what appears to be a contrary answer, we may get frustrated or even angry with God. However, as Christians, we are expected to trust in the fact that God knows what is best for us. While He always listens to our prayers and considers each and every one, He knows what we truly need. He knows the right time-table for granting our wishes, if at all. One of my favorite passages in the Bible and one I've mentioned before is Proverbs 3:5-6. Take the time to read that right now. Memorize it. If you're like me, you'll need it many times in life. It reminds us to trust in God and not to try and understand His ways. It goes on to say that if we can do that, He will lead us in the right direction. In Psalm 28:7, we are also reminded to trust in Him with our hearts. Another favorite Scripture is found in Philippians 4:6-7. This passage reminds us to make all of our requests known to God. It then says "the peace of God, which surpasses all understanding, will guard your hearts and your minds in Christ Jesus."

The Little Mermaid is another Disney hit due to another great story with a wonderful message and many life applications. Ariel's mistake of not listening to her father cost her dearly. It almost cost her father's life and hers as well. Luckily, in true Disney fashion, all things worked out in the end. However, life is not always like Disney, and mistakes can cost us. If we choose not to listen to our Heavenly father and continue to defy and disobey by approaching that line of sin, it may cost us our life as well. Recommit today to trust in God. You may not agree or understand Him sometimes. You may even get angry or frustrated at Him sometimes. However, the fact is that He knows what's best, and He loves you. Those are two facts you cannot deny.

DEVOTIONAL #77

"Walt Disney Presents"

We have but one more show to go here at the Studios, but before we get there, there's one more attraction I want to talk about. It's an attraction unlike any other. It's not a ride or a show although there is a film involved. Some people may skip it. Some people may not even know about it. Some people may think it's a waste of time. I strongly disagree. This attraction is one of the most important at this park or any park for that matter. It's not a thrilling ride or exciting show, but it's important and it needs to be a part of Disney. It's all about the history of the man who was Walt Disney.

Walt Disney Presents is an exhibit on Mickey Avenue at Hollywood Studios all about the man, Walt Disney. It's a display of his personal possessions, ideas, visions and dreams for all to see. It's a room full of the documented history of Walt Disney and the path he took to bring the Disney franchise to life. It also includes previews for upcoming additions, refurbishments and new attractions. It's a fascinating walk through his life, and I tend to learn something new each time I visit. Walt Disney Presents opened as One Man's Dream on October 1, 2001. It just recently changed its name in the fall of 2017. It was created and opened for what would've been Walt Disney's 100th birthday and was a part of the "100 years of magic" celebration that Disney had in 2001. Walt was born in 1901 and died in 1966, just a few days after his 65th birthday. The attraction includes a large room full of nearly 400 items and displays all about Walt Disney. It also includes a 15 minute film about him as well. The film was originally hosted by Michael Eisner who was CEO of Disney at the time of opening. When Eisner left that role, the film was changed and is now hosted by Julie Andrews, who is of course Mary Poppins herself. The exhibit also includes several models of rides, lands and various parts of Disney. There is even a model of Main Street, U.S.A. from the Magic Kingdom. In addition, you can see Walt Disney's Oscars that he won for *Snow White* and *20,000 Leagues Under the Sea*. He won a total of 48 Oscars as well as 7 Emmy Awards. It is said that while inside the attraction, you can find a cast member and ask them for a trivia quiz about Walt Disney. If you get the answers correct, you get a special certificate. Walt Disney only went to one year of high school before dropping out. For that reason, many might've considered him lazy or a failure, but I'd say he proved everyone wrong. He grew his famous mustache at age 25 and was never without it after that. Some other interesting things you'll see inside are his very own desk from 2nd grade with "WD" that he carved into it. You'll also see a clock inside that is stopped at 9:30am, the time of his death. When Disney Imagineers decided to plan and open this attraction, they had all the items flown on a giant, FedEx airbus and all items were carefully monitored.

There are a couple of ways most people do this attraction. Some choose a quick walk through and are done in 5-10 minutes. Others prefer to take their time and really read and focus on the various items. I prefer the latter. I also preferred the former title, One Man's Dream because that's what it really was. Walt Disney had a dream. What about you? Do you have a dream? I think it's pretty safe to say that in life, most people have dreams. Many people spend many hours daydreaming about what they want to become or accomplish in life. Unfortunately, most of these dreams tend to fall by the wayside and are never brought to life. Walt Disney was the exception to the rule. He had these dreams early on and worked very hard to make them a reality. Throughout my life whether in school, at a job or just in my personal walk, I have often been advised to have goals. I've even been told that it's a good practice to literally write down goals, make them attainable and measureable and stick with them. I agree that's important, and I challenge you to do just that. In Philippians 3:13-14, Paul talks about goals. He talks about forgetting what is behind and working hard to attain what is ahead. He also mentions the ultimate goal of Heaven. When I used to coach Cross Country, I once had a runner at the beginning of the season tell me that he was going to win an award at the end of the season. He didn't brag about it or say it in a boastful way, but he set a goal for himself to win a character award from me. Guess what? He did just that, and I certainly didn't give it to him because of what he said. I gave it to him because he worked very hard, earned and deserved it. I was impressed and proud of him. He set a goal and did what it took to accomplish it. That's what we all need to do in life.

I hope you take the time to enjoy Walt Disney Presents. It is a very important attraction that needs to remain in place. It's so important to remember the history of the man who made all of this come true. Hopefully it will inspire you to accomplish your goals and dreams as well. I also hope your main goal is like Paul said, to obtain Heaven with our Father. Proverbs 16:3 says that if we commit to the Lord whatever we do, he will establish our plans. That means God will help us accomplish our goals if we involve Him. I commit today to set goals, work hard to accomplish them and involve God in every step of the process. Please join me in doing the same.

DEVOTIONAL #78

"Fantasmic"

Now we've come to the very last attraction at Hollywood Studios. It just so happens to be my favorite attraction at this park, and I would say it's actually my favorite in all of Disney World! It is another show and it is a fantastic one! It's the closing show for HS each night. There was a time several years ago when they didn't show it every night. They only showed it on weekends and special occasions. Luckily, there was a small protest among seasoned guests, including myself. I, along with several others apparently, wrote a few emails basically begging them to return to nightly showings. I'm sure it was one of my elegantly worded emails that caused them to change their mind. They did bring it back to nightly showings, and the nation breathed a sigh of relief. Ok, maybe that's a slight exaggeration, but I sure did. It's too good to not show every night, and it always brings in huge crowds. Ok, enough introduction—Let's go watch Fantasmic!

Fantasmic is an eye-opening, jaw-dropping and magical (to use the Disney cliché) show that has been around for several years. It began in Disneyland in 1992. It was brought to Hollywood Studios in 1998 and is also shown in Tokyo Disney. In Disneyland, the show takes place on Tom Sawyer Island. However, in Florida, a new set was built complete with a 58 foot tall mountain surrounded by a 6900 seat theater. The mountain used is the 4th highest mountain at WDW and the theater also accommodates 3000 standing making it nearly a 10,000 capacity crowd. There are nearly 2 million gallons of water surrounding the mountain ranging from 1.5 to 6 feet deep in the middle. The show lasts 26 minutes, although there is also a shortened 4 minute version used during inclement weather. I've never seen this version but I can't imagine they could do much in 4 minutes! Fantasmic uses 46 performers and 78 costumes throughout the show. Near the beginning of the show, you'll see 3 large mists of water on which various movie scenes are projected. These large mists use 800 gallons of water per minute. Near the end of the show, you'll see a giant Maleficent dragon which is 50 feet high with a 50 foot wingspan and weighs over 32,000 lbs. The final scene, and my personal favorite, features 26 characters on a giant river boat which is actually bigger than the boats Columbus used in discovering America.

There are so many reasons why this show is my favorite attraction. I love the music. I love the water effects. I love the fireworks, the characters and the action. However, the main reason I love this show is the final scene. I love to see that giant boat come out with one character driving the ship only to have 25 other characters appear from out of seemingly nowhere to join him, dancing along to the music. It's that one character that really does it for me though. That lone character that starts the scene is Steamboat Willie, or technically Mickey Mouse as Steamboat Willie. In case you don't know, Steamboat Willie is Walt Disney's original Mickey Mouse cartoon. It was of course in black and white and the character in Fantasmic is also. I love that bit of creativity that the Imagineers placed in the show. I love that nod to the history of Disney and his famous first character. I think that is so important and the nostalgia of it is very powerful. I'm glad Disney takes this small moment to remember its past. We should also do the same.

Much of our Christian lives and instructions include looking to the future, planning for Heaven and making sure our lives are on the right track. However, it's also important to remember where you came from and make note of your past. 2 Thessalonians 2:15 reminds us to hold fast to the teachings of our past. Paul is reminding us that our past is important. Remembering where we came from helps us to stand firm and not waiver from our faith and beliefs. Deuteronomy 4:9 also tells us to not to forget what we've been taught but to instead teach them to our children and their children after that. Also, take some time to read Psalm 78. It is also a very important reminder of our past and what we can learn from past generations.

Fantasmic is a magnificent presentation. I would be satisfied with a Disney trip to see that show alone. For me, it encompasses all of what Disney World is. I love so much about it, but especially its reminder of the past. Our past is important. While we shouldn't dwell on it or let it ruin our future, we should remember the good things we've learned growing up. We should use what we've been taught about God and His plan and continue that message to future generations. We are all an important link in the chain to keep God's Word going strong and making sure everyone has a chance to respond to the gospel of Christ.

DEVOTIONAL #79

"Disney Bus System"

It's that time once again to travel to another park, our last one: Animal Kingdom. Before we discuss that park, just like before we have to travel there. We took a monorail between our first two parks and then a boat between the next two. So how do we now get from Hollywood Studios to Animal Kingdom? Unfortunately, we can't use either of those methods again. It's either car or bus this time unless we want to walk. I don't think you are even allowed to walk that route, but no thanks anyways. Let's try the bus instead this time. Maybe it's not quite as fun as the other two methods of transportation, but it's still a huge and important part of Disney World. The Disney bus system transports thousands daily and is a necessary component to keep Disney running. So let's take a devotional today and talk about the Disney bus system.

Disney World has nearly 400 buses in their fleet making it the 3rd largest bus system in Florida. Most of the drivers use this as a second job or a retirement job on the side as it pays around $10-12 per hour. Many just do it for fun, to make a little spending money or just to have something to do. There is a bus that runs from every Disney resort hotel to every park and to Disney Springs. You can also travel to the two water parks via the buses from each resort. Most of the buses began around an hour before the park opens and run up to an hour after the park closes. The Disney Springs bus finishes at 2am! Disney has recently put visual screens at the resorts showing guests how long it will be until the next bus arrives. These new systems track the buses through GPS so they can give an exact time of arrival. This has helped to calm some of the frustration and confusion about when buses are scheduled. In some places, Disney has installed special lanes just for the buses and some even get special traffic signal patterns to allow for better traffic flow. Disney has also begun testing using electric buses instead of diesel fuel. It is thought that at some point in the future, all Disney buses will be electric. Disney has a very special use of buses in their Magical Express system. This is the perk each Disney resort guest receives that allows them a free ride between the airport and their resort and back. The Magical Express began in 2005 and now takes 2.3 million people annually to and from their hotel. In contrast, Universal

Studios charges a fee for a shuttle and guests must carry their own luggage. On Disney's Magical Express, carrying luggage is an option. Disney will also transport your luggage from the plane to your resort room for free if you wish.

As I mentioned above, most of the Disney bus drivers are not using this job as their main source of income as it most likely wouldn't be enough. Most of them do it for fun or as a side job. I personally could see me doing this in my retirement. I do hold a CDL or bus driver license, and I think I'd enjoy driving families to the parks watching their excitement along the way. However, I do think I'd enjoy actually working inside the parks more. I have been to Disney several times and I have ridden numerous Disney buses. I have met and observed all types of drivers. Most of the drivers, I'd say 95%, have been pleasant and positive with a good attitude. However, I have had on occasion a driver that I could tell wasn't having a very good day. Sometimes, especially at night when the day is closing, I have seen a driver get frustrated or get a little harsh with his or her voice. I'm sure Disney strongly discourages this, but sometimes their aggravation can get the best of them. I'm sure it would be easier said than done, but they would have to work really hard to constantly have a positive attitude and a cheerful personality. There is one driver in particular that stands out to me and one I will never forget. We were on our way from our hotel to the Magic Kingdom one early morning and this driver not only greeted us with a smile but asked us trivia questions on the way, told some jokes, and made everyone smile and laugh. It would've been really easy that early in the morning to be grumpy or sleepy (am I naming dwarfs?), but he instead chose to make the best of the situation and work extra hard to make it a memorable ride for us.

What does Scripture say about attitude? Philippians 2:14-15 speaks of our attitude when it says "do all things without grumbling or disputing that you may be blameless and innocent." Some versions even say do all things without "complaining." Proverbs 17:22 is also a good reminder which reads "a joyful heart is good medicine but a crushed spirit dries up the bones." We are reminded to try and be joyful in all situations. It's not always easy, and we are certainly allowed to get frustrated and even angry. However, the way we handle our anger and frustration determines our attitude and how we come across to others. It's not always easy to go to work or do a job when we are tired or angry, but if we work hard, we can make the best of it and have a good attitude about it. A great majority of the bus drivers at Disney World seem to handle this very well. Next time you ride a Disney bus, take note of your driver's attitude. Better yet, check your own and greet them with a friendly hello!

DEVOTIONAL #80

"Animal Kingdom"

It's hard to believe, but we are finally in the last park at Walt Disney World! We've ridden the bus over to Animal Kingdom. This is Disney's newest park, and it also happens to be their largest park. Actually it is the largest theme park in the world taking up around 580 acres. Before we get to any of the rides or attractions, let's once again explore the park in general and discuss some facts and history about the Animal Kingdom.

Animal Kingdom opened on April 22, 1998 which happens to be Earth Day. In 2017, it was the 3rd most visited park in the United States and 6th in the world. This park is so large that the entire Magic Kingdom could fit into just one of the attractions here, Kilimanjaro Safaris which we'll discuss later. For two years straight while building this park, there were 60 dump trucks of dirt brought in every day. On opening day, the parking lot closed to capacity 20 minutes after park opening as most people got there very early. This park has 7 different land divisions which are The Oasis, Pandora-World of Avatar, Rafiki's Planet Watch, Discovery Island, Dinoland USA, Asia, and Africa. The park was originally going to have a land called "Beastly Kingdom" which would've featured mythological animals. This idea was scrapped, but this is the reason for the dragon featured on the park's sign. On opening day, there were two dozen protesters that picketed for about two hours and PETA also tried to boycott the park. However, Disney is known for taking special care of all the animals and giving them a very nice habitat. There are no plastic straws, lids or balloons offered in the park to prevent these items from harming the animals. There are 250 species of animals featured in the park with over 1000 live animals. Disney uses 4 tons of food per day to feed them all. The first birth at the park was a Kudu, a type of large African antelope. The park also has the world's most expensive roller coaster which we will discuss later as well.

For today's devotional thought, let's discuss the obvious here at this park. Let's talk about animals! What does the Bible say about them? The answer is a lot! Animals are featured in the very first chapter of the Bible. In Genesis 1, God created the animals, and in verses 26-28, He gives man the right to rule over them. Read Psalm 8:6-9 which reemphasizes this very thought of man being given permission to rule over the animals. Finally in James 3:7, it says that man can tame all kinds of animals. The Bible makes it pretty clear that the animals here on Earth are a gift from God. Can you imagine the Earth without animals? It certainly wouldn't be as fun and beautiful. I know our family really enjoys traveling to our local zoo several times a year. There is just something fascinating about observing and learning about animals.

I enjoy the Animal Kingdom a lot. I've always said Epcot is my favorite, but I may have to reconsider as the recent additions have certainly given it a boost. This park is one I always look forward to visiting. One of the reasons I love this park is that it has so much space and potential. It's so large and I know that in the years to come, Disney will continue to add to it and make it even better. It already has some phenomenal rides and shows that we'll talk about soon. I hope you also enjoy your next visit to the Animal Kingdom. Take some time while there to thank God for the gift of animals. They are beautiful to look at and learn about and are intriguing to watch. They are just another one of the many blessings from God we can be thankful for, and we should consider it an honor to take care of them.

DEVOTIONAL #81

"Tree of Life"

We've discussed Animal Kingdom in general, and we are now finally inside our last park. We've come so far and yet we still have a lot of great attractions to go! Now that we're in the AK, where do we go first? Most people head to one of the many exciting rides here. With this being the largest park, you'll have to do a lot of walking (or running if you're in our family) no matter which way you head first. However, we're actually not going to a ride yet, because there is something else we can't miss on the way to any of the popular attractions. It's that giant thing right in front of us that you absolutely can't miss. Take a look at that massive and enormous tree that is the icon of the Animal Kingdom. Let's take today and talk about the Tree of Life.

The Tree of Life cannot be missed. It's 145 feet high and is at the center of the park, much like Cinderella Castle at Magic Kingdom. Animal Kingdom is home to 4 million living plants, but this isn't one of them. This man-made tree is 50 feet wide at the base and is covered with 325 carvings of both existing and even extinct animals. When Disney Imagineers were constructing this park on paper, they knew they wanted to have some sort of icon at the center. It seemed natural to build an enormous tree, something from nature since this was more of a nature park with a focus on animals. Imagineers obtained an old oil platform and built the tree around it using it as the foundation. They also decided to put an attraction inside the tree which we'll discuss later. The tree is located on what is known as Discovery Island. There used to be another island on Disney property with the same name. It was an island close to the Magic Kingdom on Bay Lake that guests could visit. When Disney shut that island down and built this new park, they decided to pay tribute to the former attraction and name this new island after it. The tree has 8000 branches and 102,000 man-made leaves, each a foot long. It took 18 months to build the tree alone, and as mentioned, it contains hundreds of animal carvings. As you wait in line for the attraction inside, you can get a good view of many of the animals. There is also a secret path that most guests miss that leads up to the tree. Guests are welcome to travel this path to get a better look at the carvings as well. When famous animalist Jane

Goodall visited the park under construction, she noticed that among the many animals, there was no chimp. Goodall is famous for working with chimps and therefore, a chimp was quickly carved to look like David Graybeard, of the famous chimps she worked with. Finally, it is said that you can see this park icon from the top of Mount Gushmore, an attraction at Blizzard Beach as well as from the California Grille, the restaurant at the top of the Contemporary Resort.

Seeing the Tree of Life for the first time is breathtaking. Its immense size is remarkable as you can see if from virtually anywhere inside the park. Think about trees for a few minutes today. Have you ever climbed a tree? What kinds of trees do you like most? Can you think of a story in the Bible that revolves around trees? God created trees on day 3 in the story of creation in Genesis. They are mentioned specifically and played a key role in the Garden of Eden story with Adam and Eve. Consider also the story of Zaccheus in the New Testamant in the beginning of Luke 19. He climbed up a sycamore tree to get a better view of Jesus and was consequently visited by Christ at his home. There are many other stories of trees in the Bible. The story of Jonah involves a tree. You could argue that Jesus was crucified on a tree. The passage I want to focus on however, comes from John 15. Read that chapter if you have some time. It is Jesus talking, and He is reminding us how God's plan works and His purpose in our lives. In John 15 verse 5, He says "I am the vine; you are the branches. Whoever abides in me and I in him, he it is that bears much fruit, for apart from me you can do nothing." Think about a how a tree branch works. Could the tree produce anything if there weren't branches to connect the fruit to the trunk? The branches allow water and nutrients to flow through to produce the fruit or seeds. Jesus is the same way. We cannot truly bear fruit, which means serving others, and live correctly with God if we don't go through Jesus. If we follow Jesus and let Him live inside us, we know how to live, how to bear fruit and bring others to God. What a beautiful comparison Jesus makes to how a tree works!

The Tree of Life is truly a memorable Disney icon. I would like next time to explore it more and truly look at all the carvings. I have heard of families doing a scavenger hunt to see how many animals they can truly find on the tree. Hopefully when any of us see it next, we will think of God. Think of the beauty of His creation and His trees. Think also of God as the base of that tree, think of yourself as the leaves, and think of those connecting branches as Jesus Christ. Jesus is the only way to get to the Father. Jesus is the only way we can truly know our purpose in life. Finally, Jesus is the only way that we can truly know how to serve others and bear fruit for God.

DEVOTIONAL #82

"Avatar Flight of Passage"

Now that we've entered the Animal Kingdom and stopped to gaze at the colossal tree, let's get to our first ride. In years past, our family would've hastily made our way to one of the more popular attractions at either of the back corners of the park. However, that has all changed very recently with the addition of a brand new land here at AK. Pandora—World of Avatar opened in May of 2017 to a lot of anticipation and huge crowds. This newest land covers 12 acres and includes two new rides, two new places to eat and a merchandise store that includes items from the actual *Avatar* film. This film is the number one movie of all time as far as money earned taking in around 2.7 billion dollars! Disney decided to capitalize on its success and the fact that there are several sequels planned and coming soon. As mentioned, this land includes two rides, and we are going to tackle the most popular today. This ride has consistently had wait times over two hours since its opening over a year ago. Let's hopefully grab a fastpass and go ride Avatar Flight of Passage.

This beautiful and breath-taking new land of Pandora at AK cost 500 million dollars to build, and this ride was no doubt a large portion of that. This incredible experience is a 3D flying simulator that is similar to Soarin' at Epcot but greatly enhanced. During the pre-show, you are shown your Avatar which is what you will look like in the world of Pandora. If you've seen the film, this makes a lot more sense. You are then tasked with riding on the back of a Banshee, a flying, mountain creature also from the film. During the 4½ minute ride, you soar across the beautiful landscape of Pandora and experience exhilarating effects such as the wind, water mist and incredible sounds. This ride has been very well reviewed and has quickly become the favorite ride among many, including my two sons. I love it too and may have to move it into the number one spot as well. For now, that spot belongs to another ride we'll get to soon. Flight of Passage is amazing though. The fact that you are sitting on a motorcycle-like device with 3D glasses but feel as if you truly are riding this creature in the world of Pandora is truly Disney creativity at work. I understand why this ride has some of the most consistently long lines in WDW history. It's a ride you can't do just once. There is so much to see and experience that you'll want to do it over and over. My oldest son loved it so much that he chose to wait nearly 3 hours for a second ride. One of the most amazing details about this ride that my wife and I both noticed was the fact that as you are "riding the Banshee" you can actually feel it "breathing" between your legs. That alone was such a clever touch and very impressive to us.

I want to spend a little time today talking about breathing. Believe it or not, breathing is mentioned several times in the Bible. It starts in Genesis when chapter 2 verse 7 says that God "breathed into his nostrils the breath of life" speaking of the first man, Adam. In Psalm 150:6, we are told that everything that has breath should praise the Lord. In 2 Timothy 3:16, a passage we've looked at before, we are told that God breathed out all Scripture, meaning every word of the Bible is inspired by Him. Finally, speaking of Jesus on the cross, Luke 23:46 says, "Then Jesus, calling out with a loud voice, said, "Father, into your hands I commit my spirit!" And having said this he breathed his last." These are all very important passages that talk about or mention breathing.

Flight of Passage is truly an ingenious attraction. I've ridden it three times now and can't wait to ride it again. You really do get the sense of being on the back of a flying creature. The feeling of his breathing just adds to the realistic sensation. See if you can feel it next time. Remember how important breathing is. It gives us life and allows us to speak. With it we can praise God as we are instructed. With it we can tell others about Him. With it, God himself gave us his Word, gave us life and taught us the way to Him through His Son. Thank you God for truly blessing us with the breath of life, both here on Earth and eternally.

DEVOTIONAL #83

"Na'vi River Journey"

Today we are going to try the other new ride in the land of Pandora at Animal Kingdom. We've ridden the most popular and intense one. Now let's move to the more peaceful and scenic one. It's a picturesque boat ride that takes you through the Kaspavan River from the *Avatar* film. It still has decently long wait times, but they are typically a fraction of the ride next door. This indoor, dark ride that is also 4½ minutes long is a wonderful tribute to the award-winning scenery from the film and is worth doing if the wait isn't too crazy. Let's enjoy a nice, relaxing ride on the Na'vi River Journey.

You begin by boarding your raft which is actually two sewn together. A total of 12 or possibly up to 16 if there are a lot of small kids, can fit comfortably in each vehicle. In addition to life-size scenery, this ride also uses a lot of screens and projection mapping. One criticism this ride has received is that there is no real story to it. You are simply flowing through the river, but there is no plot or even a voice guide to explain the sights. If you haven't seen the film, you won't have any idea what you are seeing along the way. For that reason, you are advised to check out the movie before riding if possible. You do come face to face with one of the most realistic and impressive audio-animatronics at WDW toward the end of the ride.

One thing is for certain about this ride. It is visually stunning and the beauty of it is remarkable. As I mentioned above, the movie Avatar won several awards including Oscars for cinematography, art direction and visual effects. The movie is known for its beautiful scenes of this "new world" of Pandora. While visiting the land, you'll feel as if you're there especially at night with the bioluminescent decorations. I enjoyed the film, especially the second time I saw it. I don't think I fully understood it the first time and it's quite possible I fell asleep as I tend to do. I actually rented it again right before visiting the new land for the first time. I really enjoyed it a lot more the second time around. Do I think it's the best movie ever? No, I don't, but it's a good movie and the visual effects were extremely impressive.

Think about the most beautiful place on Earth you've ever seen. Is it the beach, the mountains or somewhere else? Maybe it's Disney

World? I remember being amazed at the beauty of the Grand Canyon the first time I saw it. As you think about those places that you've seen in person or in pictures, consider the fact that none of them will compare with the beauty of Heaven. Revelation 21:1-2 compares the beauty of Heaven with the beauty of a bride being presented for her husband. A little later in Revelation 22:1-5, the beauty of Heaven is described further. It mentions beautiful rivers, trees, fruit and much more. Take some time to read this passage. It and many other scriptures talk about what we will all hopefully see one day. I can't wait. How about you? Are you excited to see the beauty of Heaven? It's something we should all look forward to and prepare for. I am so grateful to God that He has given us so much beauty to look at while we're here. However, we should always keep in mind that He's saved the best for last and as my wife always says, "the best is yet to be!" The next time you get to ride the Na'vi River Journey and witness the extraordinary visuals, think about the beauty of Heaven and the amazing gift God has waiting for us because of the sacrifice of His Son.

DEVOTIONAL #84

"Kilimanjaro Safaris"

Yes, there's a lot of hype over this new land of Pandora, but there is a lot more this park has to offer. Let's travel to another great ride today. Before Pandora existed, most people typically started with one of two rides. To go to one, you have to go to the African land in the back left of the park. To go to the other, you have to go to the Asian land in the back right of the park. They are completely opposite of each other so you have to be firm in your choice because it's a long way between them. You can't just do one right after the other, at least not without a decent trek in between. So do we go right or left? Our family typically chooses left. There's no wrong answer. They are both great rides, and we'll talk about the other next. Were gonna go left today for a pretty good reason that I'll explain shortly. Let's talk about Kilimanjaro Safaris!

Kilimanjaro Safaris opened with the park in 1998. This is a one of a kind ride that is again truly unique to Disney. It's a definite must do at AK and is typically enjoyed by all guests which you can't say about most rides. The Safari is a 22 minute ride through the African savannah to see many different types of animals. You are placed in a 32-rider open bus-like vehicle and see animals out both sides throughout your journey. The land used for this ride is extremely vast. It is the largest attraction in all the Disney parks. In fact, the entire Magic Kingdom could fit inside this ride's space. This attraction is 110 acres while the MK is 107. This ride is similar to what Walt Disney had in mind when he created the Jungle Cruise at the MK. As I mentioned several entries ago, Walt wanted to put live animals in that ride. It didn't work out, but it's safe to say he would probably approve of this ride. The ride features many animals that are too many to list here. There were zebras featured on this ride when the park opened but they were soon removed due to their aggressiveness. They were later reinstated. Also when the ride first opened, there were several animal deaths from disease, toxic exposure, maternal killings and park vehicles. It sounds like it took a little while for Disney to work out the kinks. On one occasion the ride was closed for 40 minutes due to a hippopotamus death from pneumonia. One fun thing to look for on this ride is the small island that houses the flamingoes. The island is a large hidden mickey. Disney Imagineers were very clever in creating this ride. They used temperature tricks such as cool or heated rocks to coax animals near the road so guests would be able to see them. At the same time, there are hidden barriers to keep the animals from getting too close. This is said to be one of the most popular and competitive rides for cast members to work. While riding, you will see a few fake baobab trees. There are no real ones on the ride. Real ones of that size would be thousands of years old. These fake ones hold cameras to observe the ride in action. The only real baobab tree is near the Tusker House restaurant near the entrance to the Safari. When the ride first opened, there was a whole story attached to this ride about animal poaching. Early tests even showed a fake corpse of an elephant, but this proved to be too dark so a happy ending was added where the poachers are caught. This story line, however, was removed a few years ago.

One reason our family tries to do this ride early in the morning is because we like to get the first look at the animals. They seem to be more active and visible in the morning. I've done Safaris as all times of day. One thing I love about this ride is that you can ride it several times a day and never have the same ride. The animals are never in the same place or doing the same thing. This ride is always changing. Again, you can't say that about most other rides, if any. Unlike this ride which is ever changing, God doesn't change. Unfortunately in the world we live in today, many people, even strong Christians, think the God will change for them. Many think God will cater to their needs and understand if they want to change or tweak His Word. However, listen to what 2 Timothy 4:3-4 says. It reads, "For the time is coming when people will not endure sound teaching, but having itching ears they will accumulate for themselves teachers to suit their own passions, and will turn away from listening to the truth and wander off into myths." I think that time is now. Hebrews 13:8 says that Jesus is the same yesterday, today and forever. Numbers 23:19 tells us that God doesn't change his mind like man, and Isaiah 40:8 says that the Bible will stand forever.

Change can be good. I particularly like the Safari ride because it does change each time. No two rides are the same meaning I could ride it repeatedly with different experiences. God is not like that. He won't change His Word or His plan to cater to our needs. We must remember this and study His Word diligently to know what He wants for us. I hope you enjoy the Safari as much as I do. It's also a great reminder of God's creation. Keep in mind as you ride that the same God who created all those animals, trees and beautiful landscapes is the same God who created you and me. He will be that same God forever, without change!

DEVOTIONAL #85

"Expedition Everest"

Having enjoyed the Safari, let's trek over to the other side of the park to another very popular ride. Expedition Everest is a fairly uncommon Disney roller coaster that opened in April of 2006. It was one of the most expensive rides Disney ever created at a price tag of 100 million dollars. In fact it held the 2011 Guinness Record for the most expensive roller coaster ever created. Disney doesn't build a whole lot of roller coasters, at least not like their competitors at say a Six Flags park. Therefore they went all out on this one. It goes 50 mph, includes an 80 foot drop and goes both backwards and forwards, the first Disney ride to do so. The ride takes nearly 3 minutes and accommodates approximately 2000 riders per hour. The ride resembles the tallest mountain in the world, Mt. Everest, although Disney's mountain is 199.5 feet high. This makes it Disney's tallest ride and still allows it to avoid the light required by the FAA for structures at 200 feet or higher. There is a popular rumor out there that Disney's Everest is the tallest "mountain" in Florida, although this is not true. Actually, Britton Hill in the panhandle on the Florida-Alabama line is the tallest at 345 feet. The ride also includes the fictional Yeti, although many claim it's authenticity. The Yeti is shown in shadow form but also as a gigantic audio-animatronic. This giant creature used to move when the ride first opened but hasn't worked since a few months after opening. The framing holding the beast split soon after the ride became operational and operating it would cause a major risk. For that reason, all you see now is the giant creature in a strobe light to make it appear as though he's moving. Many dedicated Disney fans have pushed for his repair for years. I actually read a report where the Imagineer in charge of building this ride said that one day the Yeti will be fixed. However, that quote was from 2013 so don't get your hopes up. The coaster resembles a steam train and you see actual steam which comes from special vents underneath. The steam is actually not water based to prevent the cars and track from rusting. The cast members who open and close this ride have to walk the entire length of the track each day to assure safety. Try to get in the very front or very back on this ride for a couple of reasons. If you are in the very front, when your coaster gets to the very top and stops briefly, you can see a great view of Epcot and other Disney icons from the top. Also from the front or back, you can watch the track turn over. If you're in the back, you can turn around and see it when you are stopped at the top. If you are in the front, you can see it in front of you when you are stopped watching the shadow Yeti. Also at the top, look out to see many hairbands on the side of the track. This is apparently a bizarre rider tradition to throw these out.

I used to be a 6th grade history teacher, and we would talk about Mt. Everest every year in our discussion of India. This world's tallest mountain has always fascinated me. A very small part of me would love to climb it, although I know I'd be putting my life in major jeopardy, not to mention my bank account. It's apparently very expensive and very dangerous to climb. While this particular mountain isn't mentioned in the Bible, several important ones are. Think about Mt. Sinai and Moses (Exodus 20). Think about Mt. Ararat and Noah (Genesis 8). Think about Mt. Carmel and Elijah (I Kings 18). If you are unfamiliar with any of these, take some time to read them. They are great "mountain stories" among many others in Scripture. Today I'd like to focus on Mt. Moriah. Do you know who climbed that one? This is the mountain that Abraham climbed when God told him to sacrifice his one and only son, Isaac. Just like Mt. Everest, that story has always intrigued and fascinated me. The story is found in Genesis 22. Go back and read that story as well. Take some time to truly focus on what God asked Abraham to do. Put yourself in his position. What would you do? I've often thought about that, but I don't like thinking about it. What an impossible situation! What a true test of faith! How is your faith? Would you have the faith in God to sacrifice someone you love? Isn't that exactly what God did for all of us by giving Jesus to die on the cross? Hebrews 11:6 says, "And without faith it is impossible to please him, for whoever would draw near to God must believe that he exists and that he rewards those who seek him." According to this verse, it is impossible to please God without strong faith. Life is difficult and it is sometimes hard to trust in God and His plan for us. With our trivial human minds, we like to try to do things on our own thinking we know best, but we must have faith in God to trust in His will for us.

Everest is a great ride and favorite of many. I like it a lot but can only do it a couple of times before that backwards part gets to me. I hope I can continue to ride it at least once per trip for years to come. I love the story, creativity and fun this ride brings. I also will try to continue to use the mountain as a reminder of the mountain of faith I must have in God. Abraham had tremendous faith and is an example to us all. I pray to have that same faith in my continued walk with God. I pray the same for you!

DEVOTIONAL #86

"DINOSAUR"

Stepping off of Everest, my guess is you'll be like most and want to ride it again. Ok, go ahead before the line gets too long. After that, let's move on to another ride. Today's ride is very special and actually holds quite a distinction. While Fantasmic at Hollywood Studios is my favorite show and overall attraction at WDW, I've long said and continue to say for now that this is my very favorite ride in all of Disney World. Many will disagree and think I'm crazy. Some won't even ride it. I absolutely love it and always have. Let's go ride DINOSAUR!

DINOSAUR was originally called Countdown to Extinction and opened with the park in 1998. The name was eventually changed to promote the Disney's film also called *Dinosaur*, although the ride itself had little, if anything, to do with the movie. This ride lasts slightly over 3 minutes and takes you on a "time rover" where you are tasked with bringing back a dinosaur from the past. On your journey through time, you see 11 audio-animatronic dinosaurs and many other stationary ones. McDonalds sponsored this ride from 1998-2008 and you can still see a nod to the original sponsor in the queue line. Look above your head for the red, yellow and white pipes with chemical formulas on them. Those are the formulas for ketchup, mustard and mayonnaise. Disney was originally planning on using a T-Rex as the scariest dinosaur near the end but decided to go with a Carnotaurus instead after this type of dinosaur was actually discovered during the planning of the ride. If you've ever been to Disneyland in California, you might notice that this ride is very similar to the Indiana Jones ride there. In fact, the track layout of the two rides is nearly identical. You'll also notice a fountain in front of this attraction covered by plants and trees. This fountain used to be open faced but park guests would often swim in the fountain so Disney added the greenery and a dinosaur statue to deter this tradition. Finally, when this ride first opened, dinosaurs actually jumped across the track during your ride. I'm not sure why they don't anymore, but that would be a clever addition if they ever put that back in.

So why in the world is DINOSAUR my very favorite ride you may be asking? I just love everything about it. I love the preshow film, the story, the mission, the audio-animatronics, and just the thrill of it all. Maybe another reason is because my very favorite movie is *Jurassic Park*. I've loved that movie (and its sequels) since the first time I saw it. It's a great story basically about a group of people trying to escape from dinosaurs that have taken over a theme park. So what is the message we get from that? It's actually pretty simple. In both the ride and the *Jurassic Park* movie, the goal is to escape the scary dinosaurs. Similarly in life, we are constantly trying to escape something very scary. His name is Satan, and while we unfortunately can't ever completely escape him and the sin he throws at us, we have something that can help. I Corinthians 10:13 tells us that God is faithful to us and He will not let us be tempted beyond what we can handle. It also tells us that God always provides us a way out. 2 Corinthians 1:22 tells us that God gives us the Holy Spirit in our hearts. This Spirit helps us when Satan throws his sinful darts our way. It makes us know right from wrong as well as the way out. It makes us feel guilty when we do sin. God gives this Holy Spirit to those who are faithful and follow His plan to help us escape Satan. God also gives us something else very powerful. He gives us forgiveness. I John 1:9 says that if confess our sins, God will forgive them. Like the dinosaurs, sin is scary. It pulls us away from God and makes us feel guilty and dirty. Thankfully we have a much more powerful God who has given us His Spirit to help us resist sin as well as His forgiveness when we fall short.

Fortunately, the ride and movie have a happy ending. Both offer escapes from the frightening dinosaurs. Our lives can also have a happy ending if we work hard. We can escape Satan and sin as long as we follow God. If we are faithful to Him, He will always provide a way of escape. Let's remember today to thank God for giving us a way out when we are being chased, not by dinosaurs, but the devil.

DEVOTIONAL #87

"It's Tough to Be a Bug"

Well, that's about it for what would be called thrill rides at Animal Kingdom. I guess there are one or two others that are semi-thrill, if that's a word, and we'll do those soon. Keep in mind, however, that AK is still in its childhood compared to the other parks and will most likely continue to add attractions in the years to come. For now, let's skip around and do some of the other minor attractions that AK has to offer. We'll start in the middle of the park. Remember that giant tree we talked about a few devotionals back? Well, as I mentioned, it ain't just a tree. There's something inside there! Let's go see It's Tough to be a Bug.

If you wind your way around the giant Tree of Life and explore the many animal carvings on its trunk, you'll eventually find your way to the door to the inside. Once inside, you'll be given special bug glasses as you await a one-of-a-kind film. It's Tough to be a Bug is a nine minute long film hosted by Flik of the flick (pun intended) *A Bug's Life*. The attraction is a 4D short film that includes not only 3D effects but the Disney norm 4D effects of water, smell, and much more including some surprises in your seat as well. This attraction opened with the park which coincidentally opened 7 months before the movie debuted in theaters. It's pretty interesting to me that when this attraction first opened, nobody knew who these characters were. However, when they were building the Tree of Life and knew they wanted an attraction inside, it was then CEO Michael Eisner who suggested a "preview" of sorts for the upcoming movie. As you can imagine, it's been around ever since. You will rarely find a huge line for this attraction as the film accommodates 430 guests per show which means it can host over 2500 guests per hour. There are a few scary moments during the experience that some younger guests might find too intense including spiders dropping from the ceiling and the giant audio-animatronic Hopper. This machine happens to be one of the most complex audio-animatronics that Disney has with many moving parts. As you wind your way through this queue line and enjoy the animal carvings, also notice that posters along the way. They are all puns and play on words that represent many famous movies. The songs in the show also mimic some famous Broadway music. Some of the bugs in the film are also voiced by famous actors such as Cheech Marin and Jason Alexander.

Just like the 4D experiences at the other parks, I've always enjoyed this attraction. Even though it's just a film, it's a fun experience and an entertaining show. One may ask what possible lesson we can learn from a bunch of bugs. I have seen the Bug's Life movie and while I enjoyed it, it wasn't one of my very favorites. However, there is still an important lesson we can take from the theme of the movie and the attraction. The fact is that bugs are actually pretty amazing. Have you ever studied bugs? It is estimated that on Earth there are around 10 quintillion bugs. That's a 10 with eighteen zeros after it! It is also estimated that there are approximately 91,000 different species of bugs. In a nutshell, that's a lot of bugs! Even though they are small in size, due to their sheer number, bugs are estimated to have the largest biomass of any other terrestrial animal. Bugs outnumber us as humans certainly in number but also in mass by a huge amount. So what does this have to do with God or our spiritual lives? Well, in a sense, we are like those bugs. We are God's bugs. I know that sounds funny, but think about this. Just like we look down and see the small bugs beneath our feet, God looks down upon on us. What's amazing about that is He knows each of us by name. According to Luke 12:7, He even knows the number of hairs on our head (which isn't too hard of a task for me personally being that I'm bald). While we as humans don't quite number like the bugs, there are over 7 billion of us, and He knows us all. Isaiah 43:1 says He can call us all by name. He created us all. Jeremiah 1:5 says He even knew us before He formed us in the womb. That means He knew us before we even existed!

Take the time to go enjoy the bug show. It's an entertaining film with some funny lines, good music and general fun. Make sure you stay seated until the very end too for a special surprise. As you watch and learn about the bugs, remember how many there really are! Also remember how many of us there are. Then try to comprehend that God knows us all! He loves us all! We are His bugs. He created us all, and of course He created all those actual bugs too...all 10 quintillion of them! What an amazing God!

DEVOTIONAL #88

"Primeval Whirl"

Today we move to another minor attraction that could be classified as a semi-thrill ride. We'll have to head back to Dinoland. We already rode Dinosaur, of course, but our next attraction is there as well. It's also a ride that I have to hesitate to do. I've done it a few times, and I can handle it maybe once if I'm feeling alright. My boys on the other hand really like it and can do it over and over. Enjoy it while you can boys! One day you'll be like your old man with a weak stomach too. Today we're going to ride Primeval Whirl.

Primeval Whirl is a roller coaster of sorts in Dinoland. You can't miss this ride as its unique design, brightly-colored track and creative decorations stand out in this area of the park. This ride opened about four years after the park on March 31, 2002. When boarding this attraction, you and up to three other guests board a round vehicle and are taken on a one and a half minute ride on a metal track. Your vehicle is taken up a fairly tall 30 foot hill and then you slowly wind your way back down. The unique part of this ride is that your vehicle spins in a complete circle and does so all the way down the hill. In fact, this is the only roller coaster at Disney that includes a spin motion, and it was the very first roller coaster at the Animal Kingdom. It also has one of Disney's tallest height restrictions at 48 inches due to the spinning which causes you to experience 2.5 g's during your ride. You'll notice when you see this ride that it is like Space Mountain in that there are actually two identical tracks that are both used at peak times. This ride is a very slow loader and so lines can back up if the park is crowded. It is recommended that you ride this in the morning before lines get too long. The top speed of this ride is 29mph and it is themed around a meteor that supposedly wiped out the dinosaurs. This ride does have some sad history attached to it. Not one but two cast members have died because of this ride. In 2007, a CM fell from the ride platform, hit their head and died five days later. In 2011, another CM was working on the ride and suffered severe head trauma after being hit by a ride vehicle. This person also died at the hospital. Since these two accidents, special sensors have been installed to keep the ride from working if someone is in the way of the vehicle.

As I mentioned above, the ride centers on the "fact" that the dinosaurs were wiped out by a meteor. I know that many people including scientists think that a meteor is what killed all the dinosaurs millions of years ago. Similarly, I also know that many think the world itself was created billions of years ago, and the dinosaurs lived long before any humans did. This has been a big debate, especially in the Christian world for many years. Some Christians would argue strongly that dinosaurs and humans co-existed. Some would argue that the Earth is not billions or even millions of years old, but only 6000 or so. Some Christians would get very upset about those who feel otherwise. I have a different take on it.

There are verses in the Bible that possibly talk about dinosaurs making it appear that they could have co-existed with man. Job chapters 40 and 41 mention a creature, the Behemoth which could be a dinosaur. Isaiah 27 also mentions a "Leviathan" that many scholars think may be a dinosaur. So Biblically, man and dinosaurs could've been created around the same time. Who knows? God does, that's who! But my personal opinion is, who cares? Maybe that's the wrong opinion. Maybe I should get worked up and angry when someone says the Earth is billions of years old. Maybe I should argue when told that dinosaurs were around millions of years ago and died due to a meteor. However, I choose not to. Here's my feeling on the age of the Earth and the timing of the dinosaurs. God created it! God created Earth. God created dinosaurs. God created man. When did He create these things? I don't know, and don't really care. All I care about is that God did it all. Maybe I'll find out the truth of it all one day when I get to see Him. Until then, I'll leave that as one of the God's mysteries. To me, the when is not nearly as important as the who. In my humble opinion, I think sometimes Christians get way too worked up about the when. The very first verse, Genesis 1:1, says that God created the Heavens and the Earth. Hebrews 11:3 says that the universe was created at God's command. Colossians 1:16 says all things were created by God. That's all that matters. Why do we need to get angry and worked up and turn people off to Christianity and God about something that doesn't really matter? As long as people believe who created it all, that's the important part.

Primeval Whirl is a good and imaginative ride. Next time you ride it, notice the giant pictures of meteors marking the end of the dinosaurs. Use it as a reminder not to get worked up about the fact that this may or may not be true. Instead, just remember who created our wonderful planet and all the creatures on it. More importantly, remember that it's only temporary and our real purpose is to be using our time here to prepare for eternity with God. That's what really matters!

DEVOTIONAL #89

"Triceratops Spin"

Since we are here in Dinoland, we might as well stay put, because there is another attraction right next door. It's not exactly a thrill ride, but it's a ride nonetheless. In addition to these two rides, there are several carnival type games in this area where guests can purchase tickets and play for prizes. This area is very much like a county fair type park area and for that reason, a lot of Disney enthusiasts have given negative reviews to this area. Some say it cheapens the park, and I would probably agree. It could be a lot worse, but it does seem to be more of a knockoff of other parks, and I wish Disney would do something different with the area, something uniquely Disney. That's enough of the negative, however. Let's focus on today's ride, a simple experience that the little kids especially enjoy. It's called Triceratops Spin.

Triceratops Spin opened on November 1, 2001 and is another copycat of the classic Dumbo ride from Magic Kingdom, similar to Aladdin's Magic Carpets or Astroorbiter. Actually, the only difference from Dumbo is that you are now riding in dinosaurs instead of elephants. You also have a little more control of your dinosaur which is different than Dumbo. Just like on the magic carpets, there are two sets of controllers in each dinosaur. If you sit in the front seat, you control whether the dinosaur tips forwards or backwards. If you sit in the back seat, you control whether the dinosaur goes up or down. Very near this ride, you will find two giant statues of dinosaurs named Chester and Hester. There is apparently a back story on these two. The story goes that they owned a gas station where dinosaur bones were found in the area. This find led more and more people to the area which is why the "Dino-institute" was founded. Chester and Hester decided to sell souvenirs to make extra money and also decided to make a little amusement park to further capitalize on the publicity and tourists. Sounds like someone had a lot of time on their hands to make up that story. If you look at Triceratops Spin while it's in motion, it resembles a toy top. The center of the top reveals a spinning dinosaur which rises as the ride progresses. The ride lasts one and a half minutes and includes 16 dinosaur vehicles.

As I mentioned above, this ride is somewhat of a reproduction of Dumbo, one of the more famous and well-known rides in Fantasyland at the Magic Kingdom. Yes, it looks a little different, but the experience is basically the same. It's an imitation, like it or not. The Bible also speaks of imitation. Ephesians 5:1 says that we are to be imitators of Christ. I Peter 2:21 says that Christ left us an example to follow. And in I Corinthians 11:1, Paul says, "Be imitators of me, as I am of Christ." There are many others I could share, but as you can see in all three of these verses, we are to imitate Christ. We all tend to have heroes in our lives. We have people we look up to, admire and maybe even try to imitate. The Bible makes it pretty clear that Jesus Christ is truly the only one we should really try to be just like. While we can never be as perfect or sinless as He was, we can always strive to be more and more like Him each day.

I don't mind riding good ole' Triceratops Spin. It's a nice, relaxing ride with a nice breeze. Yes, it's an imitation of Dumbo, but that makes it a good reminder that I need to do a better job in my life of imitating Christ. I need to study His life and teachings daily to know better how to live like He did. We can all do a better job of this, and I challenge you to make this a top priority!

DEVOTIONAL #90

"Finding Nemo—The Musical"

Ok, let's take a break from these exciting rides at Animal Kingdom and move to a few shows featured at this park. There are actually some really good shows at AK that I enjoy almost as much as the rides. We're going to start with my very favorite. Yes, this is my favorite show at all four parks, not including the nighttime show, Fantasmic. I cannot visit the Animal Kingdom without going to this one. It is phenomenal, and I think it could even make it as a Broadway show if it was lengthened a little. Today, we are talking about Finding Nemo—The Musical.

The "Finding Nemo Show," as we like to call it, opened in January of 2007. It takes place at the Theater in the Wild which is technically in the Dinoland portion of Animal Kingdom, although none of the three shows that have been there have ever been about dinosaurs. The first show at this theater was Journey into the Jungle Book. After that, there was a show based on the Tarzan movie called Tarzan Rocks. The theater was originally open to the elements without a roof but was given a roof when the Nemo show moved in. The current show features live actors and life sized puppets and is 35 minutes. This significantly condenses the original *Finding Nemo* movie. Unlike the movie, the show adds music with several featured songs that include the popular "Big Blue World" and "Go with the Flow". This has by far been the most well received show to grace the theater welcoming thousands of guests per day. The show is performed six times daily and the theater which holds 1500 people is full at most showings. The writers knew they had to take the popular film and condense it considerably. To do this, they focused on a single theme from the movie, the idea that the world is dangerous and beautiful. This was the first time ever that Disney based a theme park musical on a non-musical movie. Six new musical numbers were written specifically for this show. The same writers who wrote the music also wrote the music for the popular film, *Frozen*. This show is one of three Nemo based attractions in WDW. Can you name the other two that we've already discussed?

I absolutely love this show. I will be honest and say that I have gotten a lump in my throat a few times while watching it. It is a heart-warming story that includes great action, lots of humor and some wonderful and catchy songs. My favorite song from the show is called "Go with the Flow" and is sung by Crush to Nemo's dad when he thinks he's completely lost. Crush is trying to send the message to just "go with the flow" and everything will work itself out. Even though I love the song and the message is very appropriate to the story, it is the exact opposite of what we need to do as Christians. Unfortunately in today's society, a lot of people, including Christians do exactly that. They go with the flow. They cater to and adapt to the world's standards. If the world says something is ok, then they go with it. The basic premise is majority rules. However, in Philippians 2:15 we are told to be blameless and innocent children of God even in the midst of this "crooked and twisted generation." Those may sound like harsh words that Paul wrote, but unfortunately they are true. This world is full of evil, but because it is so much easier, a lot of Christians choose the path of conforming to what the world says is acceptable. Don't forget what Paul says in Romans 12:2 that we are not to conform to the world but instead be transformed by the renewing of our minds.

If you've never seen the Finding Nemo show, go see it! It's been a while since I've seen it myself, and I can't wait to see it again. The actors and puppeteers do a great job! It's a wonderful show and the music is fantastic. See if you enjoy the "Go with the Flow" song as much as I do. Also keep in mind that in our Christian lives we are not to go with the flow. We need to be different from the world. We need to follow God's Word no matter what. It doesn't matter what's popular or accepted by the world. What matters is what God says. That's the flow we need to go with.

DEVOTIONAL #91

"Festival of the Lion King"

From one show to another, let's head over to another really good one on the other side of the park. This one doesn't really have a story but is more about stunts, exciting visuals, and music. Today let's focus on the Festival of the Lion King!

Again, we tend to shorten the name of this one and refer to it as the "Lion King Show". It takes place in the Africa section of the park, but used to be shown in Camp Mickey-Minnie when it opened with the park in 1998. Camp Mickey-Minnie land is no more. That land has been completely transformed and is now Pandora. Therefore in 2014, they moved this show to Africa and built a brand new theater to house it. This show also takes place at Hong Kong Disneyland. It is in the form of a musical revue and is not just a condensed version of the film or the Broadway show. However, some of the performers in the show have gone on to perform on Broadway. Entering the 1500 seat theater, you will notice it divided into four sections, each based on a certain animal. The four animals are Warthog, Elephant, Giraffe, and Lion. Based on where they sit, guests cheer for one of these animals and even have to act them a few times during the show. The 30 minute show involves 136 costumes and is shown 7-10 times per day. It involves floats based on each of the four animals above. The floats were previously used during a Disneyland parade to promote the film when it first came out. This show was originally supposed to be temporary as was the land it was in. The plan was to eventually put in Beastly Kingdom in this part of AK to highlight mythical and fantasy creatures. However, the land and especially this show were quite popular and became a permanent fixture instead. When the show moved to Africa a couple of years ago, the Timon character from the film received an upgrade. He now blinks his eyes and his mouth actually moves when you hear his voice. There have been a couple of incidents with this show. On March 21, 2016, a small electrical fire began beneath the elephant float during a performance. The fire was quickly extinguished and nobody was hurt. The show resumed the next day and the other three floats continued to be used while the elephant float was repaired. Another incident involved three of the performers who were fired for refusing to wear the costumes that other performers wore. They complained of the costumes being dirty and sweaty. Apparently Disney didn't agree with their reasoning, and they got the magical boot.

Have you seen the *Lion King* movie? Has anyone not seen it? In a word, it's a classic with a great story and music. What would you say is the lesson from the movie? Disney films always tend to have a good message though they may be subtle. In this movie, Simba runs away from his home and family when he thinks he is responsible for his father's death. He grows up far away from home and finds happiness in a new place. However, when his friend from childhood finds him and tells him how much trouble his home land is in, he has a dilemma. Simba isn't sure if he can go back home. He doesn't believe he has the courage and strength to defeat his evil uncle and make things good again. Of course it's Disney so there has to be a happy ending, right? Simba does eventually make the decision to go back home and he finds the courage to defeat the power of evil a.k.a. Uncle Scar. I would say that the main lesson from this film is to believe in yourself, and stand up for your beliefs. In our last devotional, we talked about how we need to be different from the world. Today's message is similar, but we're going to take it a step further and say that we also need to stand up to the world and be bold as you do what's right.

Sometimes in the struggles of this world, it's hard to have that courage. It's hard to believe in ourselves and stand up for what we know is true. It's much easier to conform to the world and stay quiet. However, that is not what we are called to do. Isaiah 41:10 says that God will strengthen and uphold us. It also tells us not to fear for God is with us. Psalm 18:32 says that it is God who arms us with strength. Obviously we need God to give us courage and strength, especially in times of fear. However we are also told in 2 Timothy 1:7 that God gave us His Spirit and it does not make us timid but instead makes us powerful. In other words, God has given us the power to be strong when the world is scary. His Spirit inside of us gives us the ability to stand up for our beliefs and believe in ourselves.

The Lion King show is an entertaining show. The music is good of course, and the stunts are pretty impressive. In my opinion, the movie is even better, and the message displayed is one we can take to heart. We all need to remember to believe in ourselves. There is no doubt that God will give us strength if we are in need. We can always pray to God for more strength and courage. Just remember that we already have that strength inside us through the power of His Spirit. We all need to make sure we are not letting our fears get the best of us, but instead are using that God-given power to further His kingdom.

DEVOTIONAL #92

"UP! A Great Bird Adventure"

For today's devotional, we're going to one more show here at Animal Kingdom before we get back to a ride. This is a different kind of show than the ones we are used to. It's more of a platform to teach and display living, breathing creatures. It is not based on a Disney film or feature famous Disney songs. However, they did just recently add couple of familiar characters to it. Let's go see the bird show which is officially named Up! A Great Bird Adventure.

The bird show opened with the park in 1998 and was originally called Flights of Wonder. This is the only attraction in Asia that has survived since day one. It has just recently been refurbished and now uses the characters Russell and Doug from the Disney film *Up*. It is a 25-minute show that includes several species of birds including a peacock, toucan, crane and eagle among several others. These various birds perform tricks and stunts and demonstrate their abilities. This is an audience participation show as well as a few guests are invited to participate in the show. This show takes place at the Caravan Stage Theater which is in the Asia section of the park. This theater has a brand new roof added in 2016. It had been just a canopy for many years. There are conservation messages interspersed throughout the show trying to teach the audience to take care of the birds' habitat. The show has a host, a cast member who is also a bird trainer. There are 3 other trainers featured in the show as well, but a total of 20 were involved in training the birds and rehearsing for this show . The show also typically includes some humor, both intended and unexpected as you never know exactly what the birds will do. There is also a talking parrot in the show that is quite entertaining. One of the parrots they have used over the years is named "Groucho." He is quite famous for his talking and singing having appeared on the Tonight Show and the Ellen show. He is 30 years old having been born in Kalamazoo, Michigan in 1986.

I really enjoy this show, although I haven't seen the updated version yet. For many years, I avoided this show due to time or because I figured I wouldn't enjoy it. One year we decided to give it a try and I was immediately hooked. I have seen it several times now, and I enjoy it each time. It's pretty amazing to see what these birds can do. At one point, they allow some of the birds to fly throughout the audience. If you are in just the right spot, the bird will fly within inches of your head. If you are afraid of birds, this might not be the show for you. The lesson for today from this show is simple.

The birds used in this show are obviously well-trained. There has clearly been hours of time and effort put into perfecting the tricks and stunts these birds do. As I mentioned, sometimes the birds are allowed to fly throughout the theater. I suppose if the birds wanted to, they could escape or at least fly somewhere they weren't supposed to. However, they always come back. They always do what they are told or expected to do. At least they always have when I've been to the shows. So my question for today's thought is this...are you trained? In a sense we are also allowed to fly. We are given freedom in life to do what we want to do. We can go whatever direction we choose, but do we always come back to God? The fact is we can't make it on our own forever. My guess is that if the birds in this show did fly away, they wouldn't last long. They aren't trained to survive on their own. They've always been provided food and shelter. We also can't survive on our own. Oh, most of us can physically survive with food, water and shelter, but we must have God in our lives to survive spiritually. Revelation 2:5 tells us to repent when we fall and come back to God. Acts 3:19 says basically the same in for us to repent and come back so our sins may be wiped away. Also remember the parable of the Lost Son in Luke 15. Remember how far away from his father that boy got, but he was able to come back to see his father welcome him with open arms.

Go try the bird show at Animal Kingdom, especially if you've never checked it out. I think you will be impressed. Watch how the birds do what they are told for the most part and always fly back to their trainers. Keep in mind that we always need to do the same. It doesn't matter how far away you've flown. You can always fly back. God will always welcome you with His arms wide open. What a forgiving and loving God we have!

DEVOTIONAL #93

"Kali River Rapids"

There are only a few rides and attractions left here in the Animal Kingdom. Today, I want to focus on a ride that I don't choose to do very often. In fact, I think I've only ridden it two or three times. There's a very good reason I don't choose to ride it more often. It's because I don't like being wet or at least having to walk around the park wet. This particular ride at Animal Kingdom always, and I mean always, gets you very wet. The sign in the line queue even says, "you will get wet". There's no "may" about it like most water rides. This ride typically has a decent line so I guess some people like getting that wet. I guess if I ever choose to ride it again, I'll need to wait and make it close to the last ride of the day. I also need to make sure it's not too cold outside, because the only thing worse than being wet, is being cold and wet. Let's brave it today and go ride Kali River Rapids!

Kali River Rapids opened less than a year after the park in March of 1999. This ride is located in the Asia section of the park and lasts around 5 minutes. There are 20 boats that hold up to 12 riders each. The ride begins with a 90 foot uphill climb and includes a 30 foot drop which is just one of the places you will most likely get wet. In addition to getting wet from the splashing water, you can also get wet in other ways such as water dripping on you from caves as well as from another interesting feature. At one point there are some elephants that shoot water at you that are controlled by guests standing on an overlooking bridge. Originally, the Imagineers planned to put an Asian safari in this area to counter-balance the safari ride in the Africa section. However, they later decided that a water ride would provide better variety. This ride was originally going to be named Tiger Rapids Run or Tiger River Run. It was also planned that riders would look at live animals as you went through the water ride. However, it was determined that the screams from guests and fast speed of the ride would not work well with live animals. This ride has very similar sister rides at Disney's California Adventure called Grizzly River Run and at Shanghai Disney called Roaring Rapids. On May 29, 2007, this ride closed when the evacuation platform malfunctioned and injured 5 guests and one cast member. A final fun fact of this ride is that there are certain scents pumped in as you ride similar to other Disney rides. If you pay attention, you will smell jasmine and ginger as you go up the hill and you will smell a burning smoke smell during the logging section.

As I mentioned above, you WILL get wet on this ride. The signs say it. The riders show it. There are some water rides in Disney World where you MAY get wet such as Splash Mountain or Pirates of the Caribbean, but this one is different. Getting wet is inevitable meaning it's going to happen no matter what. What else in life is inevitable? What can you say is going to happen in your life without a doubt? There's not much if you think about it. Most of your life is ruled by choices, your choices that you get to make. God knows what you will choose, but He does let you choose. The only thing that we can know without a doubt that is going to happen no matter what is our death and our eternity. Sorry to be so grim but the truth is you will die. Everyone dies, and unless Jesus returns before that day, it will happen. It's inevitable. Eternity is also unavoidable. It's a fact that you will either go to Heaven or Hell. They are real places. I'm sure you've heard John 3:16, but remember that it says that whoever believes in Jesus will have eternal life. We also need to remember Mark 16:16 that says whoever believes and is baptized will be saved. In John 14:1-3, Jesus tries to comfort His disciples by telling them about Heaven and what it will be like. There are numerous verses in Scripture about Heaven and Hell. The entire book of Revelation is John's account of God showing him what Heaven will be like.

I probably need to man up and ride Kali River Rapids again. I commit here and now to riding it next time I'm at Animal Kingdom. If it's not too cold, and if it's the end of the day, and if the line isn't too long, and if someone pays me, and if...ok, I'll stop. I guess sometimes you just have to get wet. If you ride Kali, you will. If you believe in God, you have to believe in eternity and His description of it. So the real question is...are you preparing for it? Are you absolutely confident in your inevitable placement after death? If not, start today and make sure that you know where you are going. The Bible says we can know. Remember that the sign says "you WILL get wet." Make sure your sign says, "you WILL go to Heaven."

DEVOTIONAL #94

"Gorilla Falls Exploration Trail"

Stepping off Kali River Rapids, we will need some time to dry off. Hopefully it's a bright sunny day, and we can dry off as we stroll through this next attraction. This attraction is maybe not as exciting as a ride or show, but it's still worth your time. It's a walking tour of sorts that you can do at your own pace, but there are some wonderful things to see. For today's devotional, we're going to explore the Gorilla Falls Exploration Trail.

This trail, found next to Kilimanjaro Safaris in the Africa section of the park, opened with the park. Four months after opening, it changed its name to Pangani Forest Exploration Trail. "Pangani" is Swahili for "Place of Enchantment." However, in May of 2016, it was announced that the original name would return. This attraction is a 3/8 of a mile trail that you simply walk through with many animals and exhibits along the way. The path is actually staffed with cast members spread out along the way. The CM's will give you information and fun facts as well as teach you about certain animals. Some of the many animals you can see are okapi, tarantulas, monkeys, mole rats, hippos, meerkats, snakes, gorillas and lots of birds. The hippos you see are actually the same ones seen in the Kilimanjaro Safari ride. This trail was built and designed to be an epilogue to the Safari and it was expected that guests would take the trail immediately after riding the Safari. I do remember being encouraged several times to take the trail by our Safari hosts. For the longest time, we never did it, but I finally tried it on a recent trip. Originally, Safari guests were told that since they successfully stopped the poachers in the Safari, they were given "exclusive access" to this trail where they could learn more. I guess this was to try and lure guests over to the trail. The idea for this trail came when a group of Imagineers took a trip to Kenya while Animal Kingdom was being built. To walk the entire trail typically takes around 20-30 minutes depending on how long you stop at each exhibit. There is a famous hidden Mickey on the trail which is not Mickey at all. Instead, it is a giant rock formation that looks like Jafar from Aladdin.

I know the idea of walking for 20-30 minutes is not as exciting as say a ride or show, but I enjoyed taking this trail and saw some really interesting things. Sometimes it can be fun to explore new places and often we find something we really enjoy that we weren't expecting. Did you know that we are called every day to be explorers? I don't mean on trails at Animal Kingdom but right in our homes. We are to explore God's Word each and every day. In the same way, we tend to find something new every time we explore Scripture and it can be an exciting adventure. Acts 17:11 talks about how a group of people called the "Bereans" explored Scripture daily, and they are called noble because of it. In 2 Timothy 2:15 we are told in a familiar passage to do our best to present ourselves to God as one approved who knows the Word of God. Finally, in Colossians 3:16, we are told to let the words of Christ dwell in us as we teach others. How can we know the words of Christ unless we read and study them? Several other verses in Scripture strongly encourage us to explore the Word of God so that we can not only know it ourselves, but teach others.

Exploring a new place can be enjoyable. You may discover something nobody has ever seen. You will at least find something that you've never seen, and it might just be appealing to you. While I don't know how exciting the Gorilla Trail will be to you, I can guarantee that exploring the Bible will be indeed motivating and beneficial to you. You will most definitely find something new every time you open up that Book. Additionally, God will use your study to help you grow closer to Him and be better equipped to talk to others about Him. Try to make time every single day to do some Biblical exploration. It will be a journey you will be glad you made!

DEVOTIONAL #95

"Wildlife Express Train"

We're really getting close to the end here. There are only three real attractions to go here at the Animal Kingdom, and the one for today's devotional is the last ride. It's not a super exciting ride, but I suppose it does qualify as a ride. It's unique in that you must ride it if you want to visit the next attraction that we'll talk about in the next devotional. So for today, let's embark on our last ride and board the Wildlife Express Train.

The Wildlife Express Train is located in the Africa section of the park and is the only way to get to another attraction, Rafiki's Planet Watch. I have only ridden this train a couple of times that I remember, but I definitely do remember it because the way it is ridden is quite unique. Everyone that takes this ride faces sideways. In other words, you are looking out the side of the train rather than forwards or backwards. You actually can't even see what is behind you, because there is a solid wall to your back. Disney did this on purpose to hide some of the less than attractive backstage buildings and storage areas. However, you do get to see some behind the scenes sights anyways during your 1.2 mile round trip journey. This train was original with the park opening, and it takes seven minutes to travel out to Rafiki's Planet Watch. It then takes 5 minutes to come back. You don't have to get off at the one and only stop as some just ride it round trip. It is nice and relaxing and you do get to see some of the holdings of the rhinos and elephants. Early plans for this train called for a steam engine actually traveling through the African savannah, but there were soon concerns about the safety of the animals. The train is designed to look like it's been traveling in Africa for 100 years, the dust and grime being part of the décor. The red and green bins on top of the train represent luggage that travelers on this "old train" have brought with them. The train cars were actually built in England in 1997 just a few miles from Shakespeare's home. A final train tidbit is that if you watch carefully while riding, you can see Pride Rock from the safari and maybe even the lions.

As mentioned above, the Wildlife Express Train is the ONLY way to get to the Rafiki's Planet Watch section of the park. You are not allowed to walk there, and it isn't accessible any other way. This makes it a unique attraction in that you have to ride one to see the other. If you happened to be scared of trains or didn't want to ride one, you wouldn't be able to enjoy the 2nd attraction. It's the only way. Can you see where I'm going with this? There is also only one way to get to God. I remember watching a clip from a popular daytime talk show a few years ago where the very popular host was having a discussion with the audience about Heaven. As expected with the world these days, many in the audience talked about different religions and different beliefs about Heaven. One very bold and courageous audience member spoke up and reminded everyone how we are told in Scripture that there is only one way to God and that is through Jesus Christ. The talk show host then basically chastised the woman and said "there can't possibly be only one way to God. There has to be several ways to get there." I believe this host was wrong, and I strongly admire the woman in the audience for her boldness and for speaking the truth. We are told in John 14:6 by Jesus himself that nobody gets to the Father except through Jesus Christ. It may not sound fair or easy or possible to some, but again, if you believe in the Bible, you have to believe it's the truth. If Jesus said it, it must be important. Jesus also said in John 10:9 that He is a gate and anyone who enters through Him will be saved. Finally in John 3:36 Jesus says "whoever believes in the Son has eternal life but whoever rejects Him will not see life." He's talking about eternal life in Heaven.

I wouldn't mind riding the Wildlife Express Train again. I don't really remember what I saw last time, and I'd like to explore it further. I think it's always fun to just relax on a nice, peaceful train ride. I also think it's interesting that it is the only way to get to a pretty important area of the park. The fact is I want to go to Heaven. I want to go there very badly, and I believe what Jesus said. I know that I'll only get to Heaven through Him. I have to follow in His footsteps, follow His commands, and follow the path He laid out for us. I really hope and pray that you want to get there too. I think you do. Make sure you also travel there by way of Jesus. It's the only way!

DEVOTIONAL #96

"Rafiki's Planet Watch"

Can you believe this is our 96th devotional? We only have four more to go, and we'll be finished. You can probably figure out where we are going today, especially if you read the last devotional. I mentioned in the last one that you had to ride the Wildlife Express Train to get to Rafiki's Planet Watch so let's go there today and explore what all there is to see!

Rafiki's Planet Watch is really not an attraction by itself but instead is considered to be a separate section of the park like Africa, Asia and Discovery Island. It technically includes three separate stations that could all be considered attractions, but we'll combine them in this entry. This used to be called Conservation Station when the park first opened. It is the only section of the park not connected to the central hub of Discovery Island. It is only connected to Africa by way of the train. The three sections include Habitat Habit, Conservation Station and Affection Section. The first two are basic behind-the-scenes looks at how animals are cared for. The latter is a petting zoo of sorts where you can interact with the animals. I read one piece of advice that stated if you are going to do this section of the park, get there early as in first thing in the morning. The reason is because morning is when everything gets done such as feeding the animals, giving them their meds, etc. Sometimes in the morning you can even find Rafiki himself meditating on the floor to start the day. RPW also includes several endangered species that you can learn about. Altogether there are 29 endangered species featured at Animal Kingdom. As expected, RPW includes tons of Hidden Mickeys that can search for. You can also see gorilla training as well as try your hand at controlling special cameras in different animals' habitats to see if you can search out the ones that are hiding.

As I mentioned, RPW includes 29 different endangered species. An endangered species is one that has been classified by the IUCN (International Union for Conservation of Nature) as likely to become extinct. I remember as a child when the bald eagle got put on the endangered list and it was a big deal. People all around our country feared our national animal becoming extinct. Strict guidelines were put into place to protect these birds, and subsequently they have officially been removed from the list as is announced during the *Up* bird show. Unfortunately, many animals don't make it off the list and do indeed become extinct. Disney is doing a service by letting the public know about these unfortunate creatures and educating guests on how they can help. So here's a question to consider today...are Christians an endangered species?

It seems to be that Christians in this world are becoming less and less of an influence. The world in general seems to be more and more tolerant every day of worldly views and ideas that are not of the Bible. The world seems to be more accepting of sinful practices as time moves on and the voice of Christians and God's Word is become less accepted or even considered. One recent article published on the Internet stated that "Christians are the most endangered minority in the world." That statement shocked and scared me, particularly because of the word "minority." Why have we gone from a Christian majority to an endangered minority? Aren't Christians supposed to be vocal and stand up for their beliefs? Jesus told us in John 15:19 that we are not of the world. In fact He says that the world hates us. We are also told in Colossians 3:5 to put to death anything earthly inside of us. I think sometimes we, myself included, think that as long as we don't partake in worldly practices, we are fine. However, we have to go further that and share and tell others the message of Christ as well.

I need to take the time to really explore this area next trip as I haven't really spent a lot of time here. I know I would enjoy it and learn a lot. It is unfortunate that many animals featured are endangered and will most likely become extinct one day. My hope and prayer today is that Christians don't follow suit. We all need to do our part to follow the first and second commandment of God stated in Luke 10:27. We need to love God first and love our neighbor second. Part of loving our neighbor includes telling them what is right and wrong and helping them with any struggles. It's not an easy task, but it's so important so that we can spread Christianity and keep it from becoming extinct.

DEVOTIONAL #97

"Rivers of Light"

Take out your handkerchief and prepare for tears, because it's time for our final park attraction. Before we leave the Animal Kingdom, we're going to watch their fairly new nighttime show. For a long time, AK didn't have a nighttime show for whatever reason. The general belief was that fireworks would scare the animals so what else could they do? Well, after many years, they figured it out. It's not my favorite night show, but it is very good. Once again, they have gotten very creative and created something visually stunning and exciting to watch. Let's watch and discuss the Rivers of Light show.

This 15-minute show began in February 2017 on the river surrounding the Tree of Life. There is a new 5000-seat amphitheater located between Discovery Island and Expedition Everest where you can sit and watch. You can also find a place anywhere around the water in that area, although the sound is not as good unless you are right in front of it. This show has the smallest audience capacity of any of the four park's nighttime shows, so you have to get there early for a decent seat. It is even recommended you get a fast pass to confirm your viewing.

The ROL show features water fountains, mist screens, floating lanterns, fire effects, lasers, lights, fog, projection mapping and live performers. It incorporates the Tree of Life into the show as well. This show was set to premier on Earth Day, April 22 in 2016 which was also the 18th anniversary of the park. However, it was delayed and a Jungle Book show based on the new live action film was opened instead. When the show finally opened in 2017, it featured eleven large barges with performances and displays. This show is generally shown every night and sometimes twice during peak seasons. This show is definitely different from the other parks in that there is no real story or plot and, as mentioned, no big fireworks-type moments. Instead, this show focuses more on color, imagery, music and beauty. It is a celebration of all living things with representations of earth, water, sky and fire. For this reason and due to the fact it doesn't really feature anything "Disney," it has gotten some less than perfect reviews.

I have seen this show only once, and while I enjoyed it and would like to see it again, it's my least favorite closing show of the four parks.

I like fireworks and explosive performances. Of course, I understand why they don't have them here. I actually appreciate the fact that Disney is choosing to take care of the animals by not scaring them with loud noises. While it would probably make for a better show, they are doing the right thing in considering the needs of the animals instead. This reminds me of something that we are supposed to do according to scripture. I Corinthians 8:13 talks about how if something we are doing causes someone else to fall meaning sin, we should stop doing it. Romans 12:18 tells us to "live peacefully with everyone" as much as is possible.

A huge fault of many humans, and I don't exclude myself, is being selfish and thinking only of what makes us happy or what pleases us. We instead have to consider others' needs and feelings when we do something. If we are offending others or especially causing them to sin, we need to change our ways. This is something we have to consciously think about often so we can make adjustments to how we live if needed. Even if something doesn't seem like a big deal to us, it may be to someone else and as a Christian, we have to consider that.

Check out the Rivers of Light show, and see if you enjoy it. Like I said, the visuals are pretty amazing and they do a great job with it. Don't expect fireworks or any loud noises though. They might make for a better show, but Disney chooses not to have them because of the animals. We need to do the same and make good choices that positively influence others, even if it is not our first choice. We must try and pattern our lives in a way where others aren't offended or are persuaded to sin. We are tasked with leading others to God, not away from Him.

DEVOTIONAL #98

"Disney Springs"

We've got three devotionals to go, but we are done with all the rides, shows and attractions in the parks. I guess I could've stopped with 97, but I think that would've driven us OCD'ers crazy, myself included. Surely we can find three more things at Disney to talk about, right? Of course we can! For this devotional, I have chosen to include a very important area of Walt Disney World that many people really enjoy. Our family didn't used to visit this area much when our kids were younger, but we've actually rediscovered it here in the last few years and try to visit each time. I'm talking of course about Disney Springs. So let's take some time today to discuss this very large area of WDW where there is much to see and do.

Disney Springs as it came to be known recently in 2015 has had many names over the years. It opened officially in 1975 and was known as Lake Buena Vista Shopping Village. I'm kind of glad that one didn't stick. It's way too long! It has also been known as Walt Disney World Village (1977), Disney Village Marketplace (1989) and Downtown Disney (1997). It is 120 acres full of shops, restaurants and entertainment venues. It currently includes four distinct areas: The Marketplace, The Landing, The West Side and Town Center. All four are connected by a spring that runs through them (hence the new name). In 1984, the area had a major renovation when Disney executives decided that they really wanted to try to keep guests on property at all times. Apparently, many people were leaving Disney property at night to find better entertainment. Therefore, they added Pleasure Island to this area to try and lure guests back to Disney property at night. They also eventually added new bridges to link the area to a Disney resort, Saratoga Springs, again hoping that people would stay on property. There are currently over 150 different venues at Disney Springs which include 25 different entertainment acts every night. It is also home to the largest Disney merchandise store in the world, World of Disney. I will also personally give a shout out to my favorite place to eat on Disney property, Earl of Sandwich. The location at Disney Springs just happens to be the first ever of its kind as this was the site of the original. This very good restaurant, in my humble opinion, eventually became a chain and has spread out all over the world. Now if I could just get them to put one here in Nashville, TN!

You may be wondering how I make a devotional out of Disney Springs? There aren't a lot of Scriptures about shops and business. However, there is one very important Bible story found in Matthew 21 and John 2 that does involve people buying and selling goods in a marketplace of sorts. Read that story if you have a few minutes. In those chapters, you'll find the story of Jesus cleaning out the temple. I realize that Disney Springs is hardly a temple, but I would argue that it is definitely a marketplace. Think about the fact that there are over 150 different venues at Disney Springs. Think how much money is exchanged, spent and used at this area every day. It has to be hundreds of thousands, if not millions of dollars. I read online that Disney makes approximately 36 million dollars per day in profit. Obviously a lot of this is from the parks and admission fees but food, merchandise and entertainment have to be a large part as well. As fun and exciting as Disney is, it is definitely a business. I'm sure most Disney executives would say that the main goal of Disney, if they're being honest, is to make money. Our family has certainly contributed a good amount toward their goal. There is a time and place in this world for making money. God talks in the Bible about being a good steward and working for your money. There is nothing wrong with what Disney is doing. There was nothing wrong with what the buyers and sellers were doing in the two Biblical passages. However, it WAS wrong that they chose the temple in which to conduct their business, and this is why Jesus was so angry. They had completely forgotten the point of that structure. They had gotten their priorities all mixed up and had put greed and selfishness above worship and reverence. I'm wondering if we do the same.

In I Corinthians 6:19, we are told that our bodies are now the temple of God. We are also told in Romans 12:1 to offer our bodies as a living sacrifice to God, and that is how we truly worship Him. We are to respect, take care of and use our bodies in service to God. How often do we instead put greed, selfishness and our personal desires ahead of God? How often do we use our bodies in ways that God would disapprove and therefore sin against him? While there is certainly a time for places like Disney Springs where there is fun, exchanging money and business, let's make sure that our first priority is loving God and using our bodies in His service. Let's not turn the temple He gave us into a marketplace.

DEVOTIONAL #99

"Disney's Water Parks"

It's time for the next to the last devotional! With my work schedule and sending these out periodically, it's taken us almost a year to go through all these. Therefore, it's hard to believe they are almost done. We'll just have to find another topic that I can write one hundred devotionals on, won't we? So where do we go for this one? Again, we are done with all the parks, rides and attractions. So for tonight, I'd like to talk about another Disney area that is very important to WDW but is not one of the four parks. It's an area that I wish we could explore a little bit. I'm talking of course about the two water parks included at WDW. They are Typhoon Lagoon and Blizzard Beach. I have actually been to Typhoon Lagoon. I think it was 1990 or 91. I went with my mom and sister while my dad was doing business somewhere in Orlando. We also visited Hollywood Studios for the first time ever on that trip. I was 14 or 15 years old, but I barely remember visiting the water park. Therefore, we need to go back and explore them both. Let's do just that tonight through this devotional.

The first water park at WDW actually wasn't even one of those two. It was called Disney's River Country. I think you're mom has been there when she was younger. This park opened on June 20, 1976 and was located next to the Fort Wilderness Resort and Campground. Actually, it still is located there but is shut down and is somewhat of a deserted park. There are YouTube videos of people sneaking in that are actually fun to watch. This waterpark closed indefinitely on November 2, 2001. It will be interesting to see if Disney ever does anything with this space. On June 1, 1989, Disney opened Typhoon Lagoon. It is 61 acres of water-based fun. It includes one of the world's largest wave pools. I actually remember that pool from my early trip. It is the 2nd most visited water park in the world, behind one in China which had about 600,000 more visitors last year. TL also includes a 2100 foot lazy river. On April 1, 1995, Disney opened a 2nd water park called Blizzard Beach. It is 66 acres making it the largest water park on property. It is the 3rd most visited water park in the world. It features a chair lift that takes you to the top of Mt. Gushmore where many of the best attractions are. It includes 21 slides, the most famous of which is Summit Plummet which is 120 feet tall and where riders reach speeds of 55 mph. This makes it the tallest water ride in the USA. It also has a 3000 foot lazy river. That's over half a mile long! All of the water at both water parks is heated which means at least one of these parks is open year round.

It's a lot easier to make a devotional from a water park than it was for a shopping area last time. Water is prevalent all throughout the Bible. I'm sure you can name at least one and probably several Bible stories based on, in or around water. I thought of Jonah, Noah, Moses, Peter, and of course Jesus who found themselves in water. I could talk about many other stories and how important water was. I could talk about God showing his power through water. I could talk about living water and the woman at the well in John 4. I could talk about creation and God creating water very early on in Genesis 1. I will choose instead to talk about one of the most important things that we experience through water. In Mark 1:9-11, we are given the example of Jesus being baptized in water by John the Baptist. In Acts 2:38, we are commanded to be baptized for the forgiveness of our sins so that we too may receive the Holy Spirit. In Matthew 28:19, we are commanded to go out into the world and baptize others. I can honestly say the greatest joys in my life are the three times in which I've gotten to baptize someone. I will never forget these times, especially baptizing you two, my amazing sons. I will never forget my own baptism at age 11. Baptism is something very special that God created as a symbol of our dedication to Him. It not only washes our sins away and shows our devotion and commitment to God, but also recreates the death, burial and resurrection of our Lord and Savior Jesus Christ. I am so proud that my entire family has been baptized and did so with full knowledge of what they were doing. I am so proud that each of us is dedicated to God and although we all sin daily, we are all trying to do what God says and Heaven is our ultimate goal. I am so grateful that God created baptism so that despite our many sins, we can be saved by His grace and forgiveness.

Think about water tonight. Think about how important it is to our lives. We couldn't survive without it. We need it to drink, to keep clean, and even to have fun at Disney water parks. We also of course need it for baptism. There are some that may say that baptism is good, but not necessary. My answer for that is always why wouldn't I do it if my Lord and Savior Jesus Christ did it? Why wouldn't I follow the command God gave in I Peter 3:21, Mark 16:16, John 3:5 and many other verses? I always want to follow the example of Jesus and the commands God has given me. Don't you? Let us never forget that we are baptized Christians, that we have the gift of the Holy Spirit through our baptism, and that we need to share the importance of baptism with others.

DEVOTIONAL #100

"Partners"

Well, here it is! The grand finale! Devotional #100! I have truly loved writing these and have learned so much about Disney. I hope you have had fun, enjoyed them, and learned a lot about Disney as well. More importantly, I hope you've learned more about God through these. I know I have, and it has been a true blessing.

This last one is important! It needs to be something special right? I've actually had this one planned from day one to be the very last devotional. It's not a ride. It's not a show. It's not an attraction, park, store or restaurant. It's simply a spot with a small landmark, and for me and many others, I think it's truly something very special to Walt Disney World. If you don't know what it is, based on the title up there, I'll give you a hint. It's probably the most photographed spot in all of WDW and maybe in America for that matter. It also happens to be my favorite spot in all the parks. I could stand there all day. I really could. Of course I'd be missing out on a lot, so I usually don't stand there very long. Have you figured it out yet? Today for our final devotional, we are going to be talking about the statue right in front of Cinderella castle at the Magic Kingdom. It is a statue displaying the true partnership and friendship of Walt Disney and Mickey Mouse, and it's appropriately named "Partners."

I've always loved that statue. I love where it located. It's the perfect spot in the Magic Kingdom. You have a perfect view of the castle as well as the ability to turn around and look all the way down Main Street to the front of the park. It also provides the perfect opportunity for a photo which is why it is usually a very crowded spot. This statue was first placed at Disneyland in 1993 to celebrate Mickey's birthday. It was then placed in the Orlando park in 1995. There are now five of the Partners statues around the world in various Disney parks. It was created by Disney legend Blaine Gibson, and it took him one year to create it. He is also the artist credited with creating nearly all of the animatronics in the Hall of Presidents. One early sketch that he made of the Partners statue had Mickey holding an ice cream cone, but this was later changed. He also decided to have Walt Disney smiling to show that he's enjoying watching people have fun at his park. Mr. Gibson knew he couldn't have created this statue while Walt was alive.

Walt Disney was known to not want a statue of himself anywhere in the park. In fact, in 1962, Mr. Gibson created a small bust of Walt Disney and presented it to him as a gift. However, Mr. Disney was less than grateful and stated “What am I gonna do with this? Statues are for dead people.” For this reason, the living members of Disney’s family were very hesitant to let this project happen and almost refused. At 6 feet 5 inches the statue is 7 inches taller than Walt Disney’s actual height. If you look closely on his tie, you will find the initials S.T.R. This stands for Smoke Tree Ranch which was an area in Palm Springs, California where Walt once owned a vacation home.

Are you wondering why I chose this famed statue for our final devotional? Well, like I said, I love it. I have a small replica of it on our Disney display in the basement. I would like a larger version one day. I’d even take life size, although I’m not sure where we’d put it. I love what the statue represents; a partnership that created the magic that is today Walt Disney World. I love the smile on Walt Disney’s face. I do believe that Walt Disney would be happy to know that so many people every year enjoy his parks. I also chose this for our final devotional because I think it’s easy to make a spiritual reference. It’s easy to see in the statue that Walt and Mickey were “best friends.” Walt created Mickey. Mickey in turn helped Walt to create this empire that has grown astronomically in a relatively short time. They are friends, and they are partners. We have the same relationship with our Lord and Savior Jesus Christ. Proverbs 18:24 says “A man of many companions may come to ruin, but there is a friend who sticks closer than a brother.” In John 15:15, Jesus himself says he has called us friends. Jesus in not only our Savior and Brother, He is also our friend. We sing many songs at church and can find many scriptures about Jesus being our friend. Think about the friends you have. Do you have a best friend? Do you have a friend that would do anything for you or that you would do anything for? Would that friend die for you? Would you do the same? It’s hard to say. It’s NOT hard to say that Jesus would do that for you. In fact, He already did! Jesus is the best friend we will ever have. He loved us so much that He gave his life for us even without knowing us. It is His supreme sacrifice that gives us so much hope for our future and eternal life in Heaven. There can never be a friend like Him.

The next time you go to Magic Kingdom, take just a second to study the Partners statue. Look at the smiles on Walt Disney and Mickey Mouse’s face. Think about their friendship and their partnership. Then think about how we have the exact same in Jesus. That’s something we absolutely must take pride in and tell others about. As much as I love you, my sweet wife and incredible sons, please understand that Jesus loves you even more. What a friend we have in Jesus!

About the Author

After 16 years as a school teacher and coach, Albert took a leap of faith and went back to school to pursue his dream of being a paramedic. He is also active at his church where he has served as a deacon, Bible class teacher, and assistant youth minister. In his free time, he can often be found planning his next Disney vacation, buying another Disney souvenir to add to his collection, or listening to a Disney podcast. He has completed the Goofy Challenge Marathon Event at Walt Disney World and continues to visit the parks several times each year. He works full-time as a paramedic in Nashville, Tennessee, where he resides with his wife, two teenage sons, and their dog, Molly.

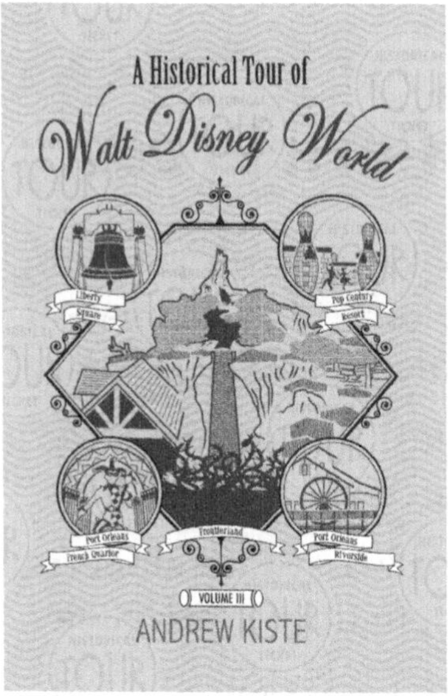

Read more about these books
and our many other titles at:

www.ThemeParkPress.com

Made in the USA
Monee, IL
13 December 2019

18615457R00118